Macedonia

For my Father

Macedonia

Warlords and Rebels in the Balkans

John Phillips

Yale University Press
New Haven and London

First published in the United States in 2004 by Yale University Press

First published in Great Britain in 2004 by I.B.Tauris & Co Ltd

Copyright © 2004 by John Phillips.

Typeset in Sabon by Steve Tribe, Andover
Printed in Great Britain by MPG Books Ltd, Bodmin

Library of Congress Control Number: 2004101435

ISBN 0-300-10268-2 (cloth: alk. paper)

A catalogue record for this book is available from the British
Library.

The paper in this book meets the guidelines for permanence and
durability of the Committee on Production Guidelines for Book
Longevity of the Council on Library Resources.

10 9 8 7 6 5 4 3 2 1

Contents

Preface

MACEDONIA: WARLORDS AND REBELS *in the Balkans* attempts to explain
how and why armed conflict broke out in Macedonia, threatening to
plunge the Balkans into a fifth war a decade after Skopje seceded
peacefully from Yugoslavia.

The former Yugoslav republic's smooth transition to independence
contrasted impressively with the violent secessions of Slovenia, Croatia
and Bosnia. A decade ago, the preoccupation of western journalists'
with Bosnia and Croatia meant that events in Macedonia received
scant mention.

When I returned to the Balkans to report on the demise of Slobodan
Milosevic in September 2000, it was expected that any further fighting
that broke out in the former Yugoslavia would most likely take place
in Montenegro. The ousting of Milosevic in a bloodless uprising
curtailed the tension between Belgrade and Milo Djukanovic, the
Montenegrin leader, but as fighting flared between ethnic Albanians
and Yugoslav soldiers in southern Serbia it became clear not only that
NATO's bombing of Yugoslavia had not resolved the status of Kosovo
but also that Albanian nationalism was now potentially as much a major
destabilising force in the region as Serbian nationalism had been hitherto.

This book examines the roots of the crisis in Macedonia's history
and experience as a Yugoslav republic. The insurgents' links to the
Kosovo Liberation Army and the rise of Macedonian nationalism and
its warlords' connections with paramilitary activities and alleged war
crimes are traced. Where possible, the rebel campaign and the
Macedonian authorities' response are described from the point of view
of the people who witnessed the drama.

The later chapters describe how the West intervened diplomatically
and militarily to halt the killing in Macedonia and enforce a peace
settlement that was still functioning in the autumn of 2003. This was

a success for the international community, compared to its poor record elsewhere in the former Yugoslavia. It is clear, however, that Macedonia will not become a stable country until the West makes a determined effort to resolve the future of Kosovo, a challenge that so far neither the European Union nor the United States of America has shown much willingness to tackle.

The ethnic communities of Macedonia, meanwhile, remain far apart in spite of the Macedonian Parliament passing most of the reforms needed to meet the grievances of ethnic Albanians envisaged in the Ohrid peace agreement. The country will need new leaders if it is to revive the multicultural society that flourished briefly in the early years after independence.

I gained much for this book from the interviews and discussions that I had with the following persons: Ali Ahmeti, Bob Churcher, Charles Crawford, the late Zoran Djindjic, Milo Djukanovic, Michael Evans, Douglas Hamilton, Violina Hristova, Zoran Jachev, Vojislav Kostunica, Mark Laity, Stepan Mesic, Saso Ordanovski, Richard Potter and Dessa Trevisan.

Many friends and colleagues freely gave suggestions and encouragement, including Richard Beeston, Jeff Bieley, Aleks Brkic, Charlotte Eager, Janine di Giovanni, John Heinemann, Tim Judah, Michael Keats, Andrew Lycett, Julian O'Halloran, Richard Owen, Valerio Pellizzari, Peggy Polk, Norman Roberson, Irena Sutic, Philip Willan and Giuseppe Zaccharia.

I am grateful to editors at the London foreign desk of *The Times* for their encouragement, especially Martin Ivens, Bronwen Maddox, Denis Tailor and David Watts.

I am indebted to Professor James Pettifer, Dr Hugh Poulson, Dr Brendan Simms and Slobodan Markovic for reading drafts of this book and generously giving scholarly advice. My colleagues Jacek Palasinski, Farley Clinton and Dragan Petrovic also read many chapters and made helpful criticisms. I also owe thanks to Dragan for ensuring that my transliteration of names and places from Macedonian Cyrillic is consistent with the Serbo-Croat Latin system.

Turi Munthe, my editor at I.B.Tauris, deserves praise for believing in and supporting this project from the beginning. Hanako Birks, also at I.B.Tauris, and Steve Tribe were vital in ensuring that it saw the light of day.

My greatest debts are to my wife, Maristella, and my children, Margaux and Suzanne, who made this book possible by helping me in so many ways.

Any errors are my own.

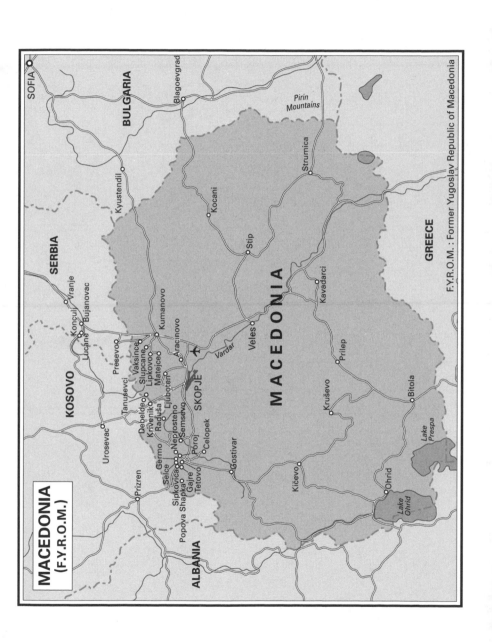

MACEDONIA
(F.Y.R.O.M.)

F.Y.R.O.M. : Former Yugoslav Republic of Macedonia

SOFIA

BULGARIA

Blagoevgrad

Pirin
Mountains

Strumica

Kyustendil

Kocani

Stip

SERBIA

Vranje

Konculi
Bujanovac

Lucane

Presevo

Kumanovo

Aracinovo

Kavadarci

Vardar

Veles

MACEDONIA

GREECE

Vaksince
Slupcane
Lipkovo
Matejced

Tanusevci

SKOPJE

Urosevac

Debelde
Kriveni
Raduša
Ljuboten
Neprosteno
Semsevo

Prilep

Krusevo

Bitola

Prizren

Germo
Selce
Sipkovica
Popova Shapka
Gajre
Tetovo

Poroj

Celopek

Gostivar

Lake
Prespa

Kicevo

Lake
Ohrid

Ohrid

KOSOVO

ALBANIA

THE FORMER YUGOSLAVIA

AUSTRIA

SLOVENIA
○
LJUBLJANA

○ ZAGREB

HUNGARY

CROATIA

VOJVODINA

Novi Sad ○

ROMANIA

○ Banja Luka

BELGRADE ○

BOSNIA-
HERZEGOVINA

SARAJEVO ○

SERBIA

BULG.

○ Split

○ Mostar

○ Nis

Kosovska
Mitrovica
○

Zadar

○

MONTENEGRO

Pec ○

Pristina
○

○ Vranje

Adriatic
Sea

Dubrovnik ○

Podgorica
○

KOSOVO

Koncul]

○○ Bujanovac

○ Prizren

○ Kumanovo

Bar ○

Tetovo
○

○ SKOPJE

ITALY

MACEDONIA

ALBANIA

GREECE

1 Southern Serbian Prelude

*He felt a pang of pain for Black Peter and his band of shaggy
ruffians whose devotion to a lost cause had led them to sudden
and ignominious death in the fastnesses of Serbia.*
Lawrence Durrell, White Eagles Over Serbia

IN NOVEMBER 2000, I travelled to the Presevo valley to report on a
miniature army of quixotic Albanian guerrillas fighting for a swathe
of Serbia that they hoped to seize for an independent Kosovo.

Entering Presevo on the road from Pristina required hours of
negotiations with the Russian peacekeeping troops controlling access
to the buffer zone separating Kosovo from Serbia proper. After at last
receiving verbal permission from their commanding officer to leave
the little province, we drove past Russian paratroopers swaggering
around the frontier post with heavy machine guns on their shoulders
and sped through deserted, flat fertile country for about an hour before
nudging past an elated young sentry into the eerie, battle-torn town of
Konculj. We soon met a platoon of fighters from the Liberation Army
of Presevo-Medvedja-Bujanovac (UCPMB) with the Albanian double-
eagle symbol on their shoulders.

The rebel units, many of them made up of teenage raw recruits,
were short of transport, relying on a Land Rover with a hole sawn out
of the roof for a machine gun to protrude from and battered utility
cars. The letters UCPMB had been daubed on the Land Rover with
red paint and a captured Yugoslav Army half-track packed with
guerrillas trundled behind it on a hill above the bleak town. They
were hungry for publicity.

'Don't sell those pictures to anyone,' Shefket Musliu, the bearded rebel commander, shouted at a photographer,[1] waving an Uzi machine pistol from the half-track to emphasise the point. 'Make the others come here to take some more.' The hard core of the men in black fatigues who gathered to celebrate Albanian flag day on Konculj's windswept football pitch were obviously well-disciplined and trained former soldiers of the Kosovo Liberation Army (KLA), seasoned from the struggle they had waged against the Yugoslav Army and paramilitary forces before and during the NATO bombardment of Kosovo launched to counter a crackdown on ethnic Albanian civilians by Slobodan Milosevic, the former Yugoslav President who had been deposed by a popular uprising in October 2000.

The day before our visit, Serb MUP police forces operating with light weapons in Presevo – a demilitarised buffer zone between Kosovo and Serbia proper established under the terms of the NATO-brokered treaty ending the Kosovo conflict – had retreated from Konculj a day after an eight-day house-to-house battle in which the Albanian insurgents killed several police officers.

Commander Plaki, a middle-aged, bearded and bandoliered officer carrying a Chinese-made sub-machine gun, vowed that the rebels would capitalise on their seizure of Konculj to capture Bujanovac, a southern Serbian county that, like Presevo, had an ethnic Albanian majority population. 'The Serbs fought badly, they are not well trained and their morale is bad,' he said in good Italian. 'Because we are guerrillas we are not afraid of any deployment by the Yugoslav Army. We are not afraid of anyone except God.'

Commander Plaki said that he had fought in Bosnia and worked in Western Europe. He had also been Konculj's village schoolteacher. He acknowledged that the genesis of the UCPMB was cryptic, however, and he was evidently reluctant to explain its origins. A report four months later in The Observer produced plausible evidence suggesting that the 'bastard army' was a creature of the Central Intelligence Agency (CIA).[2]

American intelligence was active in Serbia and Kosovo but its operatives were evidently struggling to come to terms with the new era ushered in by the demise of Milosevic's brutal regime. An ethnic Albanian arrested by British troops for a bomb attack on a busload of Serb civilians in northern Kosovo, Florim Ejupi, was identified credibly as a CIA-trained agent months later after he vanished from American custody, for example.[3]

Conspiracy theories abound in the Balkans but so do conspirators. Many analysts believe that American intelligence nurtured the UCPMB as part of efforts to prepare for a possible Yugoslav Army attack that Washington had feared might be launched to regain control of Kosovo.

A paper for Sandhurst's Conflict Studies Research Centre by Bob Churcher described how:

> based on their behaviour and tactics, it would appear that the UCPMB may have benefited from US-style training or trainers (though not necessarily funded by the US, of course). This training could have occurred after NATO entered Kosovo and before Milosevic was overthrown, and it has been suggested that it was part of a plan for destabilising the Milosevic regime.[4]

Churcher, a former British serviceman, added that the American military style of their training:

> became apparent both from the style of marching, complete with US-type marching songs, and the infantry tactics used. (The effectiveness of this was seen in November 2000 when a series of well-coordinated infantry attacks demonstrated the UCPMB's ability to coordinate the use of 82 mm mortars and to effectively 're-organise on the objective' – something that the Bosnian army never learnt in three years.)

Whatever the truth about the maestro who trained their voices, the guerrillas acquired a number of 120 mm mortars and 79 mm recoilless anti-tank weapons. The first Serb soldier had been killed by the UCPMB by the end of January 2001, when the Yugoslav Army shelled villages in what is now southern Serbia for the first time.

In February, Albanian gunmen and bomb teams also stepped up revenge attacks on the minority Serbs in Kosovo. Buses were attacked by Kosovar Albanian extremists on 13 and 16 February, with 10 people, many of them Serbian women and children, killed in the second incident. The guerrillas unleashed a heavy assault on 10 March, designed to forestall a NATO-backed deployment by Yugoslav forces in the buffer zone, part of which also borders with Macedonia.

In fact, many of the UCPMB men came from the *Trupat Mbrojtese te Kosoves*, or Kosovo Protection Corps (KPC), which was created when the KLA was dissolved. Officially consisting of 3,000 men and 2,000 reservists, the Corps has access to a large part of the KLA's former weaponry hidden in Albania. Officially a civil defence force, the KPC sees itself as the future army of an independent Kosovo. The UCPMB was set up a year before Milosevic was overthrown.

Formal rebel operations in southern Serbia started in January 2000 with a political wing and local spokesmen operating out of Pristina and Gjilane and a militia journal, *Ushtima e Maleve*, on sale in Kosovo providing news of the little war. Ethnic Albanian men in uniform appeared that month at the funeral of two brothers, Isa Saqipi, 36, and Shaip Saqipi, 32, allegedly killed by Serb forces while they were driving a tractor.

In the spring of 2001, I drove 200 miles down to Bujanovac from Belgrade with Aleks Brkic, our fixer in the Serbian capital, to write about the climax of the UCPMB's nine-month military campaign. The sun shone brightly as the immaculate porters from the Moskva Hotel stowed our bags in Aleks's red Golf. Belgrade was enjoying its first spring since Milosevic's regime had been swept away. Beautiful girls crowded the Moskva's pavement café, discussing their adventures in the seductive city's night world the previous evening. Our maternal interpreter from Sarajevo, Irena Sutic, called to wish us a safe trip. We left the Belgraders to enjoy the revolution after their harsh winter and headed south toward the warfront, joining an ever-increasing flow of Yugoslav military traffic.

A former star of Yugoslavia's national judo team, Aleks is ideal company for that kind of trip. We had already made a sortie to Bujanovac on Boxing Day, interviewing the local police chief who presented us with 'Extremism', an extraordinary book published by the Interior Ministry, cataloguing photographic evidence of mutilations allegedly carried out on Serb policemen by the Albanian guerrillas. As I was reading its account of torture and murder, sitting in a run-down Serbian restaurant in Bujanovac after the interview, a group of friendly plain-clothes policemen at another table asked me to give them the volume, insisting that I inscribe it with an appropriate dedication.

As we passed the nervous Serb police in blue flak jackets manning checkpoints on the outskirts of Bujanovac that warm spring evening, Albanian fighters fired on other police positions in the frontline town of Lucane some eight miles away, killing one Serb police officer to take the death toll in the Presevo conflict to 34. Two other policemen and three guerrillas were injured as the Albanians attacked the Serb police with mortars, 120 mm artillery and heavy machine guns. Detonations reverberated around the smoke-filled press centre in the municipal building in Bujanovac where correspondents from around the Balkans were following the conflict while simultaneously battling against the local Serb information ministry chief's clumsy use of Milosevic-era persuasion methods to ensure they sent bromides about the worsening military situation.

The following day the Albanian guerrillas pinned down a high-level target in Belgrade's new pro-western Government. Nebojsa Covic, the Serb Deputy Prime Minister with responsibility for southern Serbia and a former mayor of Belgrade, was one of the most energetic figures to emerge from the uprising against Milosevic. He was trapped by the fighting at Lucane for several hours after he drove to the town to try to finalise a ceasefire agreement to be signed between Albanian and Serb leaders. Covic's car was sprayed with bullets. The rebels made no meaningful distinction between Milosevic's clique and his opponents.

As the maelstrom in southern Serbia worsened, the guerrillas adopted some ruthless tactics, as we found out when we visited the village of Oslare and it was attacked by the UCPMB.

I made the journey to Oslare through bucolic fields of wheat and red peppers to try to interview the family of a 12-year-old Serbian boy, Ivan Velickovic, who had been wounded in the morning's bombardment unleashed by guerrillas in wooded hills overlooking Yugoslav Army positions.

Everything was peaceful in Oslare until we parked on the village outskirts, in front of an Albanian farmhouse that had also been targeted by the UCPMB. A few Yugoslav soldiers in steel helmets and full battle gear eyed us curiously from positions under trees in nearby fields.

As we walked to the building, three mortar shells exploded uncomfortably close to us, one of them perhaps 10 yards away. Fighting off panic, we dropped to the ground before scrambling behind a stone wall. There was just enough time to whip out a tourist camera and snap a souvenir picture of Emiliano Bos, a young Vatican Radio reporter in our group, as he took cover.

We ran doubled up along the wall after a long-haired Serb reporter and piled into the simple farm kitchen. There the farmer, Ilaza Jahiha, was comforting his terrified ten-year-old daughter as another blast rocked their home. The girl's grandmother, who had been busy cutting the throats of turkeys to sell at a local market, looked out stoically through the white *shami* (veil) wrapped around her hair.

The paradox of Albanians being targeted by their self-declared liberators, who perhaps relished the prospect of publicity from killing journalists, was lost on us as we sprinted for our car and sped away after an agonising three-point turn during a lull in the firing.

'We can leave but those poor people have to stay there,' Emiliano mused as our driver Saša, a Serbian photographer for the European Photo Agency, gunned his battered Opel into the relative safety of the Serb neighbourhood of the village where small boys were playing basketball.

It was good to find Aleks back at the cramped press room. 'Mr Phillips, causing trouble all over the Balkans again,' he said.

Later, after Turkish coffee and a restorative glass of rakija in one of Bujanovac's less crummy bars, we drove past Yugoslav tanks and talked our way through positions held by camouflaged Serb men and women special forces troops under Albanian sniper fire in Lucane, the scene of fierce fighting, winding our way back to the spooky, guerrilla stronghold of Konculj to watch diplomatic efforts to prevent a new war in the Balkans.

Negotiations aimed at achieving a ceasefire for the protection of civilians had previously failed when the UCPMB commanders refused to agree to Yugoslav troops entering the town of Veliki Trnovac (in Albanian Ternoc i Madh), which western diplomatic sources said had become an international centre for trafficking in narcotics, arms and illegal immigrants by Russian, Serbian and Albanian criminal gangs.

A NATO special envoy, Pieter Feith, a Dutchman about whom we would hear more later, wrangled for hours with Musliu, the UCPMB commander, during talks at an Italian-style villa. A British Army officer in the KFOR peacekeeping force escort that ferried Mr Feith to the guerrillas' mountain lair nodded to a fighter in black fatigues and gold shoulder flash fidgeting with a bayonet on an AK-47 Kalashnikov assault rifle on the road leading to the UCPMB military command. Feith had taken over negotiations from Sean Sullivan, a US political adviser to KFOR.

In the dimly lit street in front of a shop packed with singing village folk, a guerrilla commander who called himself Skorpion said the tiny liberation army made no distinction between its erstwhile enemies in the Government of Milosevic and the democratic reformers now in office in Belgrade. Many of his men were armed with modern sniper rifles bought from corrupt, badly paid soldiers in the Yugoslav Army. The bushy-bearded Musliu was equally uncompromising when he met us by the now-abandoned negotiating table decorated with Albanian, US, British and NATO flags. 'We shall fight to the last man,' he said with a mischievous grin.

The breakdown in negotiations led the Yugoslav Army to postpone its deployment into the buffer zone near the Macedonian border. Eventually a ceasefire was signed on 12 March, under which the army and Serb police agreed to withdraw heavy weapons from Lucane.

On the sand-bagged front line in Lucane, a short time after midnight, Frederick Dahl of Reuters and I met exhausted Serbian soldiers who marvelled that the ceasefire was holding. They were optimistic that the town's population was returning. 'Today we heard children's voices from the houses for the first time in eight days,' said a huge special force soldier in a black woollen cap whose nickname was John Z.

> Prayers were held at the mosque today. We have had enough of everything. I burst an eardrum when they fired rockets into this post on Friday, killing one of our comrades, but I refused to leave the line. Now our officers are sleeping. We certainly don't intend to shoot first. We just want to make ourselves comfortable and relax.

The deployment on 14 March of the Yugoslav Army in Zone C, or Zone Charlie East as the Americans know it – the nine-square-mile southern strip of the buffer zone adjoining the Macedonian border as well as Kosovo – was virtually bloodless. The UCPMB had pulled back to Konculj and other strongholds elsewhere in the buffer zone. Many of its fighters and part of the KPC began preparing for a new, more explosive struggle in Macedonia, which now became the focus for former KLA nationalists in the region, threatening to spin out of control into a full-scale Balkan war.

After the NATO bombing campaign of 1999 ended the crackdown by Serb forces on ethnic Albanians in Kosovo, many ethnic Albanians in Macedonia hoped that an independent Kosovar state would be set up to give them leverage to obtain greater rights from the Macedonian Slavs (or 'ethnic Macedonians' as they prefer to be described). Some militants hoped that ultimately Kosovo would provide a 'Piedmont' for the ethnic Albanians concentrated in western Macedonia just as the northern Italian region had spearheaded the unification of Italy in the nineteenth century.

Such aspirations were encouraged by KLA leaders such as Jakup Krasniqi, the organisation's first spokesman, a former history teacher from Cirez. 'His early pronouncements on how the KLA was intent on forming a Greater Albania, which would consist of Kosovo, Albania and Albanian-inhabited parts of Macedonia and Montenegro, did the organisation great harm,' Tim Judah noted.[5]

The KLA was founded by members of former Marxist-Leninist émigré groups from Kosovo and Macedonia who were mainly active in Switzerland and Germany in the 1970s and 1980s. These groups demanded an independent Kosovo republic that, it was envisioned, would ultimately join Albania. Initially these groups were inspired by Albania's Stalinist dictator, Enver Hoxha, but they later abandoned Marxism in favour of a purely nationalist approach.

The KLA's view on Macedonia was summed up by Pleurat Sejdiu, the head of the London branch of the People's Movement for Kosovo, or LPK, which also spawned the National Liberation Army (NLA) in Macedonia. The LPK was known to have long favoured an armed struggle to bring about Kosovo's independence and the unification of Albanians, particularly those of the former Yugoslavia. 'Kosova starts at Tivar (Bar in Montenegro) and ends in Manastir (Bitola in Macedonia). We don't care what America and England think about it, we should unite with actions, not with words.'[6]

The LPK grew out of the LPRK, the Popular Movement for the Republic of Kosovo. When the KLA was founded by the LPK in 1993, a four-man 'Special Branch' was appointed to prepare it. Among them was a man known by his pseudonym, Abaz Xhuka, who continued to live underground in Macedonia until 2001. The KLA claimed responsibility for the bombing of police stations in Prilep and Kumanovo in January 1998. Abaz Xhuka was later known as Ali Ahmeti, the NLA's political leader, who launched the ethnic Albanian rebellion of 2001. Ahmeti's closest friends still refer to him as Abaz.[7]

Alija Isam Ahmeti was born on 4 January 1959 in the village of Zajas, near Kičevo, where he attended elementary and secondary school. He was a student at the philosophy faculty in Pristina but never graduated. He entered politics as a student and at 20 was sentenced by the Yugoslav authorities to six months imprisonment, which he served in Macedonia in a prison for dissidents who rejected communist ideas. After his release, Ahmeti fled to Switzerland but later returned to Kosovo to organise demonstrations in the province with other Kosovar nationalists.

In 1980, Ahmeti joined the separatist group called Marxist-Leninists of Kosovo, organising the dramatic student demonstrations that were held in Pristina the following year. Afterwards he again emigrated to Switzerland, where he joined the banned Movement for an Albanian Socialist Republic in Yugoslavia. In 1985 he formed a sub committee for Macedonia of the Marxist-Leninists of Kosovo. Ahmeti has said that the greatest influence on him ideologically was his uncle, Fazli Veliju, an Albanologist and former high school teacher also resident in Switzerland.

Kosovo was always an important point of reference for many ethnic Albanian politicians in Macedonia. The Democratic Party of Albanians (DPA) leader, Arben Xhaferi, is from a Kosovar family with Turkish connections. A large number of other Albanian activists in Macedonia were, like Ahmeti, educated at Pristina's old Yugoslav University.

Even before the LPK special committee was set up, the idea of the KLA had been discussed at a meeting in a Zurich club attended by Ahmeti and his uncle, a minister of Kosovo's 'shadow government',

Ramush Tahiri and other Albanian activists, including Ermush Xhemaili, who went on to be the military coordinator of the National Liberation Army in Macedonia.[8]

From 1993, the KLA used areas of western Macedonia with a majority ethnic Albanian population as a natural base for their operations. Macedonia was used as a transit zone for transferring weapons from Albania and Greece to KLA fighters in Kosovo. Ahmeti returned to Macedonia that year and formed a local branch of the National Committee for Kosovo. By 1997, he was based in Tirana where he organised guerrilla groups entering Kosovo and attacking the police. Ahmeti is believed to have fought in some of the clashes in Kosovo as a KLA soldier. After the war in Kosovo ended, Ahmeti returned to Macedonia.

Hashim Thaci, the former KLA commander who went on to create the Democratic Party of Kosovo, was determined to press for independence. His biggest problem was that the UN administration in Kosovo, UNMIK, replaced the provisional government that he set up immediately after the Kosovo war. On 28 October 2000, Thaci hit another snag in his plans when the Democratic League of Kosovo led by Ibrahim Rugova, Kosovo's pacifist leader, trounced him in a landslide victory in the province's first democratic elections. The local polls showed that Thaci had only half the political support of Rugova and had little practical impact on the political structure in Kosovo.

British peacekeeping troops braced for a possible backlash by former KLA gunmen, who were bitter at the prospect of relinquishing the control of municipalities that they had been given by the UN after the Yugoslav troops withdrew. Deep divisions on the future of Kosovo opened between Britain and the USA. British irritation at what it described as 'extremely irresponsible' behaviour in the region was aroused when a senior US State Department source refused to rule out independence for Kosovo under the existing UN resolution. 'The more open-ended guarantees that we give on independence, the more we are creating potential trouble for ourselves in the future,' the commander of British peacekeeping troops in the province, Brigadier Robert Fry, told me. 'Independence for Kosovo would mean having a festering sore in the middle of the Balkans.' Reports of the American ambitions for an independent Kosovo followed a visit to the province by Richard Holbrooke, the Americans' chief policymaker in the Balkans at the time.

Against this background, the former KLA leaders had shifted the focus of the struggle for Albanian rights, and the search for territory to southern Serbia, where democratic Yugoslav forces were seeking to establish themselves after the overthrow of Milosevic. The KLA was forced to revise its objectives further after Al Gore lost the US presidential election and Holbrooke's hopes of forging an independent Kosovo as US Secretary of State were dashed.

The West increasingly leaned toward Britain's policy of opposing the creation of more mini-states in the region amid doubts that Kosovo's war-ravaged economy would be able to support an independent state. Britain had also long supported the integrity of Macedonia and for a period in the early 1990s sought to persuade it to re-join Yugoslavia or a reconstituted Yugoslav federation.

Paradoxically, the demise of Milosevic was in part a blow to the Albanian nationalists in Kosovo. They could no longer claim they were oppressed by him. In this way, western sympathy for their cause was diminished. The former KLA men moved their attention away from Kosovo's internal politics to sponsoring guerrilla activity in the Presevo valley, the demilitarised five-kilometre-wide buffer zone, established in 1999 as part of the July military-technical agreement between KFOR and the Yugoslav Army (VJ). The agreement allowed only police with small arms inside the buffer zone and forbade all VJ forces access. Heavy weapons were excluded.

The avowed aim of the UCPMB was to capture the southern Serbian counties of Presevo, Medvedja and Bujanovac which have historical ethnic Albanian majorities.[9] They began to form and operate within the buffer zone as early as November or December 1999.

The former KLA command was testing the strength of the new democratic government in Belgrade headed by Vojislav Kostunica, the Yugoslav President, a 'moderate' Serb nationalist, and was hoping to provoke a counter-revolution in favour of Milosevic, who was at large then in his villa in the Belgrade suburb of Dedinje, or to help foment a *coup d'état* by his Yugoslav Army supporters.

Hours after observing the Yugoslav deployment in the buffer zone that effectively closed down the UCPMB, I received a call from my daily newspaper assigning me to travel that night to the Macedonian city of Tetovo, 25 miles west of the capital, Skopje. Shooting had broken out in Tetovo, as 5,000 Albanians chanting slogans in favour of the KLA staged protests in support of ethnic Albanian rebels. The rebels had seized the villages of Brest and Malina Mahala in fierce fighting with elite Macedonian 'Wolves' special forces units[10] after US airborne peacekeepers on 7 March had flushed the insurgents out of Tanusevci, a village on the border with Kosovo. Heavy machine gun fire and mortar blasts were heard from the direction of the border with Kosovo.

Skirmishes had begun around Tanusevci and Debelde in late February after Belgrade ceded Tanusevci to Macedonia in a bilateral border agreement that deeply upset the former KLA. (The agreement would remain a source of tension between ethnic Albanian leaders in Kosovo and Skopje into 2003.) An ethnic Albanian was killed by a Macedonian sniper and ethnic Albanians began moving their families out of the villages. The NLA began its offensive in the area the same day that the Yugoslav Army re-entered Zone C.

In his account, Churcher argues that the events at Tanusevci followed planning for an insurrection in early 2001 by extremist Albanian political thinkers, usually of Macedonian origin, who were members of the LPK and LPCK (National Movement for the Liberation of Kosovo) parties and wanted to follow up on the war in Kosovo. However, he says it would seem that the uprising was precipitated in reaction to provocation by the ethnic Slav Macedonians, who evidently wanted to stage a small 'incident to order' in advance of a summit of Balkan Prime Ministers being held in Skopje on 22–23 February and to divert attention from a domestic scandal over unauthorised telephone tapping that was then rocking the nationalist-led Government. The Albanians certainly were not planning an insurrection in February but the Interior Ministry attack on Tanusevci precipitated the revolt.

The trouble began when a hitherto unknown Macedonian TV crew working for the well-known TV station A1 claimed to have been kidnapped by ethnic Albanians for a few hours in Tanusevci. After their release there was reportedly a one-hour fire-fight when a Macedonian unit from the border forces tried to enter the village. Villagers said that nobody returned fire at the security forces but an Albanian boy or young man from the village, Muzafer Xhaferi, was shot in the back of the neck and died. A two-hour gun battle was reported on 26 February and described by the Macedonian special forces as a major battle. Special forces officers said that 200 'black uniformed invaders' were waiting to infiltrate into Macedonia from Kosovo and Presevo.

On 4 March, two Macedonian soldiers were killed by the hitherto almost unknown National Liberation Army now occupying half of Tanusevci. By 8 March, the US KFOR forces had occupied quite a large part of Tanusevci, officially convinced that their GPS positioning devices showed them still to be in Kosovo. Two days earlier, US forces shot two Albanians apparently pointing weapons at the patrol, the first time presumed members of ethnic Albanian armed groups had been hit by KFOR troops.

On 9 March, the Macedonian Deputy Interior Minister, Refet Elmazi, and Ljube Boskovski, at the time Secretary of State for Interior Affairs, were pinned down by NLA gunmen near the village of Brest.

A Macedonian policeman was killed but Elmazi and Boskovski got back to Skopje. The incident undoubtedly contributed to the nationalist Boskovski adopting tough tactics when he became Minister of the Interior two months later. Elmazi, an Albanian whose appointment was daring for the Government given the usual total ethnic Macedonian control of the Interior Ministry, had supported the claim by the villagers that nobody had been firing on the Wolves when Xhaferi was killed.

Tanusevci, located high on a border ridge, was in origin the summer grazing village of Vitinje, now in Kosovo. Until 1947, Tanusevci and Vitinje had been part of the same administrative county (the Vardar Banovina). The new border disrupted the sheep farmers' traditional regional habits by dividing the villages that wanted to stay together.

These harbingers of the Macedonian conflict had largely been ignored by the international media, though seasoned observers such as Michael Keats, the United Nations press chief in Kosovska Mitrovica, and Dragan Petrovic, the Belgrade correspondent on *The Times*, had foreseen the situation arising.

Our Serbian taxi lurched through the deserted streets of Skopje, past the railway station clock with its hands still stuck at 5:16, the time when an earthquake erupted in the city on a morning in late July 1963, killing about 1,000 people, injuring 3,000 and leaving some 100,000 homeless. We made for the Grand Hotel, which was rapidly filling with correspondents and television crew. Across the capital, crouched in a great valley surrounded by mountains, local radio stations beamed details of the latest clashes.

A police spokesman, Stevo Pendarovski, said the trouble in Tetovo began when about 15 rebels opened fire with rifles in the suburb of Kale about 1.2 miles north of the city centre and in the nearby village of Selce. 'Police are being shot at, and they are responding,' said a Macedonian Army spokesman, Blagoja Markovski.

Thanks to the international community, an uneasy peace had returned to Southern Serbia. At one point in previous weeks, KFOR Russian and American peacekeeping troops deployed in a joint patrol beat off an attack by UCPMB gunmen, the first time the two countries' soldiers had fought together against a common enemy since the Second World War. But the Albanian nationalism subscribed to by the hard men forged by the KLA's struggle and their followers, with or without American backing, was like a brush fire. Once extinguished in one area of the Balkans, it reignited almost immediately elsewhere in the region. Churcher believes that:

behind the scenes the Skopje government was looking for a military solution, and avoiding talks with its own Albanian governing coalition partner, the DPA... In fixing the Tanusevci problem through violence the Macedonian government may well have been speeding up the process of the destruction of its own newly formed state.[11]

The DPA also may have turned a blind eye to the events on the border because the area supports its rival, the old (formerly socialist/communist partisan oriented) Party of Democratic Prosperity (PDP), he adds. 'The Macedonian units fully intended to 'go in hard', and this was undoubtedly going to leave a legacy of bitterness in the Albanian community in Macedonia.'

Now Macedonia was teetering on the edge of a civil war that threatened to engulf not only the UCPMB's former killing fields but also Kosovo itself and much of south-eastern Europe. Among those who were outraged at the prospect was Milcho Manchevski, the director of the award-winning film *Before the Rain*, a haunting prophecy of Macedonian ethnic conflict. He reflected:

> During the ten years of fighting in what was once Yugoslavia, Macedonia managed to remain unscathed, without help from the international community. After tense negotiations, the Yugoslav Army left peacefully, an admirable effort credited mainly to the first Macedonian president, Kiro Gligorov. There was tension – Gligorov himself survived an assassination attempt – but no fighting.[12]

> Albanian militants claim that they are fighting for human rights. This is a mantra which has proved to be a winning argument in the past. However this time it is a front for an armed redrawing of borders... does one fight for language recognition with mortar fire and snipers?

Manchevski's view was shared by many international observers. Western diplomats in Kosovo seeking to contain the conflict would repeatedly point to what they saw as the considerable integration of Albanian parties in the Macedonian political process. They concluded correctly that the violence was to a large extent imported. Manchevski's analysis glossed over the arrogance with which many ethnic Macedonians, especially government officials, often treated ethnic Albanians. The ethnic Albanians further claimed their status amounted to a kind of European Apartheid system that denied them essential human dignity. Throughout the conflict the dividing line between basic rights and preferential treatment would be blurred.

As Churcher implies, Manchevski also ignored a strand of adventurism at work within the nationalist ethnic Macedonian security forces' command, especially during the events of Tanusevci. Whether the insurrection could have been avoided by a softer approach to Tanusevci of course is impossible to prove.

More importantly, perhaps, a backlash against the ethnic Albanian insurgents by ethnic Macedonian hardliners in the army, security forces and Slavonic paramilitary organisations trained by Serb paramilitaries would provide fresh grievances to radicalise the Albanian population, including events in Tetovo itself.

Reporting is sometimes called writing front-line history. Working in Macedonia as it struggled to avoid civil war inspired me to try and learn more about the Macedonians' past.

2 Historical Introduction

Muravia came into existence as a result of the fear and jealousy of four countries... There's little here that any of those countries especially wanted, but no three of them would agree to let the fourth have it. The only way to settle the thing was to make a separate country out of it.
Dashiel Hammett, This King Business

MACEDONIAN ETHNICITY HAS ALWAYS been the most disputed in the Balkans. The Bulgarians asserted that Macedonia was part of great Bulgaria and the Greeks swore that it was a sacred part of Greece. The Serbs insisted it was southern Serbia and the Albanians that much of Macedonia was part of great Albania, the homeland of the ancient Illyrians. The Macedonians' true identity was contested for centuries because of their heterogeneous ethnic mix.

In the late nineteenth century, however, the Macedonian Christians began fighting for a Macedonian homeland independent from Ottoman rule. Their resistance movement, the Internal Macedonian Revolutionary Organisation (IMRO), inspired the nationalist party with the same name under which it held office in Skopje, the capital, until late 2002. The older party had a chequered history in the inter-war years, pioneering the use of urban terrorism, including the assassination of King Aleksandar of Yugoslavia in 1934. So it is hardly surprising that Macedonia sometimes appears to have such tragic potential for political violence today. And yet, as we shall see, after the Macedonians finally obtained independence they would demonstrate an impressive capacity to step back from the brink of the full-scale civil war that consumed Bosnia, Croatia and Kosovo as Yugoslavia imploded. The founders of the IMRO dreamt of a multi-ethnic Macedonia living in such relative harmony as the Macedonian state could be said to have enjoyed in the first years after it seceded from Yugoslavia in 1992.

Historians have debated how far modern Macedonia is the fulfilment of the old IMRO programme or of the aspirations of the nineteenth-century Macedonian Christians. The liberal, nationalist and official wings of the new Macedonian state insist such continuity exists. Many of their colleagues in Bulgaria, Greece and Serbia challenge this interpretation.[1] Yet, any traveller who has been fortunate enough to visit modern Macedonia and study its enchanting culture can vouch for the country's special identity separate from those of its neighbours, each of whom evidently, nevertheless, have contributed some of their best qualities to Macedonian society.

Before the First World War, Macedonia was a focus for great power rivalry. Russia encouraged Bulgarian claims to the territory under Ottoman rule. The Russians wanted to extend their influence throughout the Balkans, the area extending from the eastern Alps to the Aegean and the Black Sea, from the Dniester to the Adriatic – over the lands inhabited by Romanian, South Slav, Albanian and Greek speakers. The Russians worked through the Orthodox Church and through support for the oppressed or newly free Slav peoples in the region. Albanian nationalism developed partly in response to the Bulgarian and Serb-sponsored Macedonian patriots' agitation, contesting some of the same territory such as the southern city of Bitola.[2]

Traditionally, Macedonians feel threatened by the 'four wolves' – Albania, Bulgaria, Greece and Serbia. The Balkan wars were fought for control of Macedonia, and Serbia colonised the part of Macedonia it received after the Second Balkan war in 1913, making it part of Yugoslavia, the kingdom of the southern Serbs. Tito and Stalin, the kingdom's enemies, created the first Macedonian republic in 1944 to further Yugoslav Communism and by the 1960s Macedonian historiography had begun laying claim to the heritage of Alexander the Great. But the ethnic mix dominated by southern Slavs in modern Macedonia bears little relation to the nationalities that he commanded.

Macedonia's strategic significance as a crossroads between the northern and southern Balkans has led to fears that civil war in Macedonia could ignite a much wider war involving a scramble for territory between Bulgaria, Greece, Serbia and Albania possibly supported by its ally, Turkey. Historian R.J. Crampton has cautioned that internecine conflict in Macedonia might precipitate a fundamental change in the Balkan balance of power. In the event of Turkish intervention:

the whole of the eastern Mediterranean basin, with its access to the Suez canal and the Black Sea, would be threatened with chaos. NATO's cohesion would be endangered by Greek-Turkish disagreements and in the worst of scenarios world peace could be threatened.[3]

Since the end of the Bosnian and Kosovo wars and the overthrow of Slobodan Milosevic, Macedonia has been the most unstable country of the Balkans.

The History of Macedonia

Macedonians trace their history to Caranus, the earliest known king of the Macedonians, a tribe closely related to the Hellenes, who flourished from 808 to 778 BC. The Macedonian dynasty Argeadae originated in Argos Orestikon, a city located in the south-western Macedonian region of Orestis. Alexander I Philhellene (498–454 BC) expanded the kingdom, and by 400 BC the Macedonians had forged a unified kingdom.

Alexander III (the Great, 356–323 BC) succeeded Philip II at age 20, precipitated a revolt by the Thracians, Illyrians and the Greeks and invaded Persia. Alexander's victories at Granicus, Issus and Gaugamela put an end to the Persian Empire, which was replaced by a Macedonian Empire stretching from Europe to Egypt and India.

After Alexander's death, the Macedonian Empire was carved up between generals. The dynasty of Antigonus I took over Macedonia and Greece. Under Antigonus II, Macedonia achieved a stable monarchy and strengthened its occupation of Greece. His grandson, Philip V (222–179 BC), clashed with Rome, which was expanding eastwards, and fought the Macedonian Wars against the Romans. But after the Roman army defeated Philip in Thessaly, Macedonia was reduced to its original borders. In the third Macedonian War, Rome finally defeated the Macedonian army under the last king, Philip V's son Perseus (179–168 BC). Perseus' death in Italy marked the end of the Macedonian kingdom, and by 146 BC Macedonia had become a Roman province.

To modern Macedonian historians, however, it matters little that 'the only things that can be said with any certainty about the ancient Macedonians is that they were not of Slavic origin'.[4]

Saints Clement and Naum and the Ohrid School

The Apostle Paul brought Christianity to the Macedonian towns of Philippi, Salonika and Beroea in AD 51. The southern Slavs arrived in the hitherto mainly Greek-speaking Macedonia in the sixth century. In the next century, the Bulgars followed the Slavs into the Balkans and started their struggle against Byzantium. In the second half of the ninth century, a Bulgarian king, Tsar Boris, overran part of Macedonia.

The brothers Saints Cyrillus and Methodius of Salonika created the first Slavic alphabet and translated Christian scriptures into the language used by the local Slavs. Their disciples St. Clement and St. Naum established the first Slavic university, the Ohrid Literary School, in Ohrid's old town. Here, St. Clement probably reformed St. Cyril's alphabet, calling it the Cyrillic alphabet in honour of his teacher. The establishment of the first Slavic bishopric, later to become the Ohrid Archbishopric during the reign of Tsar Samuil, is considered by the modern Macedonian Orthodox Church as an anticipation of its own creation in 1967.

Macedonia, or parts of it, alternated between Bulgarian and Byzantine rule until the thirteenth and fourteenth centuries, when the country came under the Serbian Tsars, principally Stefan Dusan, who made Skopje his capital. In 1346, the Archbishop of Serbia declared himself 'Patriarch of the Serbs and the Greeks'. The Serbian Empire disintegrated with the death of Stefan Dusan in 1355.

After the Turks invaded the Balkans, Macedonia came under Turkish suzerainty in 1371, beginning five and a half centuries of Ottoman rule. Until the sixteenth century, the Ottoman Empire won the support of many Christians by extending privileges or local autonomies to groups who agreed to police Ottoman routes, mountain passes and river traffic along the Danube. It recognized Orthodox Christians, Jews and Armenians as separate self-governing communities on religion-related matters. There were virtually no religious revolts among the Balkan Christians until the 1590s. The patriarch of Constantinople enjoyed greater ecclesiastical and secular jurisdiction under the Ottoman sultans than under the Byzantine emperors, reflecting the Turkish desire to perpetuate the rift between the Catholic and Orthodox worlds.

In the heyday of the Ottoman Empire in the Balkans, Orthodox Christians were not subject to unmitigated tyranny and persecution as nineteenth-century nationalists would claim. The average Balkan peasant during the early Ottoman Empire tilled his land under better conditions than his opposite number in Christian Europe. When the Turks overran the Balkan peninsula, they abolished the feudal arrangements prevailing under the former Byzantine, Latin, Serbian and Bulgarian rulers. They introduced a more lenient and centralised feudal system of their own and imposed a lighter tax burden than did their Christian counterparts.

Ottoman domination isolated most of the Balkans from the rest of Europe and the Orthodox world from the rest of Christendom. In

1459, the Turks suppressed the Serbian Orthodox Patriarchate and put Church administration under the Bulgarian Archbishopric of Ohrid, extending its authority until they got into Hungary. To give some satisfaction to the Serbs and ensure they remained under a spiritual authority that he could control, the Sultan restored the Serbian Patriarchate with its seat at Ipek (Pec) in 1557. The patriarchate had its largest jurisdiction ever, from northern Macedonia and Eastern Bulgaria across Serbia, Montenegro, and Bosnia and Herzegovina to the Orthodox settlements in Hapsburg and Venetian territory. But it was suppressed once more in 1766. In 1777, the Bulgarian Archbishopric of Ohrid ceased to be an independent or 'autocephalous' church, and the Turks placed the Greek patriarchate in charge of both churches on the ground that they were looking to Rome for support. The Constantinople patriarchate reigned supreme again and would do so for as long as the Balkan peoples remained subject to Ottoman authority. In the nineteenth century, the newly independent Balkan states each gained autocephalous churches.

The Christians had a substantial degree of religious freedom under Ottoman rule but not religious equality. Non-Muslims were forbidden to ride horses or bear arms. They were required to pay a special capitation tax levied on all non-Muslim adult males in place of military service. Until the seventeenth century, the Orthodox Christians paid the tribute in children, from which the Jews and the Armenians were exempted. Their position was far from ideal and they were subject to outbursts of Muslim fanaticism. However, they arguably enjoyed more freedom than did many religious minorities in Christendom such as the Huguenots in Catholic France, the Catholics in Anglican England, the Orthodox Christians in Catholic Poland, the Muslims in Catholic Spain or the Jews in all the Christian lands.

Balkan Christianity survived the centuries of Muslim rule with remarkably few losses. But the most important conversions to Islam in the Balkans occurred in Albania and Bosnia with the majority of their populations turning away from Christianity by the middle of the seventeenth century. The Balkan Christians were never subjected to systematic and sustained proselytising. But large scale Islamisation of Albanians began after Skandenberg's revolt in alliance with Venice had been put down in 1486, along with an exodus of Catholic Albanians to southern Italy. By the eighteenth century, some two thirds of the Albanian population are estimated to have been Muslim.

The exceptional impact of Islam on the Albanians would have long-term consequences for Macedonia, setting the stage for religious conflict with the Macedonian Slavs. The Albanians expanded during the eighteenth and nineteenth centuries into 'Old Serbia', particularly the Kosovo region, Macedonia and Thessaly. Since many Serbs already had migrated northward, the Albanians were able to assimilate those that remained behind. The southern and eastern Balkans became a conglomerate – Hellenic, Slav, Romance, Turkish, Albanian – of inhabitants of frequently ambivalent identity. Kosovo would, however, remain predominantly Albanian until the twentieth century when it became part of the Yugoslav state.

The Ottoman authorities encountered so much resistance in mountainous northern Albania that in the sixteenth century they granted the area complete autonomy and tax exemption in return for contingents of fighting men. The Albanians' fierce tradition of independence would also have long-term repercussions in Macedonia.

By the early seventeenth century, the Ottoman Empire was in a state of disintegration. After the death of Suleiman the Magnificent, a succession of incapable sultans lost control of the Empire, leaving it leaderless and powerless. The Empire's administration became corrupted and its wars were increasingly defensive and unsuccessful. Taxation was farmed out to the highest bidders, imposing a crushing fiscal burden on the peasant population, Muslim as well as Christian.

Corruption spread to the Ottoman armed forces and, by the early nineteenth century, the janissaries, the infantrymen who conquered the Balkans as frontier soldiers, had become useless as a fighting force. The Ottoman economy fell far behind that of Western Europe, since it had not experienced the Commercial Revolution that had produced joint-stock companies trading on a world-wide basis. French, English and Dutch Levant companies exploited the resources of the Ottoman Empire, which suffered from marked inflation after the mid sixteenth century.

Politically, the Ottoman Empire also lagged behind Western Europe, which witnessed the rise of nationalism and the nation state along with the growth of absolute monarchies, the appearance of a middle class and the spread of literacy throughout the Renaissance. The Ottoman Empire remained a constellation of peoples, religions and conflicting loyalties that failed to command the active allegiance of all its subjects. These developments strengthened the western world and enabled it to halt the Turks at Vienna in 1683. In the eighteenth century, Austria and Russia were easily able to annex vast provinces north of the Danube. By the beginning of the nineteenth century, the Turks had lost Hungary, Transylvania, Croatia, Slavonia and Dalmatia to the Hapsburgs and the northern shore of the Black Sea to the Russians.

In the nineteenth century, the Balkan peoples thus were divided among the three empires of Eastern Europe. The lack of Ottoman nationalism left a vacuum that was filled by Balkan, Arab and even Turkish nationalisms. The Enlightenment also created a new intellectual climate in the Balkans that was not primarily religious. But the extension of Austro-Russian expansion to the south made it more difficult for the Balkan peoples to win their independence.

After the Serbian uprisings of 1804–1813 and 1815 and the Greek war of independence of 1821–1829, the great powers remained reluctant to permit the collapse of any of the empires that were products of old or pre-1789 Europe, whether Ottoman, Hapsburg or Russian. The great powers pursued a policy of 'balkanizing' the Balkans, setting limits on the viability of those states, such as Greece, Serbia, Montenegro and Bulgaria, that had arisen from the partitioning of the Ottoman Empire.

By the terms of the Congress of Berlin of 1878, the great powers prevented the establishment of a Great Bulgaria, obstructed the goal of a Great Serbia by allowing Austria-Hungary to occupy Bosnia-Herzegovina and prevented Greece from annexing Macedonia. The great powers also denied the aspirations of the Albanian elites who aspired to a Great Albania including Kosovo, Macedonia and Epirus – territories to which Serbia, Bulgaria and/or Greece also laid claim.

Macedonian Nationalism

Macedonia's geographical area is bounded, in the north by the hills north of Skopje and by the Shar mountains; in the east by the Rila and Rhodope Mountains; in the south by the Aegean coast around Salonika, by Mount Olympus, and by the Pindus mountains; in the west, by lakes Prespa and Ohrid.[5] After the Balkan wars (1912–1913), Macedonia was carved up into the areas known as Vardar Macedonia, corresponding to the modern Macedonian state with the beautiful Vardar river running through Skopje; Pirin Macedonia (now in Bulgaria and named after the Pirin Mountains); and Aegean Macedonia (now in Greece).

'No other area in the Balkans has been the subject of so much dispute and the cause of so much bloodshed,' L.S. Stavrianos wrote. 'To a very considerable degree Balkan diplomacy since 1878 has revolved around the explosive question of how Macedonia should be divided among the three neighbouring countries, Bulgaria, Greece and Serbia.'[6]

In contrast to the fictional Balkan state of Muravia immortalised by the crime-writer Dashiel Hammett in his 1924 short story *This King Business*, Macedonia's strategic and economic value have made it the focus for ruthless struggle for centuries. It commands a great corridor route which leads from Central Europe to the Mediterranean along the Morava and Vardar valleys, a route which has invited countless invaders, Roman, Gothic, Hun, Slav, and Turkish. Macedonia was also desirable because it included the great port of Salonika as well as the much-coveted fertile plains in the mountainous Balkan peninsula. Macedonia, then, is a border area where several ethnic blocs meet and overlap. Stavrianos said:

> It cannot be called a melting pot because intermarriage between the several elements has been rare. Individual villages and even various groups within a single village have retained their identity over periods of centuries. This freezing of ethnic strains explains the extraordinary assortment of peoples that have survived to the present day in an area about half the size of the state of New York.

The inhabitants of Macedonia living close to the Greek, Bulgarian and Serbian frontiers in the mid nineteenth century could be classified as being mostly Greek, Bulgarian, and Serbian. According to Stavrianos, 'The remainder of the population, with the exception of such distinct minorities as Turks, Vlachs, Jews and Albanians, may be considered as distinctively Macedonian.' They had a dialect and cultural characteristics that justify their being classed as a distinct South Slav group.

In the nineteenth century Macedonians lagged behind their neighbours in developing a sense of national consciousness and so they were claimed by the Serbians, Bulgarians and Greeks, whose nationalism was inspired by the French Revolution. 'The Balkan states coveted the remaining Ottoman territories in Europe, because expansion would help them economically,' Stevan K. Pavlowitch wrote, 'and because people there aspired, or were deemed to aspire, to join them in order to escape the sultan's crumbling rule.'[7] The Serbs and Bulgarians feared that Austria-Hungary would try to occupy Macedonia as she would Bosnia-Herzegovina in 1878.

Each of the 'wolves' had plausible reasons why they felt they should rule Macedonia. The Serbs pointed to aspects of Macedonians' grammar and to their use as proofs of their Serbian origin of the *slava* festival – the feast of the patron saint of the home or village, monastery or region, traditionally celebrated by Slavs everywhere. The Bulgarians argued that physiologically the Macedonians were closer to them than to the Serbs and that Macedonian was a Bulgarian dialect. The Greeks stressed that the Macedonians were Orthodox Christians with many under the jurisdiction of the Patriarch of Constantinople. They also claimed that many Slav-speaking Macedonians considered themselves to be Greeks and they called them 'Slavophone Greeks'.

Once the Slavonic patriarchates had been suppressed, Greek culture dominated unchallenged in Macedonia until the middle of the nineteenth century, when Bulgarian influence grew. Schools provided Greek education, the churches offered Greek liturgy and the higher ecclesiastical posts were held by Greek prelates.

Macedonia was a jigsaw of religious beliefs as well as a long-standing ethnic fault line. Under Ottoman rule villagers from Anatolia were resettled among the Christian inhabitants of the area. In Albania, as we have seen, many Christians adopted Islam en masse. Mark Mazower observed that differences of doctrine often were not very important to Macedonian farmers. Asked what religion they were, 'the cautious peasants of western Macedonia would cross themselves and say "We are Muslims, but of the Virgin Mary."'[8]

'The language spoken by the Macedonians was certainly different from Serbian,' Noel Malcolm noted. 'But on the other hand many Slavs in this whole region of the Balkans did not have any strong sense of national identity at this stage.'[9] The Macedonian generally identified himself with his village or, if he thought more widely, would style himself an Orthodox Christian to set himself apart from Catholic or Muslim neighbours.

As Greek historians see it, the Macedonians might have become completely Hellenised were it not that most of the population was illiterate. Macedonia's peasant masses were largely untouched by Greek culture and continued to speak their Slavic dialects, leaving open the possibility of a national awakening in the future.

When Bulgaria, with Russian sponsorship, became a modern state in 1878, it challenged the Greek cultural monopoly in Macedonia. The Sultan recognised the Bulgarian Church, the Exarchate, in 1870, under Russian pressure, and allowed it to appoint its bishops in some Macedonian towns. Russia had a choice of Bulgaria or Serbia through which to exert her influence in the Balkans since Greece was non-Slav. Bulgaria was nearer geographically to Russia and controlled the land approaches to Constantinople and the Aegean. Before 1878, Bulgaria had needed Russian assistance more than Serbia, which had already declared its independence. Russia's selection of Bulgaria as its chief instrument in the region set off a bitter rivalry between the Serbs and Bulgarians that would be played out in Macedonia until well after the Second World War.

The Greek Patriarch in Constantinople pronounced the new autocephalous Bulgarian Church to be schismatic and the Greeks fought Bulgarian church, cultural and national influence in Macedonia. Bulgaria's Prime Minister, Stefan Stambolov, sought to win Macedonia for Bulgaria by a policy of peaceful penetration, cooperating with the Turks in return for concessions allowing the Bulgarian Church and schools to operate.

But in spite of the wolves' activities, Macedonia's nationalist movement, based in part on Christian Orthodox traditions, grew especially strong in the 1890s, campaigning for autonomy with the slogan 'Macedonia for the Macedonians'. The nationalists, many of them Macedonian exiles living in Bulgaria, were impatient with Stambolov's policies. Western sensitivity to the cause of the Christians in the Balkans gathered pace after Gladstone published his pamphlet 'Bulgarian Horrors and the Question of the East' in September 1876. Gladstone's efforts reached a climax with the Midlothian Campaign pillorying Tory policy on Turkey.

By the late 1890s, Macedonian agitation had entered a new phase, with frequent raids by members of the 'Internal Macedonian Revolutionary Organisation' (IMRO), the terrorist group founded in Salonika in 1893. Damian ('Dame') Gruev, a student and intellectual, was walking with a friend on the Salonika seafront when they ran into a young school teacher, Ivan Hadzhinikolov. They formed a revolutionary committee, which, with the addition of more friends three days afterwards, became the Macedonian Central Revolutionary Committee (*Makedonski tsentralen revoliutsoneren komitet*). Its seal consisted of a gun and dagger crossed under a bomb with the motto *Svoboda ili smrt deve* ('Freedom or Death'). A founding congress held in the town of Resen in 1893 adopted the name Internal Macedonian Revolutionary Organisation (IMRO, also known by its Bulgarian initials, VMRO). 'Macedonia was to become the original seedground not only of modern warfare and political conflict, but of modern terrorism and clerical fanaticism as well.'[10]

Gotse Delchev, a visionary teacher who was another of the very first nationalist luminaries who went on to become their most attractive and evocative national hero after he was killed in 1903 while fighting the Turks, rejected offers of assistance from neighbours. 'Those who believe that the answer to our national liberation lies in Bulgaria, Serbia or Greece might consider themselves a good Bulgarian, good Serb or a good Greek, but not a good Macedonian.' Delchev conceived of Macedonia as a cosmopolitan homeland for all its religious and ethnic groups. The first article of its rules and regulations was: 'Everyone who lives in European Turkey, regardless of sex, nationality, or personal beliefs, may become a member of IMRO'.

Delchev, born in Kilkis in 1872, had been expelled from the military academy in Sofia because of his extreme nationalist stance and went back to Macedonia as a Bulgarian teacher in Novo Selo near Stip. In 1896, he and G. Petrov wrote the organisation's statutes, which divided Macedonia into seven regions, each with a regional structure, and a central committee in Salonika as the supreme body. The IMRO was a highly professional, ruthless conspiratorial organisation. Each regional, district and village committee was to have its own secret police to issue death sentences and other punishments against enemies.[11] The nationalists envisaged a Greater Macedonia with an opening to an Aegean port. One of their main demands was the revision of the Treaty of Berlin on the Macedonian Question.[12]

The short-lived San Stefano treaty of 1878, by which Russia gave Bulgaria nearly all of Slav Macedonia, had contributed enormously to the struggle for Macedonia. Under San Stefano, Russia obliged Turkey to give Bulgaria Vranje, Skopje, Tetovo, Gostivar, the Black Drin, Debar and Lake Ohrid, as well as a strip of what became south-east Albania, parts of modern Greek Macedonia, and a strip of the Aegean coast west of Salonika. The basis for the San Stefano concept was that Bulgaria should acquire territory in all areas where two thirds of the adult male Orthodox population chose the Bulgarian Exarchate Church.

Before the end of the year, the other great powers had forced Russia to drop San Stefano and gave back the huge swathe of Macedonian territory from Sofia to Turkey under the Treaty of Berlin. Bulgarian policy thereafter would be driven by nostalgia for the Greater Bulgaria achieved briefly under San Stefano. Bulgaria would attack the Serbs in the second Balkan war and side with Germany in two world wars to try to retrieve it.

The Bulgarian, Serb and Greek pioneer priests and teachers[13] in Macedonia were later supported by armed bands known to the Turks as *komitadjis* or 'committee men', financed unofficially by the war offices or governments of Sofia, Athens and Belgrade. The British writer Rebecca West, in her 1930s travelogue on Yugoslavia, *Black Lamb and Grey Falcon*, observed many former committee men, some of whom recall the Macedonian fighters in 2001.[14]

Sofia and other Bulgarian cities were crowded with Macedonian refugees who infiltrated Bulgarian institutions, especially the army. More than a third of Bulgarian officers were from Macedonia. Sofia had only 20,000 inhabitants but the Bulgarians made it their capital because it was nearer to Macedonia. 'The Macedonians hated Stambolov for his perceived collaboration with Turkey and for his role in the murder of key IMRO leaders.'[15]

The IMRO conspirators assassinated Bulgarian ministers, threatened Bulgarian Prince Ferdinand and encouraged peasant riots. By 1895,

Ferdinand had pushed Stambolov out of office. A mob of Macedonians murdered the former prime minister. In 1895 some of the Macedonian agitators formed a rival organisation. This was known as the External Organisation because it was founded outside Macedonia, in Sofia, dedicated to liberating Macedonia and absorbing it into Bulgaria. The IMRO's slogan was 'Macedonia for the Macedonians' but the External Organisation wanted Macedonia for Bulgaria. Dame Gruev's rival Internal Organisation called for an autonomous, self-governing Macedonia. Official Macedonian historians argue that Gruev saw an autonomous Macedonia as a stepping stone to a state separate from Bulgaria.[16]

After the Ottoman-Greek war of 1897, the western powers renewed pressure on Istanbul to reform Macedonia. A congress of Macedonians and Bulgarians in Geneva was arranged for 1899, to demand the creation of an autonomous Macedonia that would include the vilayets of Monastir and Kosovo. In reaction, Albanian notables in Kosovo started campaigning more actively for their old idea of uniting the four vilayets with Albanian populations, Kosovo, Monastir, Ioannina and Shkroda, into one Albanian province.

The St. Elijah's Day Uprising

In 1903, Macedonian Christians staged the Ilinden uprising, establishing the Kruševo Republic that was crushed after ten days. It became the most hallowed event in the mythology of modern Macedonian nationalists.

Colonel Anastas Jankov, the main External Organisation leader outside Bulgaria, prepared the revolt with 100 armed followers in his home village of Zagoricani in western Macedonia in August 1902. The EO seized 28 villages close to Bulgaria and more than 500 Turkish soldiers and scores of Macedonian fighters died. Turkey recaptured the territory within days, however, and proceeded to arrest and kill leaders of the EO, even though they had opposed the insurrection on the ground that it was premature.

An anarchist faction of the IMRO, a group known as the Gemidzhi, ratcheted up the crisis by blowing up a French freighter, the *Guadalquivir*, in the port of Salonika and derailing a train from Istanbul, again in the hope of precipitating Great Power intervention. Salonika's gas piping was sabotaged, knocking out the city's lighting. The French-run *Banque ottomane* was blown up, killing many German residents in the Kegelklub district. Muslims lynched about 60 Slavs and the city governor imposed martial law as British and French gunboats anchored outside Salonika to protect western property and lives in the fortress.

Delchev was killed in a skirmish with Ottoman troops on 4 May 1903, his 'cloak flung over his left shoulder, his white fez, wrapped in a bluish scarf, pulled down, and his gun slung across his left elbow', according to a nearby comrade, Mihail Chakov.[17] But the movement outlived its charismatic founder, whose ashes would be held first in Athens and then in Sofia before being taken to their final resting place in Skopje.

By 2 August 1903, the feast-day of St. Elijah or Ilinden, the focus of the Macedonian national struggle had shifted to the town of Kruševo, in the mountains of central-western Macedonia. In the spring, its 10,000 Christian inhabitants had asked Ottoman authorities in Monastir (Bitola) to bolster the army garrison against the activities of the *cetas*, but to no avail.

Three hundred fighters in eight *cetas* attacked Kruševo on the evening of Ilinden, seizing the barracks and setting it alight. The town was declared a republic. Most of the guerrillas withdrew two weeks later after negotiations with the Turkish commander, Bachtiar Pasha, who had gathered 5,000 Ottoman troops supported by artillery 20 miles to the east to retake the town.

Turkish forces punished the inhabitants with four days of intense shelling. *Bashi Bazouks* (irregular troops recruited by the Turks from the local Muslim populations in the Balkans) rampaged through Kruševo, raping, burning and pillaging the Vlach and Greek districts but largely leaving the Bulgarian or Slav neighbourhood intact.

In the aftermath of Ilinden, however, thousands of Christian civilians were murdered and raped, 8,400 houses were destroyed and 50,000 refugees fled to the mountains, according to Bulgarian sources. The IMRO was almost wiped out, and Greek *andartes*, led by a pistol-brandishing bishop, Germanos Karavangelis, persecuted Slav villages in western Macedonia in retaliation for intimidation of Greek settlements, forcing re-conversion of Exarchate communities to the Patriarchate. In response, Belgrade also rejoined the struggle for Macedonia. The Serbian Prime Minister, Nikola Pasic, ordered Serb guerrillas into action in Porec, Kicevo, Drimkol, Dibra and Koprulu.

In October 1903, Austria-Hungary and Russia signed the Mürzsteg agreement, designed to guarantee the status quo in Macedonia while seeking to protect the Christian communities through an internationally inspired reorganisation of the Ottoman gendarmerie. The Sultan accepted the plan and, in a harbinger of modern western intervention in the Balkans, the great powers took control of gendarmerie zones in Macedonia.

The accord included a clause envisaging changes in boundaries 'with a view to a more regular group of the different nationalities', which

Bulgaria, Serbia and Greece interpreted as giving a green light to divide up Macedonia. Each side redoubled efforts in jockeying for the day when the administrative boundaries would be drawn up. The Balkan states were still deadlocked in the struggle for hegemony over Macedonia, which acquired an unenviable reputation.

'An image of Macedonia was created concerning Macedonia and the Macedonians,' Slobodan Markovic wrote. Macedonia started to be identified as a country of brigandage.[18] Nevertheless, British sympathisers with the Macedonian cause generated general condemnation in London of the atrocities perpetrated against Christians by the Turkish army and the Albanian irregular *Bashi Bazouks* as the St. Elijah's day rising was crushed.

James Bourchier, a partially deaf former master at Eton who liked to wear Bulgarian peasant dress while in the field as Balkan correspondent of the London *Times*, tried to influence British public opinion toward intervention. But the numbers of people killed in Macedonia were not considered sufficient to warrant risking western lives. Markovic credits Bourchier with changing British attitudes to the Balkans from an 'Orientalist' view, under which the Slavs were perceived as barbarians who were unable to think for themselves, to a 'Balkan' attitude. Slavs, while still regarded as inferior beings, were seen as powerful warriors who could tip the strategic balance.

After Russia's defeat by Japan in 1905, its foreign policy focused anew on south-eastern Europe, and Macedonia, the heart of what remained of the Ottoman Empire, was the main point of conflict with Austria-Hungary. In the summer of 1908, Britain and Russia appeared about to agree a new plan to reform Macedonia. But later that year reformist Ottoman army officers in Macedonia, irate at Ottoman feebleness and western intervention, led the Young Turk revolution against the Porte (the Ottoman administration), in spite of Sultan Abdulhamid deploying thousands of agents in Macedonia to try and choke off the conspiracy. The Sultan pledged to restore the 1876 Constitution but the decline in Ottoman power was irreversible. In October 1908, King Ferdinand proclaimed the full independence of Bulgaria by agreement with Austria-Hungary. Amid outrage in Belgrade that fuelled Serbian irredentism toward Macedonia, and ultimately led to the First World War, Austria annexed Bosnia-Herzegovina, prompting the new Balkan powers to wage war at last on the Ottoman Empire with a view to liberating Christian Macedonia.

The Balkan Wars

After the Italian invasion of Libya, Turkey moved substantial forces to North Africa. Greece, Bulgaria, Serbia and Montenegro formed an alliance to drive the Turks out of Macedonia while Serbia and Bulgaria in March 1912 initialled a related agreement dividing Macedonia between them in the aftermath of the conflict.

The first Balkan war began 8 October 1912 and lasted six weeks. Ottoman forces fought against the Bulgarians, Serbs and Greeks in Macedonia and within a week the Serbs had defeated the main Turkish force at Kumanovo and seized Skopje, massacring many Albanians. In Skopje, the underground society Black Hand installed itself near the Russian consulate and organised other revenge attacks on Albanians in retaliation for Albanian attacks on Slav Christians.

The Turks were finally defeated at Bitola in the largest battle of the first Balkan war. Greek forces beat Bulgarian troops in a race to seize Salonika and southern Macedonia.

The Rise of Albanian Nationalism

Greek expansion and Serbian territorial aggrandisement had already set off fears among the Albanian Muslims that the Porte might not defend them. The League of Prizren, founded by a group of Albanian intellectuals in 1878, sought to spread the Albanian language by opening several Albanian schools in southern Albania. Sultan Abdulhamid II cracked down, making it a crime to possess material written in Albanian. The League of Prizren was banned, and its leaders fled abroad. Christian and Muslim Albanians combined in 1896 to send a joint appeal to the Great Powers demanding a single administrative unit of Albanian-inhabited lands with Monastir as its capital.

Haji Mulla Zeka founded the first politicised Albanian guerrilla movement in 1899 to resist the Bulgarian revolutionary groups. Albanian Revolutionary Committees were formed in numerous towns in Albania by 1903 to prepare the ground for an uprising against the Ottoman Empire. For a time these allied with the Young Turk movement but when it became clear that the Committee of Union and Progress was dedicated to Turkish nationalism, Albanian nationalists began to agitate for an independent state. An Albanian uprising in Kosovo for independent schools in May 1912 led to the capture of Skopje by rebels in August and an amnesty by the government on 19 August 1912, meeting many insurgent demands.

The Treaty of London at the end of the first Balkan war left the status of Albania to be decided by the Great Powers. The London Conference of Ambassadors ruled, on 20 December 1912, that the country should become an independent state because the Ottoman Empire, by losing all of Macedonia, would no longer have any territorial connection to Albania. The Conference appointed commissions to delimit the frontiers with Montenegro and Serbia and with Greece. On the northern frontier, clashes broke out between the Albanians and Serbs who occupied territory that the ambassadors had assigned to Albania. The Serbs continued to hold the territories until forced out by an Austrian ultimatum in 1913. The frontier commission had not finished work when the First World War began.

The Serbian seizure of Albanian territory to the south of what was then Serbia would rankle with Albanian nationalists until the present day, providing a powerful historical basis for the resentments that set off the Albanian insurgencies in southern Serbia and western Macedonia in 2001, as well as for the resistance in Kosovo to oppression by Milosevic's regime.

In June 1913, the second Balkan war broke out, after Bulgaria attacked Serbia. Greece and Serbia counter-attacked and Turkey and Romania also fought Bulgaria. Large parts of Macedonia became southern Serbia under the Treaty of Bucharest signed in August, setting the scene for Bulgarian and Turkish support of Austro-Hungary in the First World War. Under the Treaty, Bulgaria retained of Macedonia only the middle Struma Valley, the upper Mesta Valley, and a westward-jutting salient in the Strumica valley. Neither the Supremacists nor the IMRO federalists, many of whom had fought with Bulgarian forces, were satisfied with the outcome.

Behaviour on all sides in the second Balkan war in particular would leave inter-ethnic scars that were passed down to present-day Macedonia. Pavlowitch wrote:

> All participants had behaved in such a way as to show that their aim in Macedonia was not only to acquire territory, but to get rid of rival or antagonistic ethnic groups… All sides had destroyed villages or quarters, killed civilians, practised extortions and forced assimilation.[19]

A Carnegie Endowment international commission of enquiry arrived in Macedonia at the end of the Balkan war. It reported in detail the brutal treatment handed out by all combatants to their enemies and to the civilian population, usually by irregulars but also by regular army units. The war, and the report, spared nobody. Bulgarians mistreated Greeks and Serbs and vice versa while Albanians and Turks mistreated Christians and vice versa. The opposing Bulgarian and Serbian views on the events of the Balkan wars and their outcome, with both sides robustly blaming the other, would persist up until the twenty-first century, along with deep suspicion and hostility between the Slavs and the ethnic Albanians.

Inter-War Macedonia

At the end of the First World War, Macedonia was partitioned into three. Bulgaria was left with a small chunk of 6,798 square kilometres, while the newly named Yugoslavia, with 26,776 square kilometres, and Greece, with 34,600 square kilometres, had much larger shares. Bulgaria never renounced its claim to the territory and Sofia remained the nerve centre of the IMRO, the most violent terrorist organisation in the Balkans. The IMRO allied itself with Ante Pavelic and his fascist Ustashas in Croatia, as well as with Fascist movements in Italy and Hungary. Bulgaria's relations with Yugoslavia and Greece were to be vitriolic for the next 25 years.

In the 1920s, the Macedonians' national identity was still indistinct, as Barker, the leading British post-war authority on south-eastern Europe (considered by Macedonians to be pro-Greek like many British Foreign Office experts) wrote at the time.[20]

A Yugoslav programme in the 1920s to bring Serb colonists to Macedonia, Kosovo and the Sandzak tried to secure them 'in a fashion reminiscent of Hapsburg "populationism" in the eighteenth-century Vojvodina', John Lampe wrote. Homesteads for Serb families from Bosnia-Herzegovina, Montenegro, and the Lika region of the old Croatian Military Border were to be carved from former Albanian or Turkish lands.[21]

In the early 1930s, the IMRO, now also supported by Mussolini, carried out hundreds of murders, bombings and shootings in Sofia. It declared war on Yugoslavia with the backing of Il Duce to try and drive the Serbs from Macedonia. The Yugoslav Macedonian border with Bulgaria was heavily militarised.

Many outrages were perpetrated by Vlado 'the Chauffeur' Georgiev, who assassinated King Aleksandar of Yugoslavia in Marseille in 1934. The sequence of events was filmed and shown in cinemas around the world. 'Everyone saw the remarkable film of the assassination,' the popular American pundit John Gunther said. 'Its great quality of emotion came from the fact that the audience knew, from the time that the King stepped off the boat, that he would be dead in ninety seconds. And the King did not know this.'[22]

The Supremacists were led by Vanche or Ivan Mihailov from Stip, who sought to incorporate northern Macedonia into a Greater Bulgaria. (Georgiev was Mihailov's chauffeur. He also killed Mihailov's moderate rival Toma Levski and reputedly plotted to blow up the League of

Nations building at Geneva.) The Supremacists controlled the south-western Bulgarian region of Petrich, where they levied taxes and ran a harsh administration as a terrorist state within the Bulgarian kingdom.

Colonel Kimon Gheorgiev staged a *coup d'état* on 19 May 1934, in which Bulgaria's King Boris III was forced to abolish parliament and consent to the establishment of an authoritarian regime which at last outlawed the IMRO.

After the Italian and German invasion of Greece and Yugoslavia in April 1941, the Axis powers set about dismembering the Yugoslav kingdom. The Italians used the Albanians to annex part of Kosovo and western Macedonia where Albanian populations were already the majority. Bulgaria reclaimed Macedonia and parts of southern Serbia. Bulgarian rule of Macedonia used every pressure to convince or coerce the inhabitants into thinking they were Bulgars and, for most Macedonians, the experience ended any wish to be ruled from Sofia. Bulgaria opened as many as 800 schools in Yugoslav Macedonia and sent teachers and priests to 'Bulgarise' the people.

Bulgaria also endowed Skopje with a national theatre, a library, a museum and for higher education the King Boris University. 'The general policy of the Bulgarian occupation authorities was to win over the inhabitants... with generous treatment,' L.S. Stavrianos wrote. This evidently failed. By the end of 1943, Macedonian partisans under the leadership of the Secretary-General of the Communist party, Josip 'Tito' Broz, were staging armed resistance. 'The Bulgarian occupation forces retaliated with harsh measures which served only to fan the flames of the revolt.'[23] Bulgaria, whose king and people had successfully resisted Nazi pressure to deport their own Jewish population to Nazi death camps, connived in the deportation of Skopje's Jewish community.

Mazower's astute comment that 'nationalism could only offer a basis for rule over such a land with the aid of extreme violence and a good deal of wishful thinking' turned out to be prophetic of the events that, at the start of the twenty-first century, threatened to tear apart Macedonia's proud but fragile nation state.

By a tortuous process of elimination, Macedonian Slavs rejected attempts to rule them made by Sofia, Belgrade and Athens, making the world at last believe they wanted Macedonia for the Macedonians. But ethnic Macedonians and ethnic Albanians in Macedonia would still have to reconcile their disparate legacies from the Ottoman Empire with the cosmopolitan idealism of Delchev and his comrades.

3 Yugoslav Republic

The names in my primer are Croatian and Serbian, Slovene
and Macedonian, fairly distributed. As many Petars as Mitars,
Djordjes as Ivans.
Dubravka Ugresic, The Museum of Unconditional Surrender

TITO EFFECTIVELY ENDED THE Macedonian Question during his lifetime
by creating a separate republic of Macedonia within post-war
Yugoslavia. In this, the cynical Communist strongman was almost
certainly inspired by designs on Salonika and rivalry with his Russian-
dominated comrades in Bulgaria, to whose Macedonian populations
and territory Yugoslavia could in this way lay a stronger claim, rather
than by sympathy for the romantic Macedonian cause. Fostering
Macedonian autonomy equally gave Tito a good rationale for ruining
the pioneering Serbian landowners and former Royalist officers who
had settled in Macedonia during the inter-war years. He could seize
their lands on the pretext that they belonged to Macedonian peasants,
many of whom were in actual fact fervent Royalist supporters who
would subsequently be killed by Tito's regime when they revolted
against its oppression.

During the Second World War, Tito's adoption of the principle of
self-determination for all nationalities was a factor that helped the
Communist-led guerrillas to triumph over the nationalist resistance
led by Draza Mihailovic, the Royal Yugoslav Army officer who wanted
to lock Macedonia into a greater Serbia.

Comintern – the international Communist movement, orchestrated
from Moscow – viewed the dissatisfaction with the post-1918 political

set-up that was felt by large sections of the population in Macedonia as a tool to help bring about Marxist revolution. The Yugoslav state was seen as the creation of western imperialist forces and the disaffection of the Croats and the Slav Macedonians was potentially useful to destroy it. Comintern specifically called for an independent united Macedonia. But it took some time for this policy to be impressed firmly on the local parties in Yugoslavia, Bulgaria and Greece.

In the inter-war Yugoslav state, the Communist Party, which grew out of the Serbian Social Democratic movement, in the beginning ignored the national question. Its biggest success in the elections of November 1920 was in Macedonia, Kosovo and Montenegro, the poorest areas of Yugoslavia. In Macedonia, the communists won 36.72 per cent of all votes cast, with particular support in the areas of Kumanovo, Skopje and Tikves where they garnered 44 per cent, 44.11 and 45.9 per cent of the vote.[1] The Red successes were probably due mainly to poverty and the lack of a viable alternative protest vote (unlike in Croatia where the Croatian Peasant Party received the poor protest vote).

The Communist Party leader in Skopje was a Serb, Dusan Cekic, who had moved there from Leskovac after the Balkan wars. He was in favour of an autonomous Macedonia within a Balkan federation. At this stage, however, the first Yugoslav Communist Party head, Filip Filipovic, admitted that Serbs, Croats and Slovenes were different people but would not accept the same for the Macedonians and the Montenegrins. Comintern's adoption of the concept of an autonomous or independent Macedonia was unpopular with many Serbs.

In Bulgaria, the Comintern sought to infiltrate and split the VMRO, which claimed Macedonia for Sofia, by setting up a leftist faction, the VMRO-ob under Dimitar Vlahov. Vlahov recorded the typically high-handed Russian decision on Macedonia in 1934:

> Comintern itself wanted the Macedonian question considered as one of the consultations of its executive committee. One day I was informed that the consultation would be held. And so it was. Before it convened, the inner leadership of the committee had already reached its stand, including the question of the Macedonian nation… it was concluded that the Macedonian nation exists.[2]

As Hugh Poulton notes, Bulgarian mainstream political opinion subsequently held Comintern responsible for 'inventing' the entire idea of the Macedonian nation. By the mid 1930s, the rise of Hitler had led Comintern to adopt a policy of Popular Fronts. Moscow for a while played down its previous enthusiasm in the late 1920s for advocating the complete break-up of Yugoslavia and independence for Croatia and Slovenia as well as Macedonia.

When Tito, himself a Croat with a Slovene mother, took over the leadership of the Yugoslav Communist Party in 1937, he argued that Macedonia should exist within a federal Yugoslavia.

In 1942, Tito had developed his position in a widely published article entitled 'The National Problem in the Light of the National Liberation War'. He stated that the liberation war and the national question were 'inseparably joined' and that the different Yugoslav nations had 'the right to self-determination including the right of separation', a right that would be invoked half a century later at the cost of 300,000 lives.

During the war, Tito sent one of his trusted lieutenants, Svetozar Vukmanovic, whose *nom de guerre* was Tempo, a leading Montenegrin Communist and member of the Party's central committee, to generate and lead the Macedonian resistance. His Macedonian fighters made their first attack at the sprawling tobacco town of Prilep in October 1941.[3] At the end of the war Vukmanovic would be proclaimed a National Hero and hold high government office.

A struggle had developed between the Yugoslav and Bulgarian communist parties as to which grouping should command the Macedonian Partisans. Stavrianos recounts how in August 1941 the Comintern decided in favour of the Yugoslav party 'apparently because the Bulgarian comrades were considered too passive toward the Russo-German struggle'.

A communiqué of the Macedonian Communist command of October 1942 mentioned the 'Macedonia nation' but the first congress of the Anti-Fascist Council for the National Liberation of Yugoslavia (AVNOJ), Tito's first attempt at forming a provisional Yugoslav Government, held at Bihac in Bosnia in November 1942, did not mention the Macedonians specifically. The second AVNOJ congress in Jajce on 29 November 1943 did recognise the Macedonian nation and gave it equal status to the other five federal units: Serbia, Croatia, Slovenia, Montenegro and Bosnia-Herzegovina.

But Macedonians were sparsely represented on the central Titoist bodies of the AVNOJ, showing that the party still was weak in Macedonia. There were no Macedonians on the 17-member supreme executive body or on the provisional government (the National Liberation Committee).

Vukmanovic-Tempo obtained significant support through the Partisan programme of a federal Yugoslavia in which the Macedonian nation would enjoy full equality with other peoples. By the summer of

1943, Partisan bands were in the field and Vukmanovic-Tempo was liaising with Partisans in Greece, Albania and Bulgaria. Tito's aim seemed then to create a united Slav Macedonia which would extend beyond the pre-war Yugoslav area.

The hardships and heroism of the Partisan war were described vividly by Milovan Djilas, the tough Montenegrin ideologue of the Yugoslav revolution and future dissident, who was sent by Tito from Belgrade to lead the struggle in Montenegro as Tempo left for Bosnia en route to Macedonia.

'The uprising grew and gained strength in Macedonia as well,' Djilas recalled in his account, *Wartime*.[4] 'Svetozar Vukmanovic-Tempo arrived at Vis from Macedonia, overjoyed at the self-confident militancy of the Macedonians. He had ample personal reason for this, because it was he who had effected the transformation to armed struggle in Macedonia.'

The People's Republic of Macedonia was proclaimed on 2 August 1944, the symbolic anniversary of the Ilinden uprising, at the first Macedonian Anti-Fascist Assembly held at Prohor Pcinski monastery. This declared 'Macedonia as a federal state in the new Democratic Federation of Yugoslavia' and issued a 'manifesto' that described its position in the old Yugoslavia as that of a colony. The manifesto said it stood for equality for all the nationalities in Macedonia and urged Albanians, Turks and Vlachs to engage in the national liberation struggle.

Macedonian was made the official language of the federal state. Tito's ambitions for this entity now far exceeded those he advocated in the late 1930s of a limited Vardar Macedonia within a Yugoslav federation. It was to include Bulgaria, probably Albania and perhaps even Greece.

These ambitions were clear from a proclamation by the Macedonian Assembly (ASNOM) on 4 August 1944:

> People of Macedonia! In the course of three years of combat you have achieved your unity, developed your army and laid the basis for the federal Macedonian state. With the participation of the entire Macedonian nation in the struggle against the Fascist occupiers of Yugoslavia, Bulgaria and Greece you will achieve unification of all parts of Macedonia, divided in 1915 and 1918 by Balkan imperialists.[5]

Tito had a problem with reliability at the top level of the Macedonian party. There were only three Macedonians on the 556-member central Anti-Fascist Council in 1943: Metodije Antonov-Čento, Vladimir

Poptomorov and Mihajlo Apostolski. In August 1944, Čento became head of the newly formed Anti-Fascist Assembly of National Liberation of Macedonia (ASNOM) but later fell out with the party and was sentenced to 11 years' hard labour in 1946 for trying to call for a totally independent Macedonia. Poptomorov went to Bulgaria in 1944 and became the country's Foreign Minister in 1949.

At first, even Bulgaria's Communists complied with the Titoist policy, since it was supported by Stalin. The border between Macedonia and Serbia was re-drawn in favour of Skopje to give the Macedonians the Kumanovo area, a long-standing demand of the IMRO, some of whose members had become involved in the Macedonian Communist Party or enrolled with Tito's Partisans. Since Macedonian national unity was lacking at the end of the war, two Yugoslav army corps were moved from central Yugoslavia to Macedonia to underline Belgrade's territorial rights over Vardar Macedonia.

In a historic gesture, the ashes of Delchev, the quintessential Macedonian turn-of-the-century hero, were transported from Sofia to Skopje (they were moved to Sofia from Greece in 1923) and 3,500 books deemed of historical value to Macedonians were moved from the libraries of the Bulgarian capital to those of Skopje.

Djilas, in a speech published in Belgrade's *Politika* newspaper on 7 November 1944, stated that 'the Macedonian people has the right to unite wherever it lives', meaning that the republic laid claim to sovereignty over inhabitants in the regions of Macedonian Greece and the Pirin areas of Bulgaria.

In Sofia, Resolution X of the Bulgarian Communist Party's plenary session resolved 'to work systematically for bringing close together again culturally the Macedonian people of Pirin with the popular republic of Macedonia... for the diffusion of the study of the Macedonian language and history among the inhabitants of Pirin'.

In 1945, Bulgaria and Yugoslavia had held talks in Moscow over uniting in a proposed 'Balkan Federation' or confederation but these discussions were suspended on the eve of the Yalta agreement. This followed a Soviet-brokered meeting between Tito and a Bulgarian delegation at Craiova in Romania in October 1944. Stalin suggested a federation between Yugoslavia and Bulgaria when he met Tito for the first time in late 1944.

The Bulgarian Communist leader Georgi Dimitrov supported the idea and in November the Bulgarian party leadership, in a letter to the Yugoslav party committee, made significant concessions to Macedonian national aspirations. The party in Gorna Dzumaja (now Blagoevgrad), the capital of the Pirin region, was declared a Macedonian organisation.

Schools were named after Macedonian heroes and a Macedonian newspaper founded.

A Yugoslav politburo member, Edvard Kardelj, went to Sofia to discuss the federation but the discussions went awry. Bulgaria was interested in losing the stigma of being the only pre-war Slavonic state that joined the Axis and a federation might have helped prevent a punitive peace treaty. But Kardelj baulked at the Bulgarian suggestion that Sofia be the capital of the new entity, with Dimitrov party leader and Tito president. The Bulgarians wanted the federation to be an association of two states, while Belgrade imagined Bulgaria would become another part of Yugoslavia. In 1945, Stalin poured cold water on the scheme after Britain indicated that a threat to Greece was unacceptable.

Stalin resumed pressing Tito for the federation in 1946 but Tito then argued it was unworkable because of differences between the two countries. In Yugoslavia, power was in the hands of the Communists while in Bulgaria other parties still influenced the Government considerably.

But when Tito expressed interest in Yugoslavia acquiring Salonika and the Aegean Macedonia, Stalin was quoted as replying: 'Yes, Salonika is an old Slavic city. You need access to the Aegean.'[6]

In June 1946, Dimitrov told the Yugoslav Ambassador that Bulgaria was prepared to cede Pirin to the People's Republic of Macedonia. Bulgaria signed a peace treaty with the Allies in February 1947, removing a stumbling block to federation. In August, Dimitrov and Tito signed the Bled agreement, tantamount to the union of Pirin with Vardar Macedonia. Bulgaria's Parliament passed legislation enabling the teaching of Macedonian language and history in schools in Pirin and agreed to pay for 87 teachers to come to Pirin from the People's Republic of Macedonia for three years. A Macedonian theatre was opened in Gorna Dzumaja in November 1947 with help from the National Theatre in Skopje. Dimitrov opposed immediate formal union of the two constituent parts of Macedonia until after the proposed Balkan federation had been achieved.

Talks on this resumed with Dimitrov in 1948 but foundered when in an interview he spoke grandiosely of a Balkan federation to include Greece, Hungary, Romania, and Albania. Stalin was angered and summoned the Bulgarian and Yugoslav leaders to Moscow for a dressing down, especially for their designs on Greece. Tito declined to go, sending Kardelj. But Tito put the idea on hold that year, saying it could jeopardise the fulfilling of Yugoslavia's five-year economic plan. He also agreed to pull back a Yugoslav division that had been sent to Albania to support the Greek Communist leader Markos Vaphiadis, who, in December 1947, declared a provisional democratic government of Greece.

Relations between Belgrade and Bulgaria cooled after Moscow withdrew military and civilian advisers from Yugoslavia on 17 March 1948, the prelude to Stalin's formal excommunication of Tito and the Yugoslav leadership on 28 June 1948. Stalin had previously considered Tito a potential successor to head the world Communist movement but by now Moscow regarded the manoeuvring over Macedonia and a Balkan federation as proof he was overzealous. The Soviet-Yugoslav split put an end to the proposed unification of Macedonia and future Bulgarian leaders, after Dimitrov died in 1949, were unreceptive to the idea of a separate Macedonian consciousness.

It is important to note that Macedonia was spared the impact of the Second World War that was visited on other parts of Yugoslavia, suffering only an estimated one per cent of total casualties. Nevertheless, it had undergone a war over territory and choices of political loyalty, dividing inhabitants' loyalties between Partisan, Chetnik and pro-Bulgarian villages during the conflict.[7]

Djilas evoked the ferocity of the Partisan conflict in a section of his memoir where he described the guerrillas' methods of dealing with Germans:

Some five hundred yards ahead we stumbled onto two Germans.

'Where are the German soldiers?' I asked in German. One of them replied in good Serbian, making a circular motion with his hand, 'All around.'

This heightened my outrage at the insolence of the Germans... I unslung my rifle. Since I didn't dare fire, because the Germans were some forty yards above... I hit the German over the head. The rifle butt broke, and the German fell on his back. I pulled out my knife and with one motion slit his throat. I then handed the knife to Raja Nedeljkovic, a political worker... whose village the Germans massacred in 1941. Nedeljkovic stabbed the second German, who writhed but soon was still.[8]

Tito's policies in Macedonia met with opposition from Serb peasants and landowners, who sought to recover from the Macedonian peasants the lands that they had owned before the Second World War. Most Serb peasants received their land back but Serb pre-war army officers and owners who did not cultivate their lands directly had them confiscated by the ruthless new Communist state. From 1945 to 1947, a fierce anti-Communist opposition movement sprang up in Macedonia which was repressed harshly.

British intelligence evidently retained active contacts with anti-communist fighters still active in Macedonia. Operating as an agent in the mountains of Macedonia, close to the Albanian border, was Bob Battersby, a colourful member of the Intelligence Corps, who served in the 1946 civil war in Greece, going on to become a Conservative European MP at Strasbourg and the Tories' special adviser on Eastern Europe.

'He was repeatedly subjected to death threats, apparently from within the anti-Communist Partisan group to which he was attached, on the basis that his death might provoke a helpful increase in British support,' a tribute to Battersby recalled. 'In such treacherous territory, he learned to carry hand grenades rather than small arms as "a more effective negotiating tool."'[9]

In those two years, the Ozna, political police – *Odsek za zastitu naroda* (Department for the Protection of the People) – headed by Aleksander Rankovic, the Communist Interior Minister, arrested 600 alleged members of 'armed bands' and 100 'spies'. In 1948, 134 purported 'fascist and terrorist' organisations were uncovered in Macedonia.

Tito, evidently still hoping to obtain the use of Salonika, supported the Greek Communists, EAM/ELAS, against the Greek Government, over opposition from Stalin who had accepted Greece would remain a British and American sphere of influence.

In 1949 and 1950, peasants' uprisings took place in Macedonia and were brutally repressed in one of the most shameful chapters of Yugoslavia's history.

After the split between Yugoslavia and Bulgaria, Yugoslav Macedonia resorted to repression to eradicate pro-Bulgarian sentiment, arresting and killing large numbers of people, as the pioneering Hugh Poulton recounts.[10] Bulgarian sources claim that thousands of people were killed after 1944 and that more than 100,000 people were put in prison under 'the law for the protection of Macedonian national honour'.

About 1,200 prominent Bulgarians were reportedly killed on the orders of Vukmanovic-Tempo and Rankovic in Skopje, Veles, Kumanovo, Prilep, Bitola and Stip. In 1946, the Bulgarian politicians Dimitar Guzelev and Yordan and Dimitar Chatrov were sentenced to death and 74 people led by Angel Dimov were jailed for attempting to detach Vardar Macedonia and join it to Bulgaria. There was a series of trials throughout 1947 and 1948 of those such as Metodije Anotonov-Čento.

Communist Macedonia was largely shaped by the sword, or the secret policeman's knock on the door at dawn, with other aspects of the nation following. A literary language was agreed upon in 1947. The autocephalous Macedonian Orthodox Church was founded in 1958 and the Macedonian Academy of Sciences in 1967 to try and nurture national consciousness.

The new authorities bolstered their position by setting up a written language for the republic. At first the spoken dialect of northern Macedonia was selected as the basis for Macedonian but it was felt this was too close to Serbian and the dialects spoken in the cities of Bitola and Veles were adopted:

> These dialects were closer to the literary language of Bulgaria but because the latter was based on the eastern Bulgarian dialects, it allowed enough differentiation for the Yugoslavs to claim it as a language distinct from Bulgarian – a point which Bulgaria has bitterly contested ever since.[11]

For decades, Bulgaria would officially regard Macedonia as a test-tube country created artificially by Tito.

The Macedonian alphabet was accepted on 3 May 1945, and the orthography on 7 June 1945, and a first primer of the new language appeared in 1946. The Macedonian Department at the Faculty of Philosophy at the University of Skopje was also founded in 1946. A Macedonian literary language grammar appeared in 1952, and in 1953 the Institute for the Macedonian Language, 'Krste P. Misirkov', was set up.[12]

The Yugoslav policy of ethnogenesis in Macedonia was carefully hidden. The Macedonian national museum did not display original works by figures such as the Miladinov brothers in the vanguard of Slav consciousness in the mid nineteenth century, who it was argued were Macedonian not Bulgarian, though in some of their writings they said they were Bulgarians. Appropriately edited versions in the new language were promoted to boost the line. The history of the VMRO was bowdlerised with the Bulgarians claiming that exaggerated emphasis was placed on the activities of the autonomist wing of the organisation who wanted a separate Macedonian entity while Sofia claimed that the majority of revolutionaries wanted Macedonia to be part of Bulgaria.

An engaging interpretation of this period propounded by Kyril Drezov argues that there was a 'natural withering away' of Bulgarian identity in Vardar and Aegean Macedonia from the 1920s to the 1940s:

Although it seems that before the 1940s the majority of the population in Vardar Macedonia professed some sort of a Bulgarian identity – as a legacy from medieval history and the Bulgarian national revival in the 19th century – this same population at the very same time had also a very strong Macedonian identity – as a result of specifically Macedonian struggles for the 50 years preceding the 1940s. Once specifically Macedonian interests came to the fore under the Yugoslav communist umbrella and in direct confrontation with the Bulgarian occupation authorities, the Bulgarian part of the identity of Vardar Macedonians was destined to die out – in a process similar to the triumph of Austrian over German-Austrian identity in post-war years.[13]

A history of religious conditions in Eastern Europe by Trevor Beeson recalls that the demand for an autocephalous Macedonian Orthodox Church was made by a group of Macedonian priests, backed by the Communist authorities, 'who saw that this affirmation of Macedonian nationality would strengthen their south-eastern borders against the pressures of Bulgarian irredentism'.[14] In fact, the Macedonian Orthodox Church was unique in Christian and world history in that it was the only Christian church ever to have been set up by a Communist party and in an atheist state.

The Serb Patriarch Vikentije succeeded 'by a mixture of obduracy, evasion and procrastination, in postponing the final decision for years'.[15] The Government eventually obtained approval from the *Sabor* (assembly) of the Serb Orthodox Church for the autonomous Macedonian Church under jurisdiction of the Serbian Patriarchate. Yugoslav authorities considered the development of the Macedonian Church important enough to warrant the use of 'a mixture of blandishments and veiled threats' to persuade the *Sabor*.[16]

In 1967, the Macedonian Church split away unilaterally, cutting the uneasy relations between the two churches. Under the benevolent wing of the Macedonian Government, the Church built itself a large new Metropolitanate in Skopje. The Greek and Bulgarian Orthodox churches have always viewed the Macedonian Church as a schismatic and faked political concoction. In recent years, however, relations have warmed and some members of the Skopje hierarchy have visited Mount Athos.

The close relationship with the Skopje authorities, encouraged by a common front against the threat of Albanian nationalism and the growth of Islam, continues to this date and was exploited skilfully by the Macedonian nationalist leader, Ljubco Georgievski, and his wife, Snezana.

The new republic also moved to influence big Macedonian emigrant communities in Canada and Australia, where extreme nationalism was traditionally strong. Macedonians who left when travel restrictions were relaxed under Tito in the 1960s came into contact with older, pre-war immigrants who often tended to be pro-Bulgarian. The Yugoslav authorities founded an agency in Skopje for emigration, called *Matica*, to spread the correct form of national consciousness among emigrants. The Macedonian church also sent priests to take part in the education of Macedonians abroad.

By the 1970s, however, Belgrade was also concerned by nationalism that went beyond the official line. Dragan Bogdanovski, a future inspiration of the IMRO hardline nationalist movement after independence, was adopted by Amnesty International when he received a 13-year prison sentence in Skopje in 1979. His crime was to have headed a movement that urged the foundation of an independent Macedonia including Macedonian areas of Greece and Bulgaria. This was ironic since Delchev, proclaimed as Macedonia's greatest hero by Skopje, had himself agitated for their incorporation.[17]

The Communist authorities in textbooks claimed that the Macedonians were descended from Slav tribes in the sixth and seventh centuries AD, who were separate from the tribes who became Bulgarians. In Australia, and elsewhere in the diaspora, Macedonian nationalists began laying claim to descent from Philip of Macedon. Much of this thinking was adopted when Macedonia became independent from Yugoslavia and deep differences emerged with the Greeks over the use of the Star of Vergina on the Macedonian flag. As noted, a number of historians outside of Macedonia have accused its nationalists of looting history and backdating modern concepts.

Macedonia's Albanians under Tito

Under Tito, the Albanian minority of Macedonia was isolated from Hoxhaist Albania with which towns such as Debar had had close family and cultural ties before 1939. As Pettifer writes: 'Albanians had been forced to accept the Titoist definitions of a "Macedonian" identity within Yugoslavia on the basis of Partisan victories in the area in the Second World War.'[18]

The Albanian communities in western Macedonia faced harsh political and cultural repression under Rankovic and after Tito's death. The Islamic religion and religious institutions used by Albanians were persecuted, including the destruction of Islamic libraries such as the Bektashi *tekke* in Tetovo and the requisitioning of Islamic buildings for state use. Roads were built through the Muslim cemeteries in

Gostivar and Tetovo. This was not an entirely new policy. Rebecca West, arriving in Skopje in 1937, told how:

> We rattled down the main street to the square leading to the bridge over the Vardar, and my husband turned to crane his neck in wonder at the unique architectural horror which defiled that spot. It regrettably happened that the Yugoslavs, in their joy at turning out the Turks and becoming the masters of Macedonia, pulled down the beautiful mosque that had stood for three centuries in this commanding position, and replaced it by an Officers' Club... one of the most hideous buildings in... Europe.[19]

Until the 1980s, the plight of the Albanians in Macedonia was overshadowed internationally by events in Kosovo where violent protests in 1981 and 1989 led to martial law being imposed.

The ethnic Albanians inhabited and inhabit compact settlements in the west of the republic bordering on Albania, the north-west bordering on Kosovo and in Skopje. By 1983, they were a majority of the population in the districts of Tetovo (113,000 Albanians to 38,000 Macedonians), Gostivar (63,000 to 18,000), Kičevo (23,000 to 21,000) and Debar (10,000 to 2,500). By 1988, nearly half of Skopje's population of 560,000 were estimated by the Interior Ministry to be Albanians.[20]

The Yugoslav authorities after the Second World War promised to resolve the national problems of the country with the slogan of 'Brotherhood and Unity'. The Albanians were recognised as a nationality of Yugoslavia but not as a nation, since the Albanian national home was outside Yugoslavia.

The Albanians of Macedonia gained educational and cultural privileges. There were more than 200 Albanian schools in the Socialist Republic of Macedonia in 1951, with some 600 teachers instructing 26,000 pupils. By 1973, this had been extended to 248 schools catering for 2,150 teachers and some 60,000 pupils. In 1980, there were 2,365 Albanians at university-level institutions in the Macedonian republic. Albanians had their own newspaper, *Flaka e Vellazerimit*, programmes in Albanian were broadcast on radio and television, and there were Albanian cultural associations, theatre groups and sports clubs.

In spite of these arrangements, cohabitation between ethnic Macedonians and ethnic Albanians was far from ideal throughout the life of the socialist republic. After the demise of Rankovic and a consequent easing of the Yugoslav police state, Albanian discontent in Kosovo led to widespread demonstrations in the province in

November 1968, calling for it to be made a republic. These led to sympathy protests in Tetovo demanding that predominantly Albanian areas of Macedonia be allowed to unite with Kosovo in a republic. Macedonian authorities believed that granting such a republic would have left the remainder of the republic vulnerable to a predatory scramble for territory by Bulgaria and possibly Greece and Serbia.

In July 1981, measures were taken by the Macedonian Assembly's Commission for Intra-National Relations to crack down on Albanian nationalism in policies known as 'ideological differentiation'. School curricula and textbooks were revised and Albanian-language schools were ordered to teach more Macedonian. The Macedonian interior minister in 1984 warned of 'activity by the internal enemy from positions of Albanian nationalism and irredentism' and that ethnic Albanians were forming illegal groups.

A war of words erupted in 1988 between Tirana and Skopje, with Albanian media accusing Macedonian authorities of 'neo-Malthusian' policies to penalise ethnic Albanians with large families. The Albanian news agency ATA cited Yugoslav newspaper reports that in Tetovo 'a package of administrative measures' would be introduced in 1988 to curtail the birth rate. These included families having to pay for health services for any children after the first two were born and child allowances being withheld for those extra children.[21]

In 1987, the Tetovo Municipal Committee of the League of Communists sacked 100 Albanian civil servants from the state administration and 34 ethnic Albanian army officers in the Tetovo area were disciplined for participating at Albanian weddings where Albanian nationalist songs were chanted. Albanian League of Communist officials in Kosovo protested to the Macedonian Parliament in 1988 over a ban on sale of property in western Macedonia, to prevent Albanians buying out Macedonians, family planning restrictions 'to stop aggressive demographic expansion' and an amended law on religious teaching to prevent people under 15 receiving Islamic instruction. The Kosovar Communists charged that these steps were more repressive than anti-Albanian policies in Kosovo but they were upheld as legal by the Macedonian assembly 'to prevent the activities of Albanian nationalists and separatists'.

A number of teachers in Tetovo were expelled from the League of Communists in 1983 for not using Macedonian, as required by official regulations. Tanjug reported in October 1983 that 'a large number of pupils of Albanian nationality also followed their teachers' example by boycotting and belittling the Macedonian language'. A 1985 law restricted classes in Albanian to a minimum of 30 pupils and smaller classes were closed. The number of secondary students attending classes in Albanian in the republic was reported to have fallen from 8,200 in 1981 to 4,221 in 1989.

Compulsory instruction of ethnic Albanians in Macedonia led to protests by young Albanians in Gostivar and Kumanovo in 1988. In Kumanovo, at least 128 Albanians were detained for up to 60 days and 20 organisers of the protests were arrested and imprisoned. The harsh sentences included prison terms for three men ranging from six to 11 years and terms of four to six years for two boys and two girls aged 16 and 17 who took part in a boycott of teaching at the Pance Popovski school in Gostivar.

The Socialist Republic authorities saw Islam as intertwined with Albanian nationalism and believed it was being used to assimilate smaller Muslim groups such as the Turks, Torbeshi and Roma. *NIN* magazine in Belgrade in December 1986 reported that a considerable number of Albanians from Macedonia were receiving religious instruction in Arab countries and that 210 mosques had been built or restored in western Macedonia. Authorities began to refuse authorisation for further mosque construction.

There was little mixing between ethnic communities. A 1974 study by the sociologist Ilija Josifovski found that 95 per cent of Albanian and Macedonian and 84 per cent of Turkish heads of household in the village of Polog in western Macedonia would not let their sons marry a girl of a different nationality. As Poulton said in his groundbreaking study of this period:

> Despite the aim of 'Brotherhood and Unity' espoused by the Communist authorities, the picture was one of mistrust and increasing alienation between the Macedonians and the rapidly expanding Albanian population of the Socialist Republic of Macedonia, mirrored in everyday relations by chauvinist attitudes on both sides.[22]

In 1989, the republic's constitution was amended to define the republic as a 'nation-state of Macedonian people' instead of the previous definition of 'a state of the Macedonian people and the Albanian and Turkish minorities'.

The Emergence of Gligorov

In the early 1960s, Yugoslavia introduced self-management and decentralisation of the economy, the brainchild of Vladimir Bakaric, the most senior Croat apart from Tito in the Yugoslav Communist

Party, who wanted to devolve powers to individual republics. He was backed enthusiastically by the young Macedonian leaders, Krste Crvenkovski and Kiro Gligorov.

Gligorov was born on 3 May 1917 in the Macedonian town of Stip. He went to school at the Skopje Gymnasium and graduated in law from Belgrade University in 1938. After graduation, he returned to Skopje to work as an attorney in a private bank.

At the start of the Second World War, he became active in the resistance movement. In 1941, he joined the Communist-led Partisan organisation, the People's Liberation movement (*Narodno Osloboditelna Borba*) and was a member of the Anti-Fascist Assembly of the National Liberation Movement of Macedonia (ASNOM). He was put in charge of the finances of the ASNOM presidium when the Socialist Republic of Macedonia was proclaimed. He was also a member of the Anti-Fascist Assembly of the National Liberation Movement of Yugoslavia (AVNOJ).

In 1945, the Communist Party sent Gligorov to Belgrade where he held a string of positions in economic and financial bodies – Assistant General Secretary in the federal Yugoslav Government from 1945 to 1947, Assistant Federal Minister of Finance from 1952 to 1953, Deputy Director of the Federal Institute for Economic Planning from 1953 to 1955, Federal Secretary of Finance (1962 to 1967) and Vice President of the Federal Executive Council from 1967 to 1969.

Within 40 years, Gligorov, by now a former Yugoslav Deputy President and former Federal Finance Minister, would become the first president of independent Macedonia. He would bring to the task all the skills he had learned as an acolyte of Tito. For many ordinary Macedonians, he grew to resemble his mentor as a remarkable father figure, especially after they saw the chaos that followed the death of Tito in the other star-crossed republics of Yugoslavia.

4 Macedonian Independence and Affirmation, 1990–1999

THE MACEDONIAN PARLIAMENT (*SOBRANJE*) adopted its Declaration of Independence on 17 January 1991. Nine months later, a popular referendum confirmed Skopje's secession from Yugoslavia.

A partisan song from 1941 in the Prilep region, itself inspired by an anti-Ottoman forerunner, *A bre makedonce* ('Hey, Little Macedonian'), became popular again:

> Hey, little Macedonian,
>
> Where are you heading to?
>
> War is waiting for you,
>
> War for freedom
>
> For Macedonia,
>
> The subjugated country.
>
> So that today's tyrants
>
> finally understand:
>
> The name of Macedonia will never perish.

But most Macedonians feared war. A summer hit in 1992, *Sviri mi cigane* ('Play for me, Gypsy') by Rosana Sarik-Todorovska, expressed their trepidation:

Today we are happy and healthy, tomorrow we may not be so.[1]

Milosevic was outraged by Macedonia declaring independence, accusing Skopje of 'stabbing him in the back'.[2] Yet the break with Belgrade was peaceful, in contrast to the terrible violence accompanying the secession of Croatia, Bosnia-Herzegovina, and to a lesser extent Slovenia. The Macedonians had as far as possible prudently stayed apart from the quarrels that had, at the end of the 1980s, brought the Serbs, Croats and Slovenes into increasing conflict.

Established Macedonian politicians generally avoided agitating for the disintegration of Yugoslavia. As the historian R.J. Crampton observed:

> For Macedonia a weakening of the Yugoslav federation was a daunting prospect. It needed federal funds for its backward and impoverished economy and it needed federal protection from neighbours whom history suggested might have claims upon its territory.[3]

In addition, nearly all of Macedonia's communications links, by rail or by telephone, were routed through Serbia and Belgrade.

By May 1991, however, the domination of Serbs and Montenegrins in the federation had decided Macedonia to opt for independence if Slovenia and Croatia did so. There had been some initial support from members of the Skopje governing elite for Milosevic's rise to absolute power in Serbia because of the stance he took against the Kosovo Albanians, which reflected their own antagonism to their own large Albanian community. But most Macedonians, many of whom were called up for fighting with the Yugoslav Army (JNA) in Vukovar and other parts of Croatia, wanted to avoid further involvement in Belgrade's wars. The first JNA victim in Croatia was a young Macedonian soldier serving in Split in 1991 who was killed during anti-army demonstrations.

A group of officers within the Bitola garrison of the JNA formed the Secret Macedonia Revolutionary Organisation (TMRO-officers) with the aim of stopping Macedonian soldiers from being sent to fight in Croatia. The cause attracted wide popular support as busloads of soldiers' parents travelled from Skopje to Titograd (the future Podgorica) in September 1991, with funds provided by the Macedonian

Government, to trace their sons who were recruits and bring them back home.[4]

In January 1990, Macedonia's representatives at the 14th congress of the Yugoslav League of Communists (LCY), the renamed communist party, walked out together with the Croats in sympathy with a walk-out by the Slovenes. The Slovenes' departure was prompted by the rejection of a proposal they made for restructuring of the LCY and for devolution of more power to the republican parties. The Macedonians and Croats had no desire to be dominated by the Serbian faction in the majority because Milosevic controlled the votes of Vojvodina, Kosovo and Montenegro as well as of Serbia.

The Macedonian establishment adopted few changes to its constitution other than to sanction the multi-party elections that were being held throughout the federation and making provision for some privatisation.

The polls were held in November and December 1990. No party won outright. The nationalist Internal Macedonian Revolutionary Organisation-Democratic Party for Macedonian National Unity (VMRO-DPMNE) garnered 37 seats in the 120-member single chamber Parliament. The League of Communists of Macedonia-Party for Democratic Renewal came second with 31 seats. The two main ethnic Albanian parties obtained 25 seats and Markovic's Alliance of Reform Forces won 18 seats.

A government of experts was formed after the contest. Some of them were former communists but the administration opted to work together with the nationalists of the VMRO rather than the Albanians.

In July 1991, there were demonstrations in Skopje urging an end to inter-ethnic violence, while similar protests were also held in Belgrade and Sarajevo.

After the secession of Slovenia and Croatia, the Macedonians, together with the Bosnians, pressed for some kind of 'asymmetrical federation' of Yugoslavia in which each member would have as much sovereignty as it would like. The other republics rejected this platform.

The Macedonian referendum on independence on 8 September 1991 was supported by 71 per cent of the population. It was boycotted by the parties representing the ethnic Albanian and Serb populations and in an annexe it left open the theoretical option of rejoining a new Yugoslav federation. The referendum endorsed 'An independent and sovereign Macedonia, with the right to join the future alliance of sovereign states of Yugoslavia'.

The ethnic Albanians' boycott was in protest at what they saw as the government's non-compliance with their demands, for example for the reopening of Albanian secondary schools that had been recently closed. *Vecher*, the Skopje daily newspaper, charged that the non-participation of the ethnic Albanians showed that the Macedonian state could not rely on their loyalty and that:

> possibilities should not be ruled out for the state to set up repressive measures towards the Albanian minority in Macedonia if the PDP (the main Albanian political party) seeks the answers to its dilemmas in aggression and if a scenario of an all-Albanian referendum becomes reality.

In December 1991, Macedonia joined Bosnia-Herzegovina, Slovenia and Croatia in applying to the European Community for recognition. The Serbian Krajina in Croatia and the Kosovan Albanians also applied but were rejected. Macedonia's application was referred to the Badinter commission, headed by the French lawyer Robert Badinter, together with that of Bosnia. Slovenia and Croatia were recognised by Germany on 23 December. According to the EC criteria, the claim of Macedonia to EC recognition was just as good as that of Bosnia, if not better, but it was blocked by Greece. In April 1992, however, Belgrade acknowledged that recognition of Macedonian independence was inevitable by agreeing to re-form the Yugoslav federation out of Serbia and Montenegro.

By November 1992, and without major incident, the Yugoslav Army had left the territory that until 1941 had been part of southern Serbia, and under Tito a full republic of Yugoslavia. The most serious problem arose over the JNA's attempting to remove the radar system at Skopje airport.

Details of the withdrawal were prepared in a 16-point agreement signed in April 1992 by Gligorov and the acting Yugoslav Defence Minister, Blagoje Adzic. Skopje had been the headquarters in the Second Yugoslavia of the 3rd military district of the JNA including some 20,000 men deployed directly in Macedonia. All equipment was intended to be placed under joint JNA-Macedonian control but in the end the Yugoslav Army adopted a virtual scorched earth policy, destroying or removing facilities and equipment that was the property of the Macedonian Territorial Defence Force according to Yugoslavia's two tier system. Even military hospitals and stores buildings were withdrawn when the JNA pulled out. The radical Macedonian officers' group, the Secret Macedonian Revolutionary Organisation, staged protests over the stripping of the barracks, which it claimed violated the agreement between Gligorov and Adzic.

Yet the transition was peaceful, in part because of the economic backwardness of the republic, the output of which represented only some 5 to 7 per cent of the Yugoslav Gross Domestic Product. Government economists argued that the introduction of the *denar* as a separate currency would free the Macedonian economy from helping to bankroll the Serbian war effort and so being dragged into the hyperinflation that devastated the Yugoslav *dinar*.

There were only some 45,000 Serbs in Macedonia meaning that, as in Slovenia where the Serbs also were a small minority, Belgrade nationalists were not overly concerned by the financial or ethnic consequences of the break-up.[5] An exception was the ultra-right demagogue Vojislav Seselj, who railed against independence and spoke in the Serbian Parliament of the historic rights of Serbs over the territory, urging the army as late as April 1992 to deploy two divisions in the republic. Seselj at other times suggested Macedonia should be divided up between Serbia and Bulgaria with small areas going to Albania, or that Serbs in Macedonia should have their own Serbian Autonomous Region of the Kumanovo Valley and the Skopska Crna Gora. But these proposals never found much resonance in Belgrade. Seselj would surrender to the International War Crimes Tribunal in The Hague in 2003 for trial.

There were limited protests in February 1992 by the Association of Serbs and Montenegrins in Kumanovo and Belgrade's nationalist media grumbled when some Serbs carrying pictures of Milosevic were roughed up by Macedonian police during New Year celebrations in the village of Kuceviste at the end of 1992.

Milosevic at first encouraged Serb extremists in Macedonia, sponsoring Macedonia's Democratic Serbian Party, formed after the republic declared independence, which sought to set up a breakaway 'Karadag Republic' in the northern parts of the country where most of the Serb minority lives, in the Skopje Black Mountain and the Kumanovo Valley. According to Takis Michas: 'Although party members boasted of meeting with Ratko Mladic, the Bosnian Serb commander, in Pale, and of attending military training courses, they were unable to obtain enough support to mount an uprising.'[6]

In spite of such minor agitation, the transitional period with Serbia was remarkably smooth. The rump Yugoslavia recognised Macedonia in 1996, the first such recognition of a former Yugoslav republic by Belgrade, and an economic agreement for free exchange of goods between the two states was also reached.

'The Fox of the Balkans'

Kiro Gligorov was elected as President by Macedonia's Parliament on 27 January 1991. Nicknamed the 'Fox of the Balkans', he had been one of the last defenders of the Yugoslav federation. Trained under Tito as an old-style communist leader, he worked hard to maintain ethnic tolerance between Macedonian Slavs, ethnic Albanians and Serbs, as well as recognising the rights of other minorities such as Turks and Romas. A pragmatist, Gligorov held a series of wide-ranging talks in which all parties took part. He brought the ethnic Albanians into government, but stopped short of alienating the Slav electorate by meeting Albanian demands for decentralised administration and recognition of their independent Albanian university at Tetovo. He forged a style of informal government by consensus using procedures that had no constitutional precedent.

Gligorov's first main challenge was to deal with the violent Greek opposition that arose to the new Macedonian state. Athens accused Skopje of wanting to seize the port of Thessaloniki from Greece and objected strongly to the design of the Macedonian flag, which incorporated the Star of Vergina, the burial place of Philip of Macedon, which is in Greece.

Since 1989, hardline nationalists had been posting signs around Skopje demanding a 'united Macedonia' and reading *Solun je nas* ('Thessaloniki is ours'). As we have seen, Tito had designs on Salonika in the late 1940s and this had not been forgotten by the Greeks.[7] Macedonia was regarded as a threat to Greek national integrity, in part because a Greek province has the same name.

The Greeks recalled that in 1990 nationalist demonstrators from the then Yugoslav republic had closed border crossings into Greece, calling for recognition of the Macedonian minority on Greek territory. Part of the problem was also, as James Pettifer noted, a legacy of bitterness from the Greek Civil War in which many of the Slav-speaking minority of northern Greece became active communists and were heavily involved in the guerrilla army. Pettifer quotes estimates that there were as many as 40,000 Slav speakers in the communist forces in the last phase of the civil war that ended in 1949:

> Many went into exile in Skopje and have risen to influential positions. There is an element of revenge here in the view of some in Athens. Across the mainstream political spectrum it has been suggested that the left-wing side in the civil war was some sort of minority Slav conspiracy, rather than a mass movement that had widespread support throughout Greece only two or three years before.[8]

In reality, landlocked, friendless Macedonia with virtually no army could pose little threat to Greece, a country of 10 million people that belonged to NATO. Some Skopje Government actions were insensitive, for example a draft banknote design showing a prominent historic building in Thessaloniki as Macedonian by implication. But the Greek reaction generally was hysterical and irrational. As Tikas Michas recounts: 'It would not be an overstatement to say that Greece's foreign policy during the first half of the last decade was dominated by a single issue: Macedonia.'[9]

David Owen, the EU mediator in the former Yugoslavia, unsurprisingly felt that the Greeks had a legitimate national interest at stake but was impressed by Gligorov's determination. 'When we met President Gligorov, I realised that this was going to be a hard issue to resolve; behind an external reasonableness he hid an inner resolve and inflexibility on this issue, because for him too this was an essential national interest.'[10]

For months, hundreds of thousands of Greeks demonstrated against the Macedonians in front of the Parthenon and other areas of Athens. The Greek army carried out manoeuvres on the frontier with Macedonia. Athens prevented foreign aid reaching Macedonia. In January 1992, for example, 97 tons of medicine and food destined for Macedonia were detained in Greece in spite of a grave influenza epidemic in Macedonia. In August 1992, Athens closed the border and imposed an oil embargo. As Michas notes, throughout the early and middle 1990s, in statements by Greek politicians and the Greek press, Macedonia was referred to as 'an artificial creation', 'a counterfeit nation' and an 'invention of Tito'. Macedonians were called 'Skopjians' or 'Macedonians', in quotation marks, or 'pseudo-Macedonians'. The Macedonian language was referred to as a 'local idiom' or 'dialect' and an 'artificial construction'.[11]

Michas also argues convincingly that at the start of the 1990s the Greek Government was plotting with Milosevic to destabilise and carve up Macedonia between Athens and Belgrade. At mass rallies against Macedonia, Greeks chanted *Koina Sinora me ti Servia* ('common borders with Serbia'). 'There is now much hard evidence indicating that political leaders in Athens and Belgrade seriously entertained this adventurous scenario.'[12]

From 1991 to 1993, the Greek Prime Minister, Constantine Mitsotakis, and Foreign Minister, Antonis Samaras, met several times with Milosevic to discuss the 'Macedonian problem'. On 16 January 1992, Gligorov protested publicly that Milosevic, while in Athens, was discussing Macedonia without a Macedonian representative present.

According to Alexandros Tarkas, a senior policy adviser to Samaras, Milosevic had a long meeting with the Greek Ambassador in Belgrade, Lefteris Karagiannis, on 8 August 1991. Milosevic told the envoy: 'During the past few months I have discussed with your government the issue of Skopje. It is essential that our countries coordinate their policies.' Milosevic met Samaras a month later in Belgrade and showed the Greek Foreign Minister a map.

'Look here... in the centre of FYROM and especially in Tetovo and the surrounding areas live around 150,000 Serbs – not 40,000 as reported by the census,' Milosevic said.

The Greek Foreign Minister asked Milosevic, 'Do you mean that at one point or another they will face a problem and will have to move to another location?'

Milosevic replied, 'They will not move. Not only those but also thousands of other Serb refugees who are living in the north will move to the south toward Skopje, toward the Greek borders.'

Samaras was quoted as passing on to Mitsotakis the idea of 'exporting' Serb refugees to Macedonia though the Prime Minister did not comment on it. The following year, Mitsotakis did not object when the Greek Foreign Ministry adopted a plan involving Greece and Serbia in a common plan to destabilise Macedonia, the 'Samaras Pincer', which was designed to use economic pressure on Macedonia to provoke riots and instability, through the Greek blockade imposed on Skopje, and military pressure by the Yugoslav Army's 3rd Division, still in Macedonia at the time. Athens imposed an unofficial embargo on Macedonia in February 1992 that was covert so as to avoid European Community criticism, according to documents gathered by Michas. The embargo only became official later that summer.

Arkan, the Serb paramilitary leader, joined in the fray, declaring: 'This ghost state was created by the communist Tito in order to separate Greece from Serbia.' He said 200,000 Serbs lived in Macedonia and Serbia had a right to take the part that belonged to it. 'Of course,' he told the Greeks, 'you also have a right to take what remains. It is your natural northern border. Whatever will remain from this state will belong to you.'

In 1995, after a change of Greek Government, cooperation between Athens and Belgrade continued against Macedonia. On 16 February 1995, the Greek Prime Minister, Andreas Papandreou, decided to interrupt the transport of goods through Thessaloniki to and from Skopje. But Gligorov told Michas that Skopje did not take any possible threat of Greek military intervention seriously. 'We were always afraid of Milosevic's Serbia. We never considered Greece a real threat because we knew that she was constrained in her actions by her membership in the European Union and above all in NATO.'

The United Nations admitted Macedonia to membership on 8 April 1993, under the temporary name of the Former Yugoslav Republic of Macedonia. Macedonian satisfaction at this UN recognition was tempered by anger at the acceptance of the temporary name and there were protest rallies in Skopje, Kocani and Resen. About 600 Macedonian intellectuals demonstrated in front of the National Assembly building during a close vote on whether or not to accept the temporary name. In the end, 30 deputies voted in favour and 28 against, while 13 abstained.[13] The nationalist opposition party, the VMRO, called a vote of no-confidence over the name issue and the economy but the government survived, with 62 deputies supporting Gligorov's pragmatic diplomatic policies.

A short time before 1 January 1994, when Greece was to take over the revolving presidency of the EU, most European states also decided to recognise Macedonia as 'The Former Yugoslav Republic of Macedonia' (FYROM).

In February 1994, Greece imposed a total unilateral trade embargo, except for humanitarian items, to remind Macedonia, Papandreou said, that Athens was 'the primary guarantor of peace, stability and security' in the Balkans. This deprived the new nation of strategic access to Thessaloniki. The EU condemned this as a violation of European law and decided to institute legal proceedings in the European Court of Justice. But the Court ruled that the urgency of the case had not been established and that no decision could be expected before 1996.

The War of Maps

While much of the Greek reaction to the new state had been near hysterical, some eminent Greek scholars made forceful contributions to the debate over the nature of the Macedonian state and identified what they said were negative elements in ethnic Macedonian nationalism that later would come to the fore during the ethnic Albanian insurgency in 2001.

One of the more internationally respected Greek historians who weighed into the fray, arguing Athens' case intelligently, was Evangelos Kofos of the Institute for Balkan Studies at Thessaloniki. In a widely publicised lecture entitled 'The Vision of "Greater Macedonia"', delivered in 1994, Kofos analysed the contents of new secondary school textbooks on history and geography that the government of Gligorov introduced between 1992 and 1993.[14] 'After an examination of 12 such textbooks it has become apparent that the new leadership in

Skopje is perpetuating in its educational system certain negative features associated with the former Communist regime.' Kofos was interested in analysing the schoolbooks as a way of overcoming 'the repetition of past mistakes which have kept the Balkan peoples apart'.

Kofos expressed the hope that Greece and Macedonia might follow the example of efforts that Greece and Turkey had made in conferences held at Istanbul in 1986 and Patras in 1988 under the auspices of UNESCO's Balkan National Committee, establishing principles to be used in school textbooks particularly regarding contents referring to neighbours. Similar conferences were held by Greeks and Bulgarians in Athens in May 1990. The idea was to shake off national stereotypes even though 'obviously all the historical issues dividing the two states cannot be settled immediately'.

As Kofos saw it, Gligorov was presenting an image to the world of Macedonia as an underdog while in reality trying 'to appropriate the cultural heritage of the Greek world and to undermine and call into question Greece's supremacy in Greek Macedonia. And he is now striving to hand on to his children all that he inherited from the Tito regime'. Kofos noted that one type of map drawn up by Macedonian nationalists in the 1970s and 1980s:

> shows Greek Macedonia and the Bulgarian province of Blageovgrad ('Pirin Macedonia') as unliberated sections of a whole whose third part – the 'Socialist Republic of Macedonia' – was presented as a free entity within the framework of the Yugoslav Federation. Another series of maps, the product of extreme nationalist factions, portrayed all three sectors as under foreign occupation.
>
> Slavo-Macedonian nationalists abroad, free of local expediencies within the Balkans, proceeded to devote themselves to a nationalist 'war of maps'.

In 1992, the semi-official publishing house, Nova Makedonija, had published maps based on an inter-war Bulgarian production when Macedonia was not a state, including Slav names for Greek Macedonia. The Nova Makedonija map retained old Turkish and Slav names for places within Greece. 'This use of Slav place names can only be interpreted as a refusal on the part of the FYROM's political leaders to accept without reservation Greek sovereignty over Greek Macedonia,' Kofos concluded.

During UN negotiations in the recognition dispute, the Greek delegation submitted a copy of the Nova Makedonija production to the mediators Cyrus Vance and Lord Owen 'as indisputable proof of the irredentist tendencies prevalent in Skopje'.

The unofficial Macedonian representative in Washington at the time, Ljubica Acevska, claimed in an interview with the *New York Times* that the map was the initiative of a private publisher. However, Kofos disclosed that the maps in all new history and geography textbooks for the school year 1992–1993 were copies of that published by Nova Makedonija:

> Lest there be any doubts as to the intentions of the editors, all the maps were accompanied by the same explanations of symbols. National borders between neighbouring countries were shown by broken lines, while the solid black line designated the 'geografsko-etnitska granitsa', that is the 'geographical ethnic boundaries'.

> This second line did not outline today's FYROM as one might have expected but encircled the entire geographical territory of Macedonia to its extreme southern limit, that is the coast of the Aegean sea, the crest of Mount Olympus and continuing west to the Albanian border.

The Greek historian recalled an anecdote about a foreign diplomat at the United Nations who saw the map with Olympus divided in two and quipped that 'the FYROM's next step would probably be to demand that the gods of Olympus be re-assigned as well: six to the "Macedonians" and six to the Greeks!'

The maps were also the basis for the teaching of history in Macedonian schools so that young people in the newly independent country were educated in a spirit of 'bitterness and injustice, since 68 per cent of the lands the children have learned to regard as their own "national" territory are under foreign occupation by neighbouring states (Greece, Bulgaria, Albania),' Kofos said. 'With no opposition – for in matters of national ideology a sort of spiritual Stalinism still prevails in FYROM – it is inevitable that feelings of antagonism towards their neighbours will blow up to huge proportions in the near future.'

Kofos admitted that Greeks were especially sensitive on such matters but his exposition, although controversial, went a considerable way toward explaining why. His call for the 'political leaders of the countries of south-eastern Europe to muster the necessary courage' to resolve historiographical disputes helped to prepare the ground for an end to Athens' trade war against Skopje.

The End of the Dispute with Greece

After four years of negotiations and threats of retaliation by the EU, Greece lifted the embargo on 13 September 1995 in return for concessions from Macedonia. Skopje agreed to reform its constitution so as to adopt a new flag, a yellow eight-branched sun on a red background. It was also agreed that the provisional name, Former Yugoslav Republic of Yugoslavia, would remain until the US mediator, Cyrus Vance, resolved the dispute over what to call the state.

In 1997, the Greek foreign minister made a surprise visit to Skopje and urged cooperation between the two states in the light of the anarchy that had erupted in Albania. Greece invested considerably in Macedonia and, in November 1999, following the Kosovo crisis, the two states agreed to build an oil pipeline from Salonika to Skopje. In December of the same year, they signed a military agreement and a bilateral security accord, in part because of the ethnic Albanian insurgency in southern Serbia.

Officially, the name issue remains unresolved with negotiations still continuing in New York in April 2003. In 1993, Greece rejected suggestions by the international negotiators, Vance and Owen, of 'Nova Macedonia' and 'Upper Macedonia'. But outside of Greece 'Macedonia' has become universally accepted.

The ethnic Albanian minority in Macedonia has never become involved in the troublesome name issue. As Poulton, the expert on Macedonian minorities, noted:

> They view the name 'Republic of Macedonia' as being territorial without any special ethnic Slav connotations, and do not object to the references to antiquity by the authorities which so infuriate the Greeks.[15]

Ethnic Albanians suggested that, if the name had to be changed, an ethnically neutral 'Vardar Republic' or the ugly 'Central Balkan Republic' should be favoured. They objected to the use of Slav symbols such as pictures of Orthodox churches appearing on banknotes.

Bulgaria recognised the Macedonian state in 1992, becoming the first government to do so, but then officially still considered the Macedonian nation and language as belonging to 'western Bulgaria'. Historically, Bulgaria had long sought to reincorporate Macedonia into its territory. There were persistent reports that Bulgaria's President, Zeljo Zelev, had vetoed a Greek-Serbian plan for a Greek-Serbian-Bulgarian partition of Macedonia a short time after Macedonia declared independence.

Bulgarians professed horror when the Macedonian Prime Minister, Crvenkovski, used an interpreter when he met his Bulgarian opposite number, Berov, in Skopje in June 1993, though Bulgarian and Macedonian are mutually intelligible.

In February 1999, Bulgaria virtually recognised the existence of a Macedonian language, culture and nation separate from Bulgaria. Macedonia for its part renounced any claim on Pirin Macedonia.

The Conference on Security and Cooperation in Europe (CSCE) sent a 'spillover mission' to Macedonia in 1992 led by a US diplomat, Robert H. Frowick, who came to personify many aspects of the often bold but sometimes insensitive American policies in the region.

The mission argued that Macedonia was in grave danger of being drawn into the former-Yugoslav wars. Ironically, Frowick would controversially re-emerge as a special emissary for the Organisation for Security and Cooperation in Europe (OSCE) in Macedonia during the fighting of 2001 only to leave the country dramatically. In between, Frowick worked as head of the OSCE mission in Bosnia from 1995 to 1997, in charge of efforts to ensure the first post-Dayton elections were free and fair, and became a well-known figure promoting American interests in Albania.

The UN deployed troops on Macedonia's borders with Albania and Serbia in 1993 to prevent the conflict from the former Yugoslavia spreading. American troops deployed with this mission, the United Nations Preventative Peacekeeping Force (UNPREDEP), before they did in Bosnia. According to one report, the deployment was made after the CIA advised the Bush administration that a flare-up was imminent in Macedonia, which would definitely involve Greece and Turkey.[16]

Milosevic had met with Gligorov at Ohrid in June 1993 to try to persuade Macedonia not to accept the US troop deployment. Gligorov initially indicated he would go along with this but Skopje realised that accepting American forces would help its aspirations to become part of NATO. Macedonia was admitted as a member of the Central European Initiative, a forerunner of the Partnership for Peace, on 17 July 1993.

Macedonian politicians continued to be concerned about what they called the 'threat from the north' – that Belgrade might try to reclaim the territory. In April 1993, the defence minister, Vlado Popovski, said that Serbia still posed the greatest military threat to the new republic. That month, President Gligorov dismissed the Macedonian army chief-of-staff, General Mitre Arsovski, in part for saying while on a trip to Canada that there was no threat from the north.

The UN troops' mandate was twice extended, in 1996 and 1998, and then rescinded under a UN Security Council veto by China in retaliation for Macedonia's rash recognition of Taiwan. Poulton notes that 'this prompted speculation that it had been a US ploy to undermine the UN and thus reduce the effectiveness of the Russian and Chinese vetoes in the forthcoming war over Kosovo'.

Macedonia recognised Taiwan on 1 January 1999, in a deal in which Taipei promised aid of up to 300 million dollars in cash and more than a billion dollars over the long term. But by 2001 Skopje had received only 20 million dollars in direct investment from Taiwan and 150 million dollars in loans and technical assistance.[17]

Taiwan's improbable Alice-in-Wonderland saga in the murky waters of Macedonian politics started in 1998 during the parliamentary elections and was championed by Vasil Tupurkovski, a member for Macedonia of the previous Yugoslav collective presidency, who was of Greek origin and ran for election under the banner of his newly created Democratic Alternative (DA) Party. During the campaign, he promised that if elected he would bring 1 billion dollars in foreign investment. Tupurkovski had negotiated a deal with Taiwan and was accused by political opponents of profiting personally from the agreement – charges he strenuously denied. 'Simple greed led the Macedonians to fall into that trap,' a European diplomat in Skopje at the time commented. 'The Government was the laughing stock of the diplomatic corps.'

After Georgievski won the election and immediately recognised Taiwan, Beijing closed its embassy in Skopje and vetoed the UNPREDEP extension in the Security Council on 25 February 1999. The only other European state that had full diplomatic ties with Taipei was the Vatican.

Taiwan immediately opened an embassy in Skopje. But President Gligorov, who had been opposed to the recognition but did not have the constitutional power to block it, refused to receive the Taiwanese Ambassador, who thus was unable to present his Letters of Credentials. Taiwan had an embassy but no accredited ambassador.[18]

Tupurkovski ran for president in December 1999 but was defeated by Boris Trajkovski, who was no friend of Taiwan. By mid 2000, the DA had started to break up into opposing factions and when a new coalition government was formed the foreign minister was a member of Gligorov's party who had opposed recognition of Taiwan.

Macedonia would restore relations with China on 12 June 2001, evidently anxious to avoid Beijing vetoing UN support for Skopje in the conflict with ethnic Albanian guerrillas. Georgievski was no longer affiliated with the original DA that had recognised Taiwan and so felt no obligation in this regard.

Macedonia was denied international aid before its official recognition by the UN in April 1993. In addition to suffering the effects of the Greek embargo, Macedonia's efforts to adapt to a market economy were hindered by the international embargo against Serbia and Montenegro, depriving the country of half of its export markets and an estimated 4 billion dollars in lost income. This was only partially made up by sanctions-busting smuggling into Yugoslavia.

An austerity policy pursued from 1994 bore fruit, however. Galloping inflation was curbed from 2250 per cent in 1992 to 226 per cent in 1993 and three per cent in 1996. The budget deficit fell from 11 per cent to two per cent of GDP over the same period.

The cost of the stabilisation programme was reflected in the decline in per capita incomes, which on some estimates tumbled from an average of 800 dollars in 1989 to 400 dollars in 1996. Industrial production also fell by half. Unemployment today is still around 30 per cent officially (unofficial estimates are around 60 per cent) and the banking sector, civil service and agricultural cooperatives have been slow to adopt to the new economic environment.

Nevertheless, Macedonians remained optimistic about making the most of their unique position at a crossroads in southern Europe between the Black Sea and the Adriatic, the Aegean Sea and the Danube. American commercial interests in Macedonia, for example, centre on a project to build a trans-Balkan pipeline designed to secure a passage for oil from the Caspian Sea. The line will run from the Black Sea port of Bourgas to the Adriatic at Vlora, passing through Bulgaria, Macedonia and Albania. It is likely to become the main route to the West for the oil and gas being extracted in central Asia. It will carry 750,000 barrels a day: a throughput, at 2001 current prices, of some 600 million dollars a month.

According to a paper published by the US Trade and Development Agency in May 2000, the pipeline is important because the oil coming from the Caspian Sea 'will quickly surpass the safe capacity of the Bosphorus as a shipping lane'. The agency notes that the scheme will:

> provide a consistent source of crude oil to American refineries, ... provide American companies with a key role in developing the vital east-west corridor, ... advance the privatisation aspirations of the US government in the region... [and] facilitate rapid integration [of the Balkans] with Western Europe.

In November 1998, Bill Richardson, then US Energy Secretary, spelt out his policy on the extraction and transport of Caspian oil:

This is about America's energy security. It's also about preventing strategic inroads by those who don't share our values. We're trying to move these newly independent countries toward the West.

We've made a substantial political investment in the Caspian, and it's very important to us that both the pipeline map and the politics come out right.

The pipeline features prominently in Balkan war politics. On 9 December 1998, the Albanian president attended a meeting about the scheme in Sofia, and linked Albanian support for it inextricably to western recognition of an independent Kosovo. 'It is my personal opinion that no solution confined within Serbian borders will bring lasting peace.'

The USA sent peacekeeping troops to the Balkans in July 1993, not to the conflict zones in which civilians were being rounded up and killed, but on the northern borders of Macedonia as part of the UN deployment. Some observers have linked this to American interest in the pipeline project.

The project's manager, Edward Ferguson, the President and CEO of the Albanian, Macedonian and Bulgarian Oil Corporation, which manages the project, said on 15 February that the concern is in 'regular discussions' with Chevron Texaco Corporation and Exxon Mobil Corporation about building the 1.13 billion-dollar pipeline. AMBO, registered in the United States, has letters of acceptance from the governments of the three Balkan countries for the 898-kilometre (560-mile) underground pipeline.

The main consumers of the oil carried through the trans-Balkan pipeline would be north-western Europe and the United States rather than the Mediterranean region. 'America's own crude resources are declining rapidly and it already imports over 50 per cent of its annual needs. Europe enters in a similar situation – reserves in the north are declining and it will start running out of oil supplies around 2010.' AMBO was confident that another planned 607 million dollar pipeline sending crude from Russia to Greece via Bulgaria would not threaten its own project as the two had targeted different investors and consumers.

During the 2001 conflict, Mark Almond, a Balkan scholar at Oriel College, Oxford, also emphasised the crucial nature of pipeline interests in western intervention in Macedonia:

> Why should the West want to take over the running of a small, poor country like Macedonia with few natural resources? The answer is

strategic. The country lies on the route to be taken by oil pipelines set to run from the Black Sea coast in the east to Albania's Adriatic coast. Control of the pipeline is essential to the West's long-term energy plans.[19]

In the parliamentary elections of October and November 1994, widespread electoral fraud was alleged. The VMRO boycotted the second round of voting after it had failed to win any seats in the first, in spite of being the largest party in the outgoing assembly.

The new state's fragility also was underlined by the attempted assassination of President Gligorov on 5 October 1995, attributed by some sources in Skopje to the skulduggery of Bulgarian agents and by others to organised crime mobsters. Gligorov was treated by French, Serbian and Greek doctors who arrived rapidly in Macedonia.

The Government coalition dominated by the Social Democratic Party for Macedonian Union (SDSM), the former Communist Party, had begun to lose popularity by 1996. Liberal Party ministers squabbled with their SDSM counterparts, accusing them of running the country through corruption and the old methods of the Communist *nomenklatura*. The ministers were sacked and replaced with Albanians from the Party of Democratic Prosperity (PDP).

The anti-communist VMRO-DPMNE made sweeping gains in municipal elections held in December 1996, reaping the fruits of nationalist reaction to the PDP's increased representation and setting the stage for the nationalist victory in 1998 parliamentary elections. This would mark the first time Macedonia was not ruled by the left in more than 50 years, a sea change in the politics of the country that would have far-reaching consequences.

Macedonia's Ethnic Albanian Problem

Tension between ethnic Albanians and Macedonian Slavs grew throughout the 1990s, reflecting growing Macedonian nationalism and the strife under way between ethnic Albanians and Serbs in Kosovo.

Macedonia's Albanians became radicalised after the republic revised the constitution in 1989 to limit their citizenship rights. In 1990, 2,000 Albanians marched through Tetovo demanding independence and unity with Albania. The protest was broken up by paramilitary police.

In 1991, many ethnic Albanians refused to take part in a national census, making it hard to substantiate some radicals' claim to be as many as 35 or even 40 per cent of the population. In the 1981 Yugoslav census, the population of the Socialist Republic of Macedonia was 1,912,257, of which there were 1,281,195 (66 per cent) Macedonians,

377,726 (19.7 per cent) Albanians, 44,613 Serbs, 39,555 Pomaks, 47,233 Gypsies, 86,691 Turks, 7,190 Vlachs and 1,984 Bulgarians. By 1992, the Albanian population was estimated at up to 25 per cent – offically it is now 25.17 per cent. Because Albanians have the highest birth rate in Europe it has been estimated that ethnic Albanians could be in a majority in Macedonia within three or four decades. Put simply, the problem was that there were not enough ethnic Macedonians.

The new constitution of independent Macedonia declared in November 1991, when the nationalist VMRO was the dominant party in Parliament, went further than the 1989 changes, removing the rights of minorities to proportional representation on public bodies, a measure that had given Albanians at least some influence in the running of the old Yugoslav socialist republic.

The main claims by the ethnic Albanian parties have been threefold: to be recognised as equal by the Macedonian constitution; for Albanian to be an official language; and for a state-funded university. The Albanians said they faced an administration that was so disproportionately Macedonian that they were made to feel 'alien'. Ethnic Albanians made up only 3.1 per cent of the police force and the military until 2001.

The Government dismissed charges of discrimination, saying that such disparities were partly due to education levels among Macedonia's Albanians generally being lower than among ethnic Macedonians. But, since the 1980s, the Albanians had developed a better-educated political elite, principally among those of them who had worked as *Gastarbeiters* in Germany and other West European countries.

President Gligorov at first sought to contain the agitation by giving members of the then-moderate Party for Democratic Prosperity (PDP) four ministerial portfolios and meeting some cultural demands for representation in education and the mass media. Albanians in Government generally were given token positions as 'assistant ministers' to Slav-speakers without offices or staff and were kept out of sensitive ministries especially the Interior Ministry, which was, and is, the source of most real power in the new state.

A police crackdown in November 1992 on black-market smuggling activities in the Bit Pazar, the old Ottoman district of Skopje, led to the arrest of several ethnic Albanians and reports that one young Albanian from Ljuboten had been beaten to death in a police station. Angry crowds protested their innocence and three Albanians and one Macedonian were killed when paramilitary police opened fire on a mostly peaceful protest.

After the Bit Pazar disturbances, the EU became concerned that Macedonia might disintegrate and put pressure on President Gligorov to reintegrate with Yugoslavia. At the London Conference on former Yugoslavia in 1993, the British Foreign Secretary, Douglas Hurd, urged him to remain as close to Belgrade as possible and consider rejoining Yugoslavia after the northern Balkan wars were over.[20] British and French intelligence and security experts provided assistance to the Macedonian Interior Ministry.

Among the foreign agents operating in Macedonia was Richard Tomlinson of Britain's Secret Intelligence Service (MI6), who later dramatically fell out with his masters. He gave an intriguing but inevitably partial account of his work in Skopje in his book *The Big Breach*. In mid 1992, the only SIS offices in the former Yugoslavia were a one-man station in Zagreb and two officers in Belgrade, Tomlinson recounted:

> The Macedonian secret police were underfunded, and so were vulnerable to financial inducement. MI6 saw the opportunity and stepped in before the [German] BND or the CIA. After some paper shuffling in Whitehall an emergency aid package was negotiated... Britain would supply urgently needed medical equipment and drugs; in return Macedonia would harbour an MI6 officer'.[21]

Britain exerted special influence in Macedonia, as it does to this day, and Gligorov met again with Hurd in May 1993 to discuss security matters. British technical help was provided to the Interior Ministry as Gligorov's supporters purged it of VMRO nationalists, who were accused of being excessively pro-Bulgarian and pro-Russian. Instead pro-Serb spymasters and security chiefs were imposed and ran the ministry until the nationalist electoral victory in 1998.

In early 1993, Tomlinson was assigned to what he said was a supporting role in Macedonia to the resident MI6 officer and tasked with penetrating an ethnic Albanian party, working undercover as a journalist from the London *Spectator* magazine.

The renegade spy recalled his Skopje colleague, 'Jonathan Small', inviting him to a trip to the countryside 'to check out the station exfiltration plan', via a secret airstrip behind a copse on a hillside a few miles south of Skopje:

> The Skopje exfiltration plan differed from usual station plans in that its purpose was not to smuggle out compromised agents, but to get Small out in case the Macedonian liaison turned against him. They were a brutish lot and the political situation was not stable enough to wholly trust them. If it suited their purpose to kidnap or

imprison Small, he could not claim diplomatic immunity as officially he was not there.

The USA also bolstered its presence in Macedonia, in 1996 appointing as its first ambassador to the country Christopher Hill, a career diplomat who had been a key member of the team that had helped Richard Holbrooke negotiate the Dayton peace accord ending the 1992–1995 Bosnian War.

In his memoirs, Holbrooke recalled how Hill, 'the brilliant, fearless and argumentative country director for the Balkans', took over as his deputy from Robert Frasure, a principal negotiator with Milosevic and other key players, after Frasure died in a tragic accident on Sarajevo's Mount Igman.

Public sympathy for the Kosovar Albanians had reached fever pitch in Albania and ethnic Albanian areas of Macedonia by 1991. Albanians in western Macedonia had family and political ties to Kosovar Albanians. Their stockpiling of weapons for 'communal self-defence' in the early days after Macedonian independence led in November 1993 to criminal charges of arms smuggling and forming a paramilitary organisation being filed against members of the largest Macedonian Albanian party. Convictions in the 'arms scandal' or 'arms plot' as it was called, led to tough prison sentences.

The Arms Plot

Ten Macedonian Albanians, including Mithat Emini, former general secretary of the PDP, and Husein Haskaj, the Albanian assistant Minister of Defence, were convicted of plotting to organise an irredentist Albanian army aiming to set up a secessionist Albanian state called 'Illyrida' and were sentenced to prison terms of five to eight years. Their defence was that this was self-defence before a Macedonian army had been created. They were tried under former Yugoslav law. Members of the Government had evidently reassured PDP members they would receive light sentences of at most 18 months.[22]

Some western military sources believe that Tomlinson played a key role in fomenting the arms scandal and that French, as well as British, intelligence may have been involved in the affair. 'It would seem that the UK was involved in the arms plot,' one military source said:

> If we are to believe what Tomlinson says his activities would have been approved. The objective presumably was to stabilise Macedonia by luring the ethnic Albanian radicals into a trap: 'Nip it in the bud, old chap'. This is how our Governments' agencies operate.[23]

In his book, Tomlinson describes how he enrolled the deputy head of an ethnic Albanian party as an agent after disclosing that he was a British intelligence officer and not a journalist as he first introduced himself.

Tension with Albania in the aftermath of the affair flared up in June 1993 and threatened to set off a border war between Macedonia and Albania, according to western military sources. In June 1993, an Albanian intelligence officer, a major in the 'troops of reconnaissance' who was quite senior in Tirana's border guard, was shot and killed by Macedonian border guards and an Albanian sergeant with him was wounded, a western military attaché in Skopje at the time has disclosed.

'They left the sergeant for dead and he survived and made it back to Albania to tell what had happened. It nearly started a border war,' the diplomat told me, adding that the Macedonians had deliberately killed the Albanian officer.[24]

'This was not an accident. The Macedonians had set up a meeting on the border with the Albanian major and then instead of meeting him they shot him.' The ugly incident was only one of several unreported clashes that encouraged New York to deploy UN tripwire troops in Macedonia. 'There were quite a number of deaths of Albanians on the border at the time, more than on the Kosovo side. This led the European Union to deploy monitors on the Albanian side as well,' said the source.

In September 1993, the nationalist radical wing of the PDP, the largest of the Albanian parties in Macedonia, confronted the leadership of Nevzat Halili at its party congress, accusing him of failing to 'obtain either autonomy or the status of a "people of the state" in Macedonia'. The radicals, supported by the Albanian President, Sali Berisha, had taken control of the Tetovo party organisation in June 1993 and other branches followed.

The party split in two. By the spring of 1994, even the more moderate wing (although still coalition partners of Gligorov's SDSM) had adopted the radicals' position on the demand for 'constituent nation' status in Macedonia. The radical PDP was to become the future Democratic Party of Albanians (DPA) led by Menduh Thaci and Arben Xhaferi. These were long treated as something akin to pariahs by western diplomats in Skopje, who generally limited their contacts with Albanian politicians to the moderate PDP leader Abdurman Haliti and rarely ventured into Albanian-dominated areas in western Macedonia.

Xhaferi was born in 1948 in Tetovo, where he attended primary and secondary school. He studied at the Belgrade University faculty of philosophy and took part in leftist student demonstrations in the

Yugoslav capital in 1968. After graduating from the psychology department, he decided to become a journalist, and remained in the press industry until 1993. Before he left journalism he worked as a film editor at Pristina radio-television.

When a multi-party system was introduced in Macedonia, he became a member of the Party for Democratic Prosperity. He was elected to the Macedonian parliament in parliamentary elections in October 1994 as one of six DPA representatives in the opposition. The party also participated in local government in Tetovo and other Albanian-dominated towns and cities in western Macedonia.

The vicissitudes of the economy also accentuated ethnic resentments. Official unemployment was 28 per cent by mid 1994, and 23 per cent of those who were employed had not been paid for more than four months. 'Because this unemployment was primarily in the formal economy, Macedonians were far more affected than Albanians who congregated more in the informal sector,' Susan Woodward noted, 'and resentment at this difference was contributing to inter-ethnic tension and a rise in support for Macedonian nationalist parties.' Such resentment continues today.

Education was one of the main sources of tension in the first decade of the new Macedonian republic. Article 48 of the Constitution, adopted on 6 January 1992, enshrined the right to education in the languages of national minorities at both the primary and secondary level. But there was no such guarantee for minority-language education at the university level. Apart from a small pedagogical faculty at the University of Saints Cyril and Methodius in Skopje, the country's two state-run universities taught only in Macedonian.

The Albanian community, on its own initiative, founded the Albanian-language University of Tetovo (*Universiteti i Tetoves*) on 15 February 1995, in spite of the building originally earmarked to house it being demolished by the authorities. Initially, it comprised five faculties: law, economics, languages, education and natural sciences. Staff were recruited from the already established Albanian-language University of Pristina.

Two days after the university opened, it was closed by the Macedonian police. Street clashes led to one person killed and 15 injured. The University Rector, Dr Fadil Sulejmani, was convicted of sedition and sentenced to two-and-a-half years in prison, but was released on bail in June that year.

Britain's David Owen, who at that time led European mediation efforts in the former Yugoslavia, recalled how in Macedonia:

where Ambassador Ahrens had just visited Skopje for the third round of renewed trilateral talks between the government and the three Albanian parties, the trial in Tetovo of Prof. Sulejmani... was heightening tension. The Albanians had raised in the talks the issue of the use of their language in Parliament, to which the Minister of Justice had replied that this was a matter of 'massive sensitivity', and we in the International Conference on the Former Yugoslavia (ICFY) were trying to explore the logistics of having simultaneous translation of oral statements. In Kosovo many of the pupils involved in the 'illegal' Albanian language secondary and elementary school classes had been readmitted into the official school system. In ICFY we believed that a flare-up was now more likely in Tetovo than in Kosovo.[25]

Eleanor Pritchard wrote later that:

The university's existence remains vociferously unrecognised by the state amid accusations it is a hotbed of radical Albanian nationalism and Greater Albanian expansionist ideology. As in Kosovo, minority education has come to symbolise the struggle for all minority rights in the state.[26]

She noted that ethnic Macedonians feared recognition of the university:

Some suspect it is the first step in a programme of secessionism, aiming to sever the west of the country in order to form some kind of alliance with Albania and Kosovo. By contrast, others fear the rise of Albanians as a threat to Macedonian society per se... the widespread regional fear among Slavs of Islamic domination in the peninsula, so redolent of the ghostly Ottoman Empire, has been well documented in recent years.

In the late 1990s, Macedonia was affected by the Albanian uprising in 1997, in which President Berisha's regime in Tirana was violently overthrown. Instability in Albania first affected Macedonia in 1996, when the large Macedonian savings bank, TAT, headquartered in the city of Bitola, collapsed after it diverted money into Albanian pyramid banking schemes and thousands of Macedonian Albanians lost their savings. Arms that the insurgents in Albania seized from Albanian police and army armouries started to flow over the Macedonian border, which was controlled on parts of the Albanian side for a time by paramilitary gangs. Macedonia became increasingly infested with Albanian organised crime and narcotics smuggling rings.

Three ethnic Albanians were shot and killed when Macedonian police broke up a demonstration of several hundred in the streets of Gostivar in July 1997. The mayors of Gostivar and Tetovo, Rufi Osmani and Adem Demiri, were arrested and sentenced to several years in prison after the Albanian double-headed eagle flag was draped over the façades of their town halls. Xhaferi and the other DPA representatives in Parliament refused to take part in proceedings for six months in protest at the clashes at Gostivar.

In autumn 1997, Macedonian authorities announced as a concession that Albanian lecturers at Skopje University would be allowed to train in their own language, setting off vehement protest demonstrations by Macedonian Slav students.

If Britain and France stalwartly supported the dominant Macedonian elite, the USA and international organisations played a significant role in encouraging Albanian radicalism in Macedonia, a policy that some analysts, such as Woodward as early as 1995, had seen as inept and dangerous. 'The distinction between human rights and national rights, which all governments in the former republics were struggling to maintain, was not aided by the intervention of international actors,' she said.

> In their policies toward Macedonia during 1993, international actors… assumed that inter-ethnic conflict was a prime source of internal instability, which could escalate into armed hostility and war, so they focused on the human rights of the Albanian minority… By early 1994, however, observers already took for granted that Albanians in Macedonia had the right to territorial autonomy in the western counties and that denying this would deny their human rights. Not only were they keeping alive ambiguity over the legitimacy of Serb rule in Kosovo and signalling support for the Albanian project of separate statehood, but they also appeared to be helping this project along in its goal of linking with Albanians in Macedonia and Albania.

> On what basis, therefore, was a Macedonian state legitimate? On what basis could it defend its territorial integrity, particularly if Albanian aspirations continued to gain encouragement as well?

Not everyone agreed with Woodward, however. Misha Glenny wrote in *Foreign Affairs* in May 1995 that 'the United States has done more in the southern Balkans than anybody else and is to be congratulated for its perspicacity. This has been a quiet, if crucially unfinished, triumph for which the Clinton administration deserves due credit.'[27]

In November 1998, a right-wing 'For Change' coalition of VMRO and the Democratic Alliance headed by Tupurkovski formed a Government under Ljubco Georgievski. Tupurkovski's party drew much of its support from ex-civil war Greek families and would go back into opposition a year later. Tupurkovski had been a close associate of Gligorov and the last Macedonian member of the rotating presidency of the old Yugoslavia. His father was a communist commander in the Democratic Army in the Greek Civil War from 1946 to 1949 who went into exile in Skopje after 1950.

More innovatively, the Cabinet included members of the Democratic Party of Albanians. At the time there was a general belief in Macedonia that the Albanians should be given more representation in government and there also was international pressure to include them. Georgievski initially sought to appease the Albanians by promising money for Tetovo University and releasing Gostivar's mayor from prison where he was serving his term for displaying the Albanian flag.

President Gligorov rejected amnesty for the mayor, but Parliament overrode his veto, a sign of his declining influence. Xhaferi's party won 11 parliamentary seats in the 1998 elections and was rewarded with five ministerial posts and several deputy ministers in the Georgievski government. 'We have found the right partner,' Xhaferi said. 'This [VMRO] is not a pro-Serb party, but a party supporting pro-Macedonian ideas, and it is with this idea that we will be able to put into practice fundamental ideas that are very important for the region.'[28]

The Impact of the Kosovo War and 'Operation Horseshoe'

Hundreds of thousands of ethnic Albanians fled to Macedonia in 1999 to escape the Serb crackdown on them in Kosovo. On 2 April alone, 45,000 Albanians flooded into Macedonia.

Initially, Macedonian authorities earned international condemnation by trying to expel the refugees to other countries. On 3 April, they refused to let any in at all. This led to 65,000 being trapped at the Blace border point. The previous year, with Yugoslav agreement, they had planned a 'corridor', which would, it was hoped, be used to control the movement of refugees from Kosovo to Albania without them passing through the Albanian inhabited areas of Macedonia. But the scale of the influx had not been anticipated.

Milosevic is believed to have hoped that the influx of these Albanians, who the Yugoslav president and Macedonian authorities thought would never go home, would upset the fragile ethnic balance in Macedonia and tip the country into war between the Slav majority and Albanian minority.

According to a statement on 7 April by Joschka Fischer, the German Foreign Minister at the time, the expulsion of the ethnic Albanian population of Kosovo was part of a specific plan known as 'Operation Horseshoe'. Milosevic had told him in March that 'Serbian forces could empty Kosova within a week', but the German envoy had not taken him seriously.[29] 'The operation's title was strictly descriptive,' reported *The Observer*:

> The Serb military and police would squeeze the KLA and civilians in an attack launched from three sides, destroying the KLA's bases and fighters and driving out the population as refugees fled through the open southwestern end of the horseshoe into Macedonia and Albania.
>
> The game had been given away to western intelligence in a number of statements that should have been impossible to ignore. Most chillingly its purpose had been described to western diplomats by General Sreten Lukic, the same man who commanded the Racak operation and also – as intelligence intercepts would later make clear – its' cover-up. Lukic had described it as a massive 'clockwise' sweep across the country that would finally destroy the KLA. He had said he hoped to complete the KLA's annihilation by October.[30]

German officials provided no hard evidence of the plan, however, and, although it was widely accepted by the media at the time, its nature and existence since have been questioned. A senior US State Department source told Judah that 'Bulgaria and some other states in the region' had passed some information to the USA about 'Operation Horseshoe' and 'Operation Winter', but that it was extremely vague and not taken very seriously. Judah argues that: 'While there was without a doubt a major plan to crush the KLA which could have resulted in large numbers of refugees, until the archives are opened in Belgrade, the real picture will remain unclear.'[31]

Braca Grubacic, the respected editor of the *VIP* newsletter in Belgrade, added: 'There were vague ideas about expulsions, but I doubt that there was a real Horseshoe plan. I think that when the bombing started they just did it.'[32]

In 2000, a German general claimed the report of *Potkova* (Horseshoe) revealed by Fischer was faked. Heinz Loquai, a retired brigadier general, claimed in a book on the war that the plan was fabricated from run-of-the-mill Bulgarian intelligence reports. Loquai, then working for the OSCE, accused Scharping, the German Defence Minister at the time, of obscuring the origins of Horseshoe.[33]

Whatever the truth was, Skopje was faced with vast columns of weary, dehydrated and beaten civilians on its borders. Under western pressure, Boris Trajkovski, then a deputy foreign minister, urged that the refugees be allowed in, after initially asking the West to provide aircraft to take them away. The exact number of people who fled the province to Macedonia in all is still unclear, but reliable estimates put it at around 300,000, or one third of Kosovo's population.[34]

Even under western pressure, Macedonian policy had its limits and at times included desperate measures. In April 1999, there was a forced overnight resettlement of 40,000 Kosovar refugees from one camp in Macedonia to Albania. The authorities apparently set a limit on how many refugees should enter and remain in the country: officially the figure from March 1998 to 20 April 1999 was 127,500.[35]

Milosevic had underestimated the ability of the United Nations High Commission for Refugees (UNHCR) and western countries to react extremely quickly to the influx. On 4 April, the British Foreign Secretary, Robin Cook, called his staff and said: 'How can we cope with these people? I want an answer by 11 o'clock. Come up with the policy.'[36] An answer was found through 8,000 NATO troops being assembled in Macedonia under the command of Britain's General Jackson for peacekeeping envisaged under the Rambouillet peace package. They were ordered to build refugee camps.

In this way, the 'refugee bomb' was partially defused. Refugees were marshalled into the giant Stenkovec camps built just over the border. NATO troops also were rapidly deployed to help contain the problem in Albania with camps being built in Kukes and refugees distributed across the country.

At the same time, Christopher Hill sought to reassure Skopje that Washington was committed to Macedonian survival. 'Macedonia has an important role as a factor of stability in the Balkans... ultimately, as a multiethnic state, we very much want to see it succeed, and we're going to stand by it, and help ensure that it does succeed,' he said.[37]

But the refugee crisis continued to strain Macedonian capacity. When large numbers arrived on the border on 19 April, after an interlude in which they were prevented from arriving by Serb forces, Skopje said that only 400 of the 3,000 could be accepted. Refugee camps were filled to three times their capacity and Macedonian authorities would only allow one small extra one.

By early May, the official total was over 200,000 – more than 10 per cent of Macedonia's population. Skopje said it would not take any more and closed the border. The Democratic Party of Albanians threatened to walk out of the coalition government because of the treatment of the refugees but was persuaded to stay for fear that political instability would compromise NATO policy.

The Macedonian Albanians' anger diminished as it became clear that the UNHCR, NATO governments and dozens of non-governmental organisations were by now responding rapidly and effectively to the crisis. The camps were well run, with food and water, medical supplies, doctors and even satellite telephones. The camps were hardly comfortable but, compared to refugee camps in Africa or other parts of the Third World, they were at the luxury end of the market. The Macedonian authorities enforced a ban on people leaving the camps because they did not want refugees to move out to friends or family in Skopje or in ethnic Albanian-inhabited western Macedonia. As a result, most ordinary people ended up in tents, but middle-class and professional Kosovars and those with connections rarely went into the camps and instead travelled directly to Tetovo.

The Kosovo crisis cost the Macedonian economy an estimated 630 million dollars in lost exports over three months. Some 40,000 employees were laid off because of lost production. By November, 90 per cent of these had been rehired, but unemployment remained high with the official number of jobless, 341,500, exceeding the number of people in regular employment (313,400). The Government spent 200 million dollars on shelter for the refugees, but the Finance Ministry estimated it received only 42 million dollars in foreign aid donations to help it bear the burden.

By 1999, Macedonia's trade with the other former Yugoslav republics was only 20 per cent of the level of commercial exchange in 1990 but this had not been compensated by any significant increase in commerce with the West. Industrial production increased by an average of 15 per cent in September and October in spite of the crisis. But the balance of payments deficit was 241 million dollars in 1999 and at the end of October that year foreign exchange reserves held by the central bank in Skopje were only 412 million dollars. The average monthly wage in 1999 was around 175 dollars, a modest increase of 2.8 per cent on the previous year.[38]

During the NATO bombing of Serbia and Kosovo, Macedonia allowed thousands of NATO troops to base themselves in the country and use Macedonia's airports and road links with Greece for supply lines. Even before the bombing, NATO access to Macedonian airspace provided by the Government in Skopje gave the alliance flexibility in developing a range of options that NATO defence ministers drew up on 11 June 1998, for 'halting or disrupting a systematic campaign of violent repression and expulsion in Kosovo'.

In a show of military strength which was designed to intimidate Serb forces in Kosovo, NATO decided to carry out air exercises over Macedonia and Albania. The exercise, 'Determined Falcon', was held on 15 June 1998 and was projected as a demonstration of NATO's 'capability to project power rapidly into the region'.[39]

The incentive for Skopje was above all the apparent prospect of obtaining faster-track NATO membership, seen as all the more desirable after the Taiwan adventure backfired into the withdrawal of the vestiges of the UN tripwire force. Christopher Shapardanov, a NATO headquarters liaison officer in Skopje, noted in the spring of 1999 that Macedonia already participated in NATO's Partnership for Peace Programme and had in September 1998 been the site of a joint NATO-Macedonian military exercise, 'Operation Best Effort'. 'In the short term the alliance has provided some very strong and robust security assurances,' Shapardanov said. 'We hope that Macedonia of course will... look to membership as a very strong, long-term prospect.'[40]

Ironically, given the stance he would take during the crisis in 2001, Georgievski was bitterly criticised by the left-wing opposition for what was seen as his pro-NATO stance. In a profile, Belgrade's independent Beta news agency commented:

> Georgievski has met virtually all of the West's demands since his party came to power in 1998, turning Macedonia into a logistics base for NATO prior to the military alliance's intervention against the Federal Republic of Yugoslavia and after the NATO troops started deploying in Kosovo in the summer of 1999... His political opponents at the time criticised Georgievski, saying that he had damaged Macedonia's sovereignty by embracing the NATO troops.

Georgievski was born on 17 January 1966 in Stip, where he received primary and secondary education. He graduated from the department of literature at the Skopje University faculty of philosophy. From the start of his political career, Georgievski was a fierce advocate of a free and independent Macedonia and a staunch anti-communist. He was accused of supporting pro-Bulgarian (and hence pro-Russian) policies and of taking a hard stance toward Macedonia's other neighbours that contrasted with Gligorov's policy of equidistance.

His party won a majority of votes in the first multi-party elections in 1990 but was unable to take office because it could not find a coalition partner. In 1991, at the age of 26, Georgievski became the country's vice president. After eight months in office, he became dissatisfied with the moderate Gligorov policies and what he saw as the slow progress from communism to democracy. He resigned and returned to the opposition as a member of parliament from 1992 to 1995. He also was a successful businessman and a leading figure in the BS holding company. He ran his party with an iron hand, disbanding its executive committee in 1997 after a rift between pro- and anti-Bulgarian factions blew up.

Trajkovski, born in Strumica on 25 June 1956, was educated in law at Skopje's St. Cyril and Methodius University and then at a Protestant theological college in the USA. He specialised in commercial law and employment law and went on to head the legal department of a construction company. In 1997, he became Chief of Office of the Mayor of Kisela Voda municipality in Skopje and he was appointed Macedonia's Deputy Minister of Foreign Affairs in January 1999.

He won presidential elections against the Social Democrats' Tito Petkovshi in October and November 1999 to become head of state at the age of 43. Malpractice forced a re-vote in about a tenth of the constituencies in western Macedonia. Many ethnic Albanians, disillusioned with the former governing party led largely by ex-communists, voted for Trajkovski in a last-minute swing against Petkovshi, the first-round front-runner, and he enjoyed western support.

British support for President Trajkovski in his campaign to replace Gligorov was particularly strong. He has been a frequent visitor to an international Christian leadership organisation based at Windsor and the costumes of his Presidential Guard were redesigned to resemble British models.[41] Nevertheless, President Trajkovski was to be faced with a Herculean task. For, as Woodward commented:

> The reasons that independence movements developed later in Bosnia-Herzegovina and Macedonia, and similarly in Azerbaijan, Georgia and Tajikistan, are also reasons that violence – once it began – spread with far greater speed and intensity.
>
> Borderlands of former imperial regimes, these regions had populations that were particularly mixed ethnically and nationally. Created by outside powers as international compromises to achieve a regional balance of power, the former Yugoslav republics of Macedonia and Bosnia-Herzegovina and the former Soviet republics in the Caucasus are not easily able to achieve political autonomy.
>
> Even where their leaders pushed for their own greater autonomy within the overarching state, these lands and peoples caught in between the policies of a reforming centre and those of nationalist

separatists supported the multinational state longer because their territory and multinational security depended on it.[42]

Trajkovski failed to establish his authority over Georgievski and over the hardline interior minister in the first three years of the nationalist Government's life, Dosta Dimovska, who was seen as having a pro-Bulgarian orientation. This was to cause serious problems. In the view of a western diplomat based in Skopje:

> Trajkovski was a person who was honest, which was rare, and he was decent. But he was emotional and in character terms he was brittle, he needed a lot of support and when he didn't have enough he was out of his depth. If you look at his record he was the most important person in preventing civil war in Macedonia but he needed constant support from the international community.[43]

In the first decade of its existence, Macedonia avoided the fate of Bosnia, Croatia and Slovenia, seceding from Yugoslavia without a shot being fired. It overcame historic resistance to Macedonian statehood from Bulgaria and sweated out a long and dangerous crisis with Greece to obtain EU recognition. But internally Macedonia was deeply vulnerable to the ethnic division between Slav Macedonians and Albanians.

During elections throughout the decade, the Albanian parties skilfully used their position to exploit the balance of power between the nationalist VMRO and the pro-Serb SDSM and the fractious and fragmented situation within the Slav Macedonian elite that led, for example, to squabbling between the VMRO and the Democratic Alliance. But the supposedly radical DPA disappointed many ethnic Albanians who voted for it.

The involvement of Xhaferi's party seemed to promise rapid reforms, but little change was forthcoming even after Trajkovski replaced Gligorov in 1999. Xhaferi developed Parkinson's disease and, although he remained an influential figure, to many young ethnic Albanians it seemed as if he had lost his inspirational spark.

The influx of refugees during the Kosovo crisis underlined and heightened this weakness in Macedonian society as agitators from Pristina cafe society convinced Macedonian Albanians that they were being condemned to the permanent second-class status of the former Yugoslav *narodnost*, or national minority.

5 On the Brink of Conflict

AT THIS POINT IT is worthwhile summing up the positions of the major players in the Balkans on the Macedonian question as the conflict began.

Ethnic Macedonians
According to statistics for 1981, considered among the most reliable of those available in the past, the ethnic Macedonians of Slavonic origin made up 1.28 million (66 per cent) of the total population of the then Yugoslav republic of Macedonia of 1.912 million. The latest census, held in 2002 under the auspices of international monitors, found that Macedonia had a population of 2.022 million, of whom 64.18 per cent were ethnic Macedonians, a smaller percentage of the total population.[1] Virtually all of them are Orthodox Christians. Most lay claim to being the original inhabitants of the country but a significant number are of Bulgarian, Serb or Greek origin.

The main aims of the ethnic Macedonian political establishment were to maintain political control of the country, to prevent the Albanian minority receiving equal status with the Slavs, to crack down on the nascent Albanian guerrilla movements linked to the Kosovo Liberation Army and to take Macedonia into the European Union in order to restore living conditions to at least the level enjoyed when Macedonia was part of the Yugoslav federation.

Macedonian nationalists grouped in the VMRO (Internal Macedonian Revolutionary Organisation) led by the then Prime Minister, Ljubco Georgievski, were the strongest advocates of a hardline policy by the security forces against the ethnic Albanian radicals. The nationalists had dropped previous historic claims to territory in Bulgaria and Greece including Thessaloniki. But, as we have seen, they signed an agreement with Serbia in February 2001, under which they received a small chunk of territory that previously was part of Kosovo. Moderate nationalists in the party supported the President, Boris Trajkovski. The nationalists' main fear was that the ethnic Albanians of Kosovo would become independent and lay claim to western Macedonia, where ethnic Albanians are a majority.

The former Communist Social Democrats led by Gligorov were traditionally pro-Yugoslav and pro-Serb while the nationalists were traditionally pro-Bulgarian and to some extent pro-Russian.

Georgievski was anti-communist and, together with President Trajkovski, supported NATO's deployment in the country before and during the Kosovo crisis, for which he was criticised by the left-wing opposition. Georgievski also adopted a policy of encouraging good relations with Athens in the late 1990s.

The presence of the Democratic Party of Albanians in his government coalition did not prevent deep distrust of the ethnic Albanian population in general among hardliners in the party monitoring the rise of the Kosovo Liberation Army with trepidation.

Ethnic Albanians

The ethnic Albanians were officially 19.7 per cent of the population of Macedonia in 1981. According to the 2002 census, 25.17 per cent of Macedonians were ethnic Albanians, while 3.85 per cent were Turks, 2.66 per cent Roma and 1.78 per cent ethnic Serbs. The Albanians of Macedonia were among the huge number who remained outside Albania when it obtained its independence in 1912. As we have seen, the discontent of the ethnic Albanians was not a new phenomenon. It went back to at least the 1960s, when Macedonia was part of federal Yugoslavia. But in the 1980s and 1990s the radicalism of the Macedonian Albanians was increasingly fed by the agitation for a *Kosovo-republika*.

The ethnic Albanians' aims were for recognition as equals in the Macedonian constitution, for Albanian to be an official language and for a state-funded university. They also wanted greater representation in the police, armed forces and civil service.

When reforms promised by the Democratic Party of Albanians before it took office were slow to materialise, Macedonian Albanians who had been active in the Kosovo Liberation Army led by Ali Ahmeti, a KLA founder, made plans for an ethnic Albanian insurrection in western Macedonia to achieve greater rights for the population and eventually join an independent Kosovo.

Serbia

Modern Serbia, the larger republic of the Federal Republic of Yugoslavia, the successor to the Socialist Federal Republic of Yugoslavia, which disintegrated in 1991, renounced any claim to Macedonia. Its democratic government supported Macedonia's efforts to protect Macedonia's sovereignty against aspirations by radical ethnic Albanians that western Macedonia should be part of Kosovo or of a greater Albania. With a population of 10.5 million, Serbia remains a regional superpower, albeit one that was brought to its knees economically by the wars in Kosovo, Bosnia and Croatia.

Vojislav Kostunica, the Yugoslav President from 2000 to 2003, was a moderate nationalist who refused to renounce Yugoslav sovereignty over Kosovo. He insisted that the future of Kosovo must include allowing the return to their homes of some 300,000 Serbs who had left the province during and after the NATO invasion in 1999. Kosovo, with a population of 2.2 million, has been under international administration following the implementation of United Nations Resolution 1244 on 10 June 1999. Serbian sovereignty over Kosovo is confirmed under the resolution but it calls for greater and genuine autonomy for the province.

With many sectors of public opinion in Belgrade angry over the Serb casualties taken in southern Serbia, and wider resentment over the situation of the Kosovo Serbs, it appeared possible in spring 2001 that full-scale civil war in Macedonia might bring the Yugoslav Army into such a conflict on the side of the ethnic Macedonians.

Relations between Belgrade and Skopje had been positively transformed compared to the tense situation when Macedonia broke away from the Yugoslav federation. In the early 1990s, according to one political analyst I spoke to in Skopje in 2002:

> Serbia expressed not only political but also emotional feelings about every republic's application for independence, seeing them as a kind of betrayal – of the notion of a common motherland, of historic achievements, of the sacrifices made for this country, and, hence, of Serbia and everything it did for the Yugoslav people in the two Worlds Wars.

In fact, Serbian irritation with Macedonian nationalists went back to the mid 1980s, when they began speaking out against the traditional

Yugoslav celebrations held to commemorate the anniversary of the Balkan Wars of 1912–1913 against the Turkish occupation. The nationalists recognised that those wars had liberated Macedonia from the Turks but began to stress that this merely substituted the Ottoman Empire with Serb domination in Yugoslavia.

Serbia's relationship with Skopje had also suffered in the early 1990s from the good relationship between the Milosevic regime and Greece, Yugoslavia's main foreign supporter in Europe. Belgrade did not want to offend the Greeks by too openly supporting the new state. The UN sanctions against Yugoslavia had also hurt Macedonia. Skopje helped Belgrade mitigate the effect of the sanctions by encouraging large-scale smuggling into Yugoslavia but the nationalist VMRO saw Macedonians as the victims of a hostile Greek-Yugoslav anti-Macedonian axis.

President Gligorov repeatedly worked to ease tensions with Milosevic, humouring the Yugoslav leader over his objections to the deployment of US troops in Macedonia as part of the UN preventive force deployed there to prevent a spillover from the Bosnian conflict in 1993.

The end of the sanctions in November 1995 and the signing of the Dayton Accord ending the Bosnian War in December 1995, meaning that Skopje no longer needed to worry about being drawn into that conflict, started a new phase in relations with Belgrade climaxing with Yugoslavia's recognition of Macedonia in April 1996. This went ahead in spite of remarks by Gligorov during his first official visit to Croatia that month, in which he offended Serbs by praising the Croatian army.[2]

Albania

Albania welcomed the independence of Macedonia as a counterweight to Serbia and a nuisance to Greece. But, in the 1990s, Tirana was not particularly vehement in its protests to Skopje against conditions for the ethnic Albanians in Macedonia. It was more concerned with the Albanians in Kosovo. Albania took in 350,000 refugees during the Kosovo emergency of 1999, placing considerable strain on the impoverished country of 3.5 million people (about half the total number of Albanians worldwide).

During the Kosovo crisis, Albania followed NATO policy closely. Tirana's acute dependency on foreign assistance meant that the Albanian authorities were extremely reluctant to become involved in the crisis in western Macedonia.

However, the possibility of Albanian military involvement could not be excluded if the crisis were to spiral totally out of control. Western policymakers were concerned that, in the event of Albanian intervention in Macedonia, Tirana might seek military support from its regional ally, Turkey.

Bulgaria

As the first country to recognize Macedonia as a state in 1992, Bulgaria was in a good position to increase its influence in Macedonia by presenting itself as a protector of the Macedonians. This prompted speculation that Sofia might re-float the old idea of a Balkan Federation linking Bulgaria and Macedonia with which Tito and the Bulgarian communists had flirted in the late 1940s.

The Serb nationalist press was suspicious of Sofia in the early 1990s and accused Macedonians of not wanting genuine independence but of aspiring to be part of a Greater Bulgaria. Ever since 1878, the Bulgarians had regarded Macedonia as *Bulgara irredenta* and most Bulgarians denied that a separate Macedonian nation existed and viewed the Macedonian language as a dialect of Bulgarian.

In 1990, Sofia restored the San Stefano Day national holiday on 3 March, which had been abolished in 1946. This was interpreted as meaning that Bulgaria still aspired to all the Macedonian territory which it was awarded under the short-lived San Stefano treaty. The Bulgarian President, Zeljo Zelev, was reported to have foiled a Serbian-Greek plan for the partition of Macedonia. Part of Zelev's Union of Democratic Forces, the Bulgarian anti-communist and pro-western party founded in 1989, had good relations with Georgievski's nationalists and relations between Skopje and Sofia improved when the VMRO took power.

On 22 February 1999, the Bulgarians buried the hatchet with Skopje a short time before the Kosovo war by recognising the existence of a Macedonian language, culture and nation separate from Bulgarian. The Macedonians renounced their claim on Pirin Macedonia. This put an end to fears that Macedonia would lay claim to the area, where a handful of Bulgarians claim to be of Macedonian nationality. In March 1999, Bulgaria agreed to supply Macedonia with military equipment and the two armies held joint manoeuvres. This rapprochement enabled NATO to feel there would be stability in the area to the east and south of the Kosovo battleground.

In spring 2001, Bulgaria rushed military equipment to Macedonia and it was felt Bulgaria might be willing to go to war to protect Skopje from the Albanian rebellion. Macedonia initially rejected offers of more direct military assistance from Sofia, however. The victory in the summer of 2001 of the movement of the former Bulgarian king,

Simeon II, would have a calming effect on the region, since his populism did not fuel nationalist aspirations towards Macedonia.

When I interviewed him in Sofia during the election campaign, Simeon Saxe Coburg Gotha indicated he did not want Bulgaria to be drawn into the conflict. 'Everybody is terribly worried by the events in Macedonia,' was all he said, declining to be much drawn on such a painful subject for Bulgarians.

Bosnia and Herzegovina

Bosnia and Herzegovina is divided between the Bosnian Muslim and Croat-dominated Federation and the Bosnian Serb-dominated Republika Srpska. The Bosnian political elites have no interest in Macedonia, being absorbed instead after the Dayton peace agreement of 1995 in reconstruction, political change and relations with the international community that runs it as a protectorate. The main importance of Bosnia for the ethnic Macedonians was the fear that their country could follow the Bosnian example and end up divided between mainly Slav and predominantly Muslim entities or become involved in an equally tragic civil war. Bosniaks, or Bosnian Muslims, are a relative majority in Bosnia's population of 4 million, making up some 44 per cent against 31 per cent of Serbs and 17 per cent of Croats.

In the election of 2002, President Kostunica indicated – highly controversially – that Belgrade still hopes to obtain control eventually of the Serb-run half of Bosnia, the Republika Srpska. Some Serbs see this as potential compensation for losing control of Kosovo, which, if it were to lay claim to western Macedonia successfully, could leave the ethnic Macedonians with possible options of rejoining the rump of the Yugoslav Federation or seeking some kind of mini-state status under Bulgarian protection.

Such calculations about possible territorial changes in the Balkans were in the minds of all the actors in Macedonia to a greater or lesser extent in the turbulent spring of 2001.

6 'War in Toytown'

The town seemed like some wretch who covers his eyes with his hands and waits for blows from which he cannot defend himself.
Ivo Andric, The Bridge on the Drina

The Rise of the National Liberation Army and the Battle for Tetovo

The fighting in Tetovo set off alarm bells around the Balkans as Skopje and Belgrade advocated the creation of a five-kilometre (three-mile) strip free-fire zone running parallel to the Kosovo border inside the province. But initially the insurgency had only a limited impact on NATO and western governments.

One dramatic event, captured on celluloid from close range, brought home to policymakers the seriousness of the worsening conflict, preparing the ground for international intervention.

The first martyrs of the ethnic Albanian rebellion in Macedonia looked innocent enough when they approached the city in a battered white saloon car. What started as a routine search by local police, waving down Albanian drivers with a traffic lollipop, ended in a suicidal lunge by two men in the car who tried to strike a blow at the heart of the enemy with a grenade.

The incident in Tetovo, Macedonia's second city, on 22 March was the culmination of two months of attacks by the ethnic Albanian rebels in the north-west of the country, marking the first time the guerrillas had gone into action during daylight within Tetovo itself.

The shooting happened as the *Times* photographer Peter Nichols and I toured Macedonian positions next to a football stadium that had become a battleground in the eastern districts of Tetovo. One Macedonian stronghold, bristling with machine guns and sniper rifles supported by armoured cars, became a favourite spot for journalists watching the fighting from a side street and the stadium walls.

Each day the machine-gunners fired thousands of rounds across a main road littered with cartridges into the rebel-held forested hills above Tetovo, setting houses and trees alight. At dawn, city dustmen arrived and stuffed the cartridges into plastic sacks.

I watched as a balding, middle-aged man got out of the saloon car's passenger seat and began showing a policeman his driving licence while the elderly driver opened the car trunk for inspection. Suddenly the policeman began shouting and beating the passenger with a lollipop-shaped traffic baton as the man reached for a pocket. Now we could see the passenger was holding a grenade as the policeman wrestled with him and a second soldier in camouflage fatigues began firing an assault rifle at the car, shattering the side windows.

Other soldiers shouted to the policemen to run for cover as the passenger broke free, bent down on his knee and tried to throw the grenade over the sandbags at the machine-gun post 15 feet away. Several soldiers fired at him and his comrade, killing both almost instantly. The passenger's body twitched for two or three seconds as a young Macedonian officer emerged from the army strongpoint and finally ordered an end to the firing.

As one policeman began dragging away the bodies, others turned on the journalists, firing in the air to drive us down a dusty side street to the central Marshal Tito Square. More security troops emerged from behind the machine-gun nest and began chasing away photographers working on the first floor of a half-built house. Some young ethnic Albanian passers-by began to cry. Asaf, our teenage translator, was badly shaken.

The 'executions' were the most dramatic event inside Tetovo during a two-week assault on the city launched by the National Liberation Army (NLA). The photographs[1] and television footage of the sequence communicated to western readers and viewers for the first time the desperate lengths to which ordinary ethnic Albanians were prepared to go to challenge the Macedonian state.

Meanwhile, the battle for Tetovo continued. The Macedonian Army deployed antiquated Bulgarian T-72 tanks and rumbling Mi-24 helicopter gunships flown by Ukrainian mercenary pilots, to prevent the city falling to the rebels. Officially the pilots were Macedonians and they wore Macedonian uniforms but western military attachés speculated that Macedonian pilots could not have been trained so quickly to fly the newly acquired helicopters. This suspicion was confirmed when a Ukrainian cameraman working for Reuter Television News managed to get into the pilots' office at Skopje airport and conversed with them in fluent Ukrainian. Macedonian forces set up sandbagged positions on street corners and established a strict night curfew.

A Macedonian Air Force M-17 helicopter crashed on 17 March while ferrying elite police forces to positions at the ski resort of Popova Shapka near Tetovo. One member of the crew died and 16 policemen on board were injured, five of them seriously. The crash was good propaganda for the guerrillas who claimed they had shot down the helicopter. The Macedonian authorities denied this, saying that the aircraft had lost power after flying into draft winds and went down when it hit a funicular ski-car cable.

In a statement issued on 20 March, the rebels outlined the reasons why they had taken up arms. The statement signed by the NLA Tetovo branch said:

Macedonia's ignorant view and hypocritical disrespect of the demands and the patience of the Albanians has surpassed all limits. Our people have for decades been insulted, discriminated against and banned from all civilisation traditions in Macedonia.

These are the main reasons that forced the Albanians to take up weapons and fight for their rights. In vain we tried for years to have our rights realised through a change in government, and to have Macedonia refrain from a wrongful policy... we chose a president who we hoped would be a president for all. We gave him time and space to send us clear signals whether he was going to accept the Albanians as equals. But this did not happen. Therefore, we decided not to allow further humiliation and trampling on our dignity.

We appeal to all political and non-political Albanian figures not to delude themselves that our rights would be granted by this government. The present trend of recognition of our rights is trivial. We also appeal to all political factors, internal and external, to give their real recognition to those who are fighting to be equal, because such fighters could never be terrorists.

We are no adventurers. We had no lives to gamble away. We don't seek killings and war, because for centuries we were the victims. From this moment peace does not depend only on us.

> We urge the Macedonian authorities to make public as soon as possible whether they want this to be resolved peacefully. After this we will bear no responsibility for the future chain of events. We urge the international community to recognise our demands, which are for peace.[2]

The statement was an emotional and unsophisticated summary of the NLA's demand for ethnic Albanians to be treated as equals to ethnic Macedonians. The charge that ethnic Albanians were victims and that they had been cheated of any real reforms by electing President Trajkovski and participating in government would be heard throughout the conflict. For the moment the NLA stopped short of making detailed demands other than recognition of its existence as a political player by the Government and the international community, which the guerrillas realised was inevitably the ultimate arbiter in Macedonia. However, the unsolicited denial that their leaders were 'adventurers' invited questions about their true motivation. From the safety of Kosovo they would gamble away not their own lives but those of some of their hotheaded recruits fighting in the field as well as young Macedonians from across the Balkan ethnic spectrum.

One of the first ethnic Macedonian Slav journalists to cover the fighting was the photographer Marko Georgiev, who at one stage found himself jumping for cover in the security forces bunker in the stadium. He later recalled:

> The first few days of the clashes in Tetovo were pretty chaotic. I had the impression that no one knew where and at whom they were shooting. Crossing the open space on the street by running fast, we had no other choice but to jump ourselves in the police bunker near the football stadium in Drenovec settlement.
>
> The policemen were too busy with shooting and so scared that they only noticed us when they were reloading their weapons. The officer in charge was a bit more confident and he was constantly giving orders, screaming to the other policemen that they were frozen with fear.
>
> They were low on ammo, and badly equipped, so the commanding officer asked me, screaming to check 'with that big lens,' on one particular house if the 'red stuff' they saw was an Albanian flag or not. Using my lens I was not sure what it was, so I told the policeman and he told me to move away. He spent the next few minutes

extensively shooting at the house. When he was done, he turned to me and said, 'Now there is no more of the red stuff.'[3]

Yet it was evident that much of Tetovo's population of 200,000 (of whom about 80 per cent are ethnic Albanians) was in sympathy with the NLA. Sage Albanian patriarchs sipping Turkish coffee in bars, oblivious of the firing in the streets outside, insisted that the men shot dead at the stadium were murdered without reason. 'Look at that,' one elderly man in a white skullcap said to me, gesturing at a newspaper picture of the drama. 'What the car's passenger was holding was not a grenade. It was a mobile phone.'

The funeral of Razim Koraci, 37, and his father Ramadan, 60, drew a crowd of 300 mourners at Tetovo's Muslim cemetery. They refused to believe the two had intended to make trouble. The Macedonian Government distributed copies of a videotape of the confrontation to try to dispel any doubts that the police had acted in self-defence. But members of the dead men's community insisted they had been innocent.

'It was a horrible thing to kill people on the street like that,' said Qazim, 44, a friend of the two. 'It is not true that they had hand grenades. It was a set-up. If they had hand grenades they would have used them.'

Another family friend, Lirim, 23, said 'they were killed in a brutal way, like animals. They were innocent, that is for sure. The only victims here right now are civilians.'

During a lull in the fighting, the green coffins containing the two men's bodies were passed from one group of mourners to another, according to Muslim tradition. Sporadic machine-gun fire and the thud of mortars resumed from nearby hills as the service came to an end.

Most Macedonian newspapers published photographs in which Razim was clearly shown holding the Chinese-made grenade. But the local press could find out little about the background of the pair. Neighbours living near their well-kept, two-storey whitewashed house in the village of Drenovec, three miles north-east of the city centre, said both were taxi drivers. Ramadan had a son working in Germany, neighbours said. Washing was hanging from a line at the house but no relatives could be found.

The night before the funeral, Macedonian gunners in Tetovo blasted rebel positions near Drenovec with tanks and artillery. But there still was no sign of the major offensive that the Government had promised to unleash.

Drenovec had been shelled from positions such as the one where the two men died, with several houses in the village set on fire. The state-run television service for Albanians showed extraordinary footage of Macedonian gunners cruelly targeting civilians as they sought to retrieve furniture and other belongings from their burning homes.

In Skopje, a Government spokesman acknowledged that the security forces had also fired across the Macedonian border into Kosovo but said that the targets had been Albanian guerrillas who attacked Macedonian forces and subsequently retreated into the Serbian province. UN sources said that about 20 civilians in the area were wounded in the shelling.

In the battle for Tetovo, the Macedonian Army frequently was outmanoeuvred by the highly mobile guerrillas and their military leader, Gezim Ostreni. Born in Debar in western Macedonia, Ostreni was a veteran who had served in the Yugoslav Army and until April 2001 was a deputy commander in the Kosovo Protections Corps. Ostreni was typical of ethnic Albanians, who saw no future for themselves in the post-independence Macedonian Army whose officer corps was dominated by Slavs. Ostreni was not only a gifted tactician but also an author on military affairs who wrote a book on the partisan movement in Macedonia during the Second World War in which he examined the myth of a Slav/partisan democratic victory.

In a series of new communiqués, meanwhile, the NLA demanded more insistently that Albanians receive constituent nation status, official recognition for the Albanian language and an end to discrimination in favour of Macedonian Slavs in the police and civil service.

Even before the shooting at the stadium there had been repeated complaints by the town's ethnic Albanians about alleged attacks on civilians by the paramilitary police and special forces. Relatives of a taxi driver who was killed on the first day of the rebellion in the old Ottoman neighbourhood of Koltuk claimed the police opened fire with machine guns indiscriminately, even though the main fighting at the time was taking place 1.2 miles away, beyond the Kale, the fortress above the city, in the village of Lavce.

Marko Georgiev set up position with his cameras in Koltuk, where most residents were ethnic Macedonians or Serbs, many of whom were deeply hostile to the press:

> After a few days in Koltuk it started to become very dangerous. Partly because the locals were using every opportune moment to get rid of us, allegedly because we were there to photograph the faces of the policemen, and partly from the grenades that were falling randomly all over the place and injuring the people. When it was calmer, we would go there quite often.

One local told us a story, how a member of the army special forces, the Wolves, tried to save his life... hearing the sound of a grenade falling, the solder jumped on this civilian, in order to protect him from shelling and shrapnel, since he was equipped with a bullet proof jacket and all the protective gear. The grenade indeed fell on the street, very close to the place where they were, but luckily it did not detonate. The soldier approached the grenade, realising why it hadn't exploded, took the projectile in his hands, unscrewed the safety cap, and started towards the hill screaming 'You left the safety cap on you idiot!'

For journalists like Georgiev, covering the fighting revealed extraordinary slices of the marginalised lifestyle in which many ethnic Macedonians survived in the district.

The only civilian who had no problems talking and posing in front of the camera was Mile from Koltuk. He was a junkie and a drug dealer, released from prison just a couple of weeks ago. His house was the last one in Tetovo. From his back yard and up, there was only shooting and terrorists.

His wife seemed pretty young, not more than 25. When we arrived at their home, she was so high that for the first 10 minutes she did not even notice me photographing.

They had no running water and the sewage was running though the middle of their yard. They had one son, two years old, who still hadn't spoken a word. There was another kid hanging around the house who according to Mile was epileptic. Mile had two more kids, now in foster homes, since he couldn't look after them from jail.

Mile's wife, although high on drugs, was aware and scared of all the shooting, and begged Mile to move to another town. His response to that was that all they had to do is get another hit, and Mile himself would go up the hill to fight bare handed.

Thousands of terrified refugees streamed out of the city and surrounding villages by car, in buses or on foot. By 23 March, the UNHCR said, 20,000 people had left the country. Ljubce Klatnovski, a travel agent with an office on the edge of the main Marshal Tito Square, told me how hundreds of ethnic Albanians were planning to flee with him by bus to Istanbul. 'This is a crazy situation. We Macedonians have lived happily here with the Albanians for decades.'

As he spoke, rebel gunners from a hill just over a mile above Tetovo began pounding the Square outside with mortar fire, scattering a foreign television crew and a crowd of loafers who had been watching the fighting in the foothills of the surrounding Sar Mountains.

It was time to end our conversation. I left the travel agent's and walked hurriedly down an adjoining side street toward my car, breaking into a run as a shell exploded close behind. Our car was parked in front of an Albanian café, whose owners were closing rapidly because of the surrounding bombardment by their would-be liberators. I had hoped to find our Albanian driver, Shenasi, waiting and to speed off immediately. The café owner rapidly pulling down his shutter courteously took time to give me a box of chocolates I had bought for Shenasi's wife but left behind. But Shenasi and our other interpreter, Robert, were nowhere to be seen.

Another mortar shell crashed into the side-street, perhaps 25 metres away, spewing out shrapnel and smoke as I frantically tracked down my Albanian friends on a crackling mobile phone line. They had taken shelter in the office of the Albanian opposition grouping, the Party for Democratic Prosperity (PDP) where Robert's father was a party leader, a building they assumed reasonably that the NLA might stop short of targeting. At last the office Golf was gunned into action. We hurtled around the post office building and out of the NLA's range onto the main highway to Skopje, the capital, 25 miles away. The bracketing lasted only a few minutes, but it had been an intensely lonely experience in my bolthole behind a concrete pillar.

On the motorway, German soldiers in battle gear had set up a roadblock as part of the first NATO involvement in Macedonia's burgeoning civil war. In Berlin, Germany ordered tanks into the former Yugoslav republic after its troops, stationed on the outskirts of Tetovo as logistical support for KFOR peacekeeping forces across the Kosovo border, also were caught in the crossfire between Albanian rebels and government forces. 'We won't let anybody play games with us,' Rudolf Scharping, the German Defence Minister said. 'And also not Albanian terrorists.' The German armour, two Leopard tanks, arrived from a base in Kosovo as 'a protective measure' to defend the barracks containing 1,000 Bundeswehr troops from the NLA gunners.

In Skopje, the Government had from mid March begun to criticise NATO members for inaction in the crisis. 'Nobody in Macedonia is convinced that the United States and German governments do not know who the terrorist leaders are, and that they could not stop their actions, that is the aggression coming from Kosovo, if they wanted to,' Georgievski said. He warned that the international community must 'acknowledge failure of its operation in Kosovo as it re-examines its overall engagement' and decried Kosovo Albanians for 'replying with weapons to Macedonia's decency' by the country that embraced them during their most difficult period. Some days later, a truce was declared by the Macedonian forces to give the NLA time to meet a deadline to pull out from above Tetovo.

Marko Georgiev, continuing his work in Koltuk, found one of many elderly residents who had become trapped.

> This old woman, Ratka, had not got out of the house for six days. Her house was a few feet behind the position of the army forces who were using heavy machine guns to fire at the hill.

> We noticed her the first day of the truce, when the lady decided to go back to the small toilet at the back of her house. In Skopje, we managed to raise some money [for her], and we even found her a place to stay.

> But when we went to pick her up, we found that the security forces had started a large offensive... That was one of the most dangerous days to be in Tetovo. There was shooting from all directions, and snipers had a fun day.

As the fighting went on, the ethnic Macedonians in Tetovo and Skopje developed increasing resentment toward NATO countries in general, and Britain in particular. *Forum* magazine claimed that the NLA was trained and supported by various foreign military services including the SAS.

Forum subsequently carried a denial by Mark Dickenson, the British Ambassador in Skopje. 'It is completely untrue. If the SAS were training anyone who at this moment is fighting on the NLA side, they would be much better shots than they are,' *Forum* quoted him as saying. British military sources also strenuously denied the suggestion.

TO FIND OUT MORE about the grievances of the ethnic Albanians, I trekked into Selce, a village of 3,000 inhabitants eight miles north of Tetovo that the NLA made their base after attacking the city eight days earlier.

Villagers were building shelters and preparing first-aid stations as an ultimatum by the Government to leave the rebel-controlled area expired. Civilians worked to repair their homes after a five-hour bombardment of mortar and artillery shells in which an NLA fighter had been killed and five people wounded. They insisted they would not leave their homes, no matter how fierce the next threatened Macedonian bombardment. They complained of worsening food shortages. 'It doesn't matter what the Macedonian Government says,' Sali, a 37-year-old elementary school teacher, told us.

> Everybody is staying here in their homes, including women and children. We have nowhere else to go. It is dangerous to try to escape. All the roads are blocked. The Macedonian Government must understand that the people here are determined to obtain the rights they deserve.

In a winding village street, Afer Kadria, a farmer, surveyed the damage to his home from the mortar shells, while in his garage a rebel pasted tape on to the windows. The farmer's family hauled a steel garden gate and a wooden cable frame in front of the makeshift shelter, in which, they said, 28 relations would spend the night. Inside, a woman wearing veils tended wooden stoves for heating and cooking and another rocked a baby in a wooden crib.

The NLA sent word that foreign journalists were unwelcome as they prepared defensive positions against the coming Macedonian assault. Guerrillas in black uniforms decorated with hunting knives eyed Rory Carroll of *The Guardian* and myself with irritation after we persuaded two shepherds to help us slip into the insurgent base through their land.

A young man who said he was a student from Skopje University showed us around and questioned us for two or three hours. Then the fighters firmly ordered us out at gunpoint and we began a long march back to Tetovo through Sipkovica, another rebel stronghold.

Sipkovica was crowded with journalists, all of them hoping to get to Selce, but all had been turned back by the NLA fighters. Many of these colleagues were old Balkan hands. By now, Macedonia had become the world's top story as the Balkans braced once again for full-scale war and journalists were flooding to Tetovo.

As the Macedonian sun set, there was a scramble to find transport to return to Tetovo before the expected Macedonian Army onslaught that night. I shared one of the last taxis out of the village with a colleague from *Le Figaro*, and we were dropped off north of Gajre, another NLA-held village above Tetovo. We clambered over logs the NLA had felled to block the road, picked our way around a suspected minefield and then hitched a ride with some Australian photographers and a Greek cameraman in a soft-topped Land Rover. A crazed Macedonian had fired a pistol at the photographers' vehicle from

Tetovo's cemetery, which had become a favourite snipers' haunt, as they set out for Sipkovica that morning. Fortunately the gunman did not re-appear as we skirted the graveyard. Earlier, Rory, a Polish photographer and I had spent the night in a shepherd's house four miles away in the village of Germo as it came under Macedonian mortar fire for the first time.

Latif Latifi, the civil defence commander in Germo, said that the villagers were not capable of defending themselves against a sustained attack. 'There are fighters at the front,' he said.

> But here there are only civilians. There are old people who should go to the Tetovo hospitals but they can't. Look at these young children. How long will their trauma from these events last? This is not the war of an army against another army, but of an army against civilians.

From the start of the fighting, the NLA insisted it did not want to change Macedonia's borders to create a greater Albania. But many local people said they saw their future in one state with Kosovo Albanians. 'This is Kosovo,' our host said, pointing to the floor as we bedded down in Germo.

On the way to Germo, in the small hillside village of Poroj in no man's land, we had seen an Albanian soldier from the Macedonian Army desert to the NLA carrying his Kalashnikov. He had driven at breakneck speed into the village square in an old car. He jumped out of the vehicle, screaming 'Who will take me to fight with my brothers on the mountain?' After tearing his Macedonian Army flash from his camouflage fatigues, the deserter was whisked away in a civilian car to NLA positions. The army was paying a heavy price in desertions, most of them among Albanian reservists sent into the front line.

I dictated a story about the deserter on Rory's mobile telephone in front of a house where a doctor from Tetovo was setting up a clinic. The doctor overheard references to soldiers and front lines. He accused me of describing the village, largely de-militarised, as an NLA command post, of putting the villagers at risk from more attention from the Macedonian gunners. I offered to try to arrange for tranquillisers, antibiotics and other medicines to be sent by mule along the track we had climbed from Tetovo.

At times, the self-pity of the villagers was almost oppressive. 'They feel themselves bigger victims than Belfast Catholics,' muttered Rory, a patriotic Irishman.

As recently as 1991, another seasoned observer had noted that Macedonia's Albanians:

do not have full access to the organs of power, but the harsh repression of the pro-Serb communist leadership in Macedonia has been rapidly eroded since the elections of 1990. And yet the Albanians here seem most unwilling to shake off that past, insisting that their fate remains more terrible than that of the Kosovar Albanians, despite the common knowledge that to the north their compatriots are kept in check by one of the most militarised police forces in Europe.[4]

Once back in Tetovo from Germo, I met the head of Caritas International in Macedonia, Elvira Simoncini. She agreed to try and supply the village clinic. A Caritas convoy set off for Germo with the medicines a few days later but was forced to turn back on the outskirts of the village when it came under Macedonian sniper fire.

AT THE END OF March, the Macedonian Army at last launched a classic infantry assault on the area, chasing the rebels out of the villages around Mount Sar into the mountains beyond as the helicopter gunships clattered overhead. The NLA left considerable quantities of weapons behind them in Selce.

Airborne troops were dropped onto the mountain slopes and a mortar barrage was unleashed on suspected rebel positions. Soldiers and special police units stormed up the steep incline in the south of Tetovo, which, in more peaceful times, was used to ferry skiers by cable to the snowy slopes above.

'The fifth Balkan war in the past ten years officially broke out in the foothills above Tetovo yesterday when government troops backed by tanks, artillery and helicopter gunships seized a rebel stronghold in a day of heavy fighting,' wrote Richard Beeston, who now joined those covering the fighting for our newspaper.[5] Another colleague, Anthony Loyd, rode in by mule from Kosovo passing through a heavy bombardment at rebel headquarters at Selce. The Macedonian dawn offensive was described by one onlooker as 'the first attack by the Macedonian military since Alexander the Great.'

Munic Suleiman, a jewellery shop owner, spent the day avoiding sniper fire and trying to catch a glimpse of the battle raging above. 'I was in bed when I heard the big mortars going off and I knew then that the offensive had started,' he said.

Occasionally, groups of soldiers sweating beneath helmets and flak jackets could be seen moving under rebel sniper-fire across the alpine meadows and closing in on the village of Gajre. An estimated 300 in-experienced and ill-equipped infantry were used in the first wave, backed by elderly Soviet T-55 tanks that struggled up the twisting mountain road spewing exhaust fumes. 'This is one of the last phases of the operation we have taken for the complete expulsion of terrorists from Macedonia,' Georgi Trandafilov, the Defence Ministry spokesman, said.

Reporters who tried to enter the main hospital to check on the number of dead and wounded from the fighting were barred by a soldier and angry men in civilian clothes, suggesting that casualties were higher than the official figure of five injured.

As ever in the Balkans the main victims of the latest day's fighting were the civilians. Some 50 villagers cowered in one house as their barns were set alight by tank and mortar fire and burnt out of control. There appeared to be little attempt by either of the belligerent parties to help refugees to escape or get the injured out.

The Macedonian offensive polarised opinion further, with Macedonians jubilant that their forces had finally gone into action and Albanians angered by the heavy-handed approach of the military. 'Tell me who the terrorists are?' said Selim, a farmer who spent the night trying to stop flames consuming his house after a forest fire ignited after a rocket attack. 'The young lads who are helping to fight for our rights or the army who shoots at its own people and leaves your home to burn?'

The Party for Democratic Prosperity, the main Albanian opposition group, suspended its participation in Parliament and urged the Democratic Party of Albanians to pull out of the governing coalition. Leaders from both parties said, however, that they were willing to engage in talks over Albanian demands for equal rights, the recognition of their language as an official tongue and the establishment of an Albanian university.

Two days after the offensive began, foreign emissaries started arriving in Macedonia to put pressure on the authorities to halt the offensive and the burgeoning Balkan conflagration. As troops continued their push into the mountain villages around Tetovo, seizing eight strongholds of the NLA, Lord Robertson of Port Ellen, the NATO Secretary-General, and Javier Solana, the European Union's High Representative for Foreign Affairs, arrived in Skopje.

Western diplomats said that the Macedonian military had shown restraint in their operations, which were judged to be 'proportional' to the threat from the ethnic Albanian insurgents. Christopher Hill, one of the main architects of US policy in Macedonia, was quick to denounce the rebels. 'It's very disappointing that people who were so helped by NATO actions should now become the problem.' He said it was fair to describe the guerrillas as 'outlaws'.[6] 'Some of them believe that they can somehow sucker the international community into being left with no choice but to support them. I believe... they have done great harm to the cause that they believe they're supporting.'

Senor Solana said that the EU supported Macedonia's operations against the guerrillas and described the assault as 'reasonable' in the circumstances. After his talks with Macedonian leaders, Lord Robertson praised the authorities for acting 'with commendable restraint but also with determined fairness'. The Government in Skopje had pledged to intensify the dialogue between the divided communites, he said. He warned the country that it faced a stark choice. 'I believe that there are two options for the people of this country: it is a united Macedonia or another Balkans bloodbath.'

Western envoys would repeat such warnings over the following six months. The Macedonian Army's lacklustre performance in Tetovo, meanwhile, had raised questions as to whether it would be able to quell the uprising without additional foreign assistance.

The Macedonian Army's Inadequacy

The Government said that the army and police had scored a 'total victory' over the NLA at Tetovo. But military experts such as Zoran Kusovac, a correspondent for *Jane's Defence Weekly*, argued that this was far from true. Western military attachés sometimes referred derisively to the efforts of the ill-equipped Macedonian forces as 'war in toytown'. 'There is doubt that the Mount Sar operation can be called a total victory,' Kusovac wrote.

> After a week's procrastination and a slow troop build-up, less than 500 Army of the Republic of Macedonia (ARM) soldiers accompanied five T-55 battle tanks (MBTs) into the hills above Tetovo. Progressing slowly and meeting little opposition, government troops heavily shelled any suspected guerrilla outpost, mostly civilian houses whose inhabitants took refuge before the long-announced offensive began.[7]

ARM units, which included a substantial proportion of reservists, moved further into the hills only after helicopters strafed the heights with 57mm unguided rockets. Four Mi-8MTV transport helicopters and two Mi-24D gunships were delivered to ARM's air wing on 23 March, substantially augmenting the previous complement of only three M-17s. The helicopters, originating from Ukraine, were the first major purchase by the ARM in many years.

The inadequacy of the army went back to independence when the Yugoslav armed forces had stripped all they could from Macedonia as it left. Many Macedonians wanted to distance the new country from the militarism and xenophobia of other former Yugoslav republics and the VMRO-dominated Parliament at one stage proposed abolishing the armed forces altogether.

On paper, the Macedonian Army had some 20,000 men with 100,000 reservists but there were only about 10,000 in uniform in the summer of 1991, of whom some 7,500 were mainly untrained national service men. A large number of former JNA officers controlled what was almost a symbolic force and the officers were periodically purged according to whether the Government was dominated by pro-Bulgarian or pro-Serb factions.

President Gligorov had an uneasy relationship with many senior officers and in March 1993 he had dismissed General Mitre Arsovski as Commander in Chief. Ethnic Macedonians were also worried about building up too large an army, which might become increasingly dominated by ethnic Albanian conscripts because of the demographic structure of Macedonia.

Ethnic Albanians doing national service made up to 35 per cent of the army by 2001, while the number of non-Slav officers was only about 4 per cent of the total. The Serb community of 40,000, living mainly in Kumanovo, was disproportionately represented in the officer corps, explaining in part the concern of the ethnic Albanian population over how the armed forces would treat them.

As another military expert noted, a pro-Belgrade political and military underground has always existed in Skopje. Serb paramilitary groups, including Arkan, were active in Macedonia throughout the wartime period in ex-Yugoslavia, and had many links with the official armed forces.[8] Arkan had considerable investments in Skopje in retail and sports goods sectors. War criminals flooded into Macedonia from Kosovo after Serb forces were defeated in 1999.

The Skopje operation of Technometalvardar, an old Yugoslav metal trading company, was widely believed to have been controlled by the Serbian State Security (secret police) in the early 1990s. It was believed to be working with other organisations in Skopje to smuggle arms to Serbia through Macedonia during the Bosnian war. The company had links to the powerful Karic banking and trading organisation that backed the Milosevic regime. Technometalvardar was eventually closed down after allegations of corruption but this was not enough to assuage ethnic Albanian concerns about the Skopje military and intelligence establishments' links to Serb nationalist extremists.

Most of ARM's equipment, including virtually all battle tanks and artillery, came as aid, though two state-owned military factories produced small arms and explosives at Makedonski Brod. The army was badly affected by the arms embargo on Yugoslavia from 1992 to 1995. Bulgaria donated 150 T-55s in 1999, but only 104 of those were operational, with the rest used for spares and training. Sofia also supplied 142 pieces of Soviet-built field artillery in calibres up to 152mm. Other donations included armoured personnel carriers (APCs): 60 ex-East German BTR-70s from Germany; 63 M-113 APCs from Italy and 10 Leonidas APCs from Greece.

The Macedonian Army continues to rely on foreign aid. The US Government announced on 29 March 2001, that it would provide 13.6 million dollars in military assistance in the fiscal year 2001. Of that, equipment would account for 6.7 million dollars, including a further batch of 36 M101A1 105 mm howitzers, which would double the number of that type in service, 30 2.5 ton trucks and 707 MG3 7.62 machine guns.

David Des Roches, a spokesman for the US Defense Security Co-operation Agency, said that another 750,000 dollars was earmarked for training. Washington also pays for the consulting company Military Professional Resources International (MPRI), which advises the Macedonian Army on transformation along NATO standards and played a key role in building up the Croatian armed forces. Some experts believe that the MPRI or a similar organisation also may have been used to train the ethnic Albanian guerrillas in southern Serbia and that a significant number of these went on to fight with the NLA in Macedonia.[9] This would mean that very likely there were people on both sides of the Macedonian conflict trained with US funds to kill each other in a highly bizarre example of the contradictions sometimes afflicting American policy in the Balkans.

'Despite the aid, the ARM remains poorly equipped, badly trained and led,' *Jane's* said. Units around Tetovo were seen to be short of medical kits and field radios. The large number of reservists employed indicated that the ARM fell short of the official goal of A-class units being kept at full strength at all times. Despite claims of successful transformation, the ARM officer corps was too large, old-fashioned and top-heavy. Experienced non-commissioned officers were in short supply.

Staunch resistance by 100 NLA fighters cornered in the Gracani area after the Tetovo fighting continued to embarrass the ARM, whose infantry units seemed extremely reluctant to engage in an open battle.

Commentators in Belgrade were also concerned at the feeble performance of the Macedonian armed forces. 'The National Liberation Army has ignited a true war in northwestern Macedonia,' the independent Beta news agency noted.[10]

Macedonian forces failed in their attempts to suppress the guerrillas, who have successfully organised channels for supplying and transporting weapons from Kosovo. The guerrillas correctly foresaw that the international forces, which guard the borders, would not engage them in open armed conflict and thus put the lives of their soldiers at risk. All this led to the National Liberation Army's success in the field.

Within a month, the insurgents, after a period of respite in neighbouring Kosovo, had regrouped, killing eight Macedonian commandos on 28 April in an ambush near the mountainous northern border with Kosovo and seizing control of several mainly ethnic Albanian villages, this time in the province of Kumanovo, perilously close to the main Athens to Belgrade motorway.

This was the highest death toll in any single clash since fighting had erupted in February. Stevo Pendarovski, the Interior Ministry spokesman, said the soldiers were attacked near the village of Vejce, nine miles north of Tetovo. 'Eight are killed and two are injured. They were fired at with machine guns and rocket launchers. Macedonian forces responded, and the attackers withdrew. The situation is quiet now. It was an isolated incident.' The assumption was premature.

The slaying of the eight commandos, which was an enormous loss for a country of only two million people, provoked the first civilian backlash by Slavic Macedonians grouped in sinister new paramilitary-style, 'self-defence' organisations in the southern city of Bitola, 170 kilometres (120 miles) south of Skopje, from where four of the dead soldiers came. Ethnic Macedonian Slav crowds looted and set fire to Albanian shops. In Skopje, gunmen terrorised Albanian neighbourhoods, killing a Kosovar Albanian as he ate in a pizzeria, and attacking the Albanian Embassy.

The activities of the paramilitaries had their roots in armed groups of supporters of the nationalist VMRO-DPMNE party, the so-called 'Defence Committees' that had appeared in areas of mixed population around Ohrid and Struga and other areas of western Macedonia as far back as 1992. The chairman of the Ohrid Assembly, Blagoja Siljanovski, at first gave these groups of irregulars tacit support, saying they were helpful in keeping public order and security in the region. He later had dropped his approval and ruled out any potential official cooperation with the paramilitaries.[11]

For readers and viewers in Britain or the rest of Western Europe, the killing of the eight commandos was just another statistic and, since it happened far from the eyes of the international media, the ambush and others like it would have far less impact than the disturbing images of Razim and Ramadan dying in Tetovo.

The incident and subsequent fighting above Tetovo during the army offensive brought home to the West for the first time the danger that the conflict easily could degenerate into a new, full-scale Balkan war.

7 The Slide into Civil War

Black Peter made a short speech reminding them all of the
pledge they had taken to win through with the treasure, and
Methuen could not help reflecting that this alone betrayed the
one weakness of a Balkan soldier – forgetfulness. He must each
day be reminded of what he is fighting for and exhorted to do
his duty.
Lawrence Durrell, White Eagles Over Serbia

THE FIGHTING AROUND KUMANOVO was more protracted than in Tetovo, concluding in an effective victory for the more mobile and pugnacious National Liberation Army. For western observers, it confirmed that the Macedonian security forces lacked the military capacity to defeat the guerrillas, who were entrenched in the villages of Vaksince, Slupcane and Lipkovo near Kumanovo, itself a bastion of Macedonian nationalism and of Macedonia's Serb minority. The Macedonian Army's tactics were to blast the villages with heavy artillery and tank fire backed up with helicopters firing rockets.

For days there was little for the media to do but watch the heavy bombardment of Vaksince from a safe Macedonian position a mile and a half away, next to the main Skopje to Belgrade railway line, for all the world like eighteenth-century aristocrats peering at battles with picnic hampers, wine and a powerful telescope while on a grand tour. Occasionally a train would pass and the passengers on board would peer at the display of Macedonian fire power as the Ukrainian gunships flew over their carriages firing off flares and chaff to ward away heat-seeking ground-to-air missiles while the locomotive trundled toward the beleaguered capital.

'Are you enjoying the show?' a good-natured bus driver shouted as he slowed down to enable his passengers to take a better look. By the side of the road with fields of wheat and wild flowers on either side, a motley crowd of spectators turned out to watch the two sides do battle under a blistering Balkans sun.

In Skopje, our itinerant work back and forth from the edge of the battlefront attracted some curiosity among the few other foreigners who were still going about their business. Mercenaries, arms dealers or spies drinking whisky in the shady Holiday Inn bar studied the comings and goings of camera crews laden with flak jackets and helmets in the lobby. 'Do be careful,' a dapper British diplomat said. 'We wouldn't want you to become what we call a "consular case".'

A western military attaché explained to BBC staff how he had defeated a hangover nurtured with his Russian opposite number. Editors in London made clear their frustration at the paucity of colour and action.

In Kumanovo, crowds of ethnic Macedonian teenagers gathered in the sunshine in cafes on the town's main square, flirting and smoking as rock music blared from loudspeakers. A few miles away, ethnic Albanian women and children were cowering and some dying in cellars under the fire of these young people's army. Playing down the conflict's effect in Kumanovo was important to its citizens, who are proud of the town's historical importance for Slavs. During the first Balkan war in 1912, the Serbs defeated Turkish forces at Kumanovo, from where they were able to capture Skopje.

For some ethnic Albanians, equally, collective memories of the treatment of Albanians massacred at the time by Serbs and their underground society the Black Hand, in retaliation for Albanian attacks on Christians, fed fear during the modern siege in the villages around Kumanovo in which Macedonian authorities accused the NLA of using civilians as human shields.

The surreal quality of the spectacle near Vaksince was liable to obscure the seriousness of the conflict, which continued through the summer as the two sides fought to determine the country's fate.

A BBC reporter, Nick Wood, found a back road to the NLA headquarters at Lipkovo and visited Slupcane during a ceasefire. In spite of the truce, over-zealous Macedonian gunners decided to target his 'armour-plated' Land Rover, blowing it up with all the correspondent's kit inside as he watched aghast with the photographer Andrew Testa from a nearby NLA trench. A 17-year-old girl fighter consoled Nick by jumping out of the trench under heavy shellfire and picking a flower for his buttonhole.

The Macedonian Army was unapologetic. They had seen the Land Rover in the rebel-controlled area for four days, army sources said, and 'assumed it had been stolen by the NLA'. The vehicle was plastered with tape marking it clearly as television transport. Its destruction, equally clearly, was intended to intimidate foreign reporters. As if his close call were not enough, Nick soon was receiving stern cables from accountants irately demanding explanations for the loss of such an expensive piece of equipment, worth tens of thousands of licence-payers' pounds.

A short time later, I joined Douglas Hamilton, Reuter's NATO correspondent, as he set off in an armoured Land Rover to assess the situation in the NLA-controlled villages. After passing a series of semi-empty Albanian hamlets that I had reconnoitred a couple of days earlier with a Hungarian photographer, Bela Szandelszky, who was accompanying us, we skirted an isolated Macedonian police station close to an Orthodox monastery near the town of Matejce that would become an NLA strongpoint a fortnight later.

On a flat stretch of road we reached a checkpoint at the start of 'liberated territory.' A group of determined-looking teenage NLA fighters wearing jeans, bandannas and cowboy hats waved us through sandbagged positions they defended with Kalashnikov AK-47 assault rifles and shotguns.

A throng of civilians crowded around us to tell us about their woes. A short young fighter in black fatigues introduced himself as a press officer and jumped into the Land Rover to navigate the way to the NLA command post in the village of Lipkovo where, he said, there was a 'media centre'.

Douglas remonstrated with his Albanian colleague from Reuter's Tirana office, Benet Koleka, who was interpreting. 'No soldiers in the vehicle,' Douglas fumed. 'That's the rule. That's the way Kurt got killed.'

The memory of Kurt Schork, an American Reuter correspondent from New York who made his name during the Bosnian war only to be killed in Sierra Leone in 2000 while reporting with an army patrol, is vivid in the Balkans. Douglas's words conjured up images for me of watching Kurt working frenetically in the Reuter war office in Sarajevo's shelled-out Holiday Inn where he remained throughout the long, atrocious siege of the city.

Also on our minds at the time was the killing of a British journalist working for Associated Press Television News in Krivenik, Kosovo, just 1,200 yards from the Macedonian frontier, while covering the NLA's Tetovo offensive. A mortar shell mortally wounded Kerem Lawton, 30, when it hit his vehicle on 29 March in a village close to an NLA training camp. NATO opened an enquiry into his death to try to determine if the Macedonian Army or the rebels were responsible.

Both sides denied responsibility for the unfortunate 'consular case'. Publication of the NATO report on its investigation was repeatedly delayed amid speculation that American peacekeepers based in Kosovo had tipped off Macedonian forces about the camp, setting off the bombardment.

Lawton's widow, Elida Ramadani, a 27-year-old Kosovar Albanian, was eight months pregnant when he was killed.

Jeff Bieley, the UPI correspondent in Skopje, met reliable sources who consider it 'quite likely' that the Americans wanted the Macedonians to shell the NLA training camp. An American diplomat in Skopje said that the US military liaisons in Macedonia that normally monitored the shelling in the area with field radar batteries withdrew from the area that day. 'That allowed them to deny they knew who was shelling where,' Jeff commented.[1]

Lawton's death drew the attention of *Jane's Defence Weekly*, which hinted strongly that 'lack of training and co-ordination' in the Macedonian Army were to blame for the incident. 'At the time the Army of the Macedonian Republic was engaged in a counter-insurgency operation that relied heavily on artillery and mortar support.' KFOR sources said that Lawton and another civilian killed in Krivenik had been hit by a 120 mm mortar bomb. The NLA commander in the region said his units had no mortars above 82 mm.[2]

Lawton actually expired from his wounds at the gate of the US base, the sprawling Camp Bondsteel, in Kosovo while a civilian ambulance was awaiting clearance to take him to the base hospital. In interviews with Bieley, the ambulance driver and the doctor with Lawton blamed the US peacekeepers in part for his death, particularly as they had failed to deploy a medivac helicopter to rescue the British reporter.

It looked strongly as though Kerem Lawton's death, like the destruction of the BBC vehicle, was part of a deliberate Macedonian military policy of discouraging the foreign media. The Macedonian generals had seen the impact on world opinion of western coverage of atrocities by their former colleagues from the Yugoslav Army in Bosnia, Croatia and Kosovo. It is likely that they hoped to prevent unwelcome publicity for the ethnic Albanian side of the conflict that might stem the influx of arms, equipment and cash. On the other hand, supporters of the Macedonians argue that there was no way they could have known there were journalists in the village at the time and that, from where Macedonian artillery positions then were, the gunners could not see their targets.

Both arguments underlined the need for NATO to disclose the results of its inquiry. More than two years after the event, the report would be released once it had been made available to Lawton's widow and his employers.

Part of the delay in publication was due to the attitude of the Macedonian authorities, who insisted that the NLA was responsible, thus the original plan for a joint NATO-Macedonian report was scrubbed. Instead, according to the sources,[3] the NATO report found that:

> The basic conclusion, based on crater analysis and what we knew of the positions of both the ARM and NLA, is that the mortars were 120mm of a kind used by both sides, and that they could have been fired from an area where there were known NLA and ARM forces, and from either side of the border. So the end result is that we cannot attribute responsibility to either side.

Even before the report was officially published, however, it was circulating unofficially in diplomatic circles. One respected western military attaché who saw it dismissed it as 'a weasel-worded whitewash', or just the kind of cover-up that the NATO Secretary-General, Lord Robertson, had promised to avert.

'The NLA did not have a mortar in the area and even if they had, why would they want to shoot backwards,' said the diplomat. He described the US failure to help Lawton after he was wounded as 'pretty disgraceful', but added:

> You have to remember the Americans never wanted to get involved in patrolling the border. They only agreed to do it under strong pressure from NATO and Britain. They probably were not thinking rationally, just following the idea of force protection first and may have felt constrained by a regulation prohibiting their helicopters from carrying civilians.

A Government spokesman, Georgi Trandafilov, said at the time there was 'not the remotest possibility' that Macedonian soldiers had fired the shells.[4] This was clearly nonsense.

A KFOR statement at the time said little more. 'KFOR regrets the incident took place and that the lives of our soldiers were endangered in an area that is clearly inside Kosovo territory,' said Major Axel-Bernd Jandesek, spokesman for the peacekeepers.[5]

Hans Haekkerup, the head of the UN Mission in Kosovo, made the strongest suggestion that Macedonia was to blame, calling on the Government in Skopje to change tack. 'I deeply regret this tragedy which has cost the lives of innocent civilians. I will be raising the urgent need for restraint by Macedonian forces and for dialogue to replace shooting when I visit Skopje tomorrow.'[6]

Thereafter, Douglas, who had been working in the village where Lawton was killed a short time before the attack, and his colleagues in the Associated Press bureau in Skopje received strict dispositions from their head offices to avoid taking unnecessary risks. 'Our bosses have made it clear they don't want to be going to any more funerals,' Douglas said, as he swung the Land Rover up an almost vertical track.

This left correspondents in the field, in an awkward, rather Kafkaesque position as to how to work. The official policy in London or New York headquarters was to avoid taking risks. But in practice news editors under pressure to beat competitors still expected correspondents to perform whatever the hazards.

After dabbling in war reporting in Lebanon, Iraq, Algeria, Croatia and Bosnia, taking calculated risks and testing my courage has become a familiar experience, if never 'routine'. Still, having been obliged to leg it under mortar fire twice within a week at Oslare and Tetovo before witnessing the 'executions' at the roadblock in the city, I was not keen to push my luck.

In spite of the indiscriminate expenditure of ammunition by both sides in Macedonia, killing had not taken place on anything like the scale of Bosnia or Croatia. As we bumped through no man's land, I was nevertheless grateful that Douglas was an old colleague who exudes professionalism, coolness and trust, as well as, or perhaps most of all, for the cocooning protection, however illusory, of his Land Rover.

This time our equipment was better than when we had worked together in 1993 near Zadar, on the dazzling Dalmatian coast, during Croatia's offensive to recapture Krajina. A Croatian Army public relations trip had almost ended in disaster as our journalists' bus met Croatian troops in full battle gear retreating under Serbian fire. Film footage of Douglas was shown on CNN the next day as he dived under the bus for cover from a whining shell in what in retrospect seemed an almost comic scene captured by Mike Sposito, Visnews' frontline cameraman.

Fortunately, there was little time to dwell on the fate of our dead colleagues. We soon reached a large Albanian farmhouse and were asked to park the vehicle in the covered entrance to prevent it being spotted and possibly attacked by Macedonian helicopters.

Inside the house, we took off our shoes and entered a carpeted room lined with sofas and with pistols hanging on the bare wall. The 'press officer' spoke into a cellphone and told us to wait for the local commander, *Sokoli* (the Hawk). We were offered coffee and fruit juice with the hospitality a visitor receives all over the Balkans. The young fighters wandering in and out of the room seemed disciplined and calm.

Elsewhere in the village, there were scenes resembling those we had seen at Selce weeks earlier. We were shown groups of veiled women and children living in cellars. The rumble of tank shelling reverberated around nearby mountains. On the outskirts of the village, fighters and civilians were digging trenches.

'We came here from Slupcane three days ago to stay with relatives after my uncle, Remzi Osmani, was killed in the shelling,' a young woman, Zeliha Osmani, said. 'We have no milk here. For a week we have been living on tea and beans.'

The press officer, a native of Kumanovo, slyly parried questions until we heard the clattering of an approaching Macedonian helicopter gunship. In the farmyard we watched the copter pass over a forested mountain some two kilometres away, fortunately carrying its deadly cargo of rockets elsewhere.

Sokoli, a tall, appropriately aquiline man of around 35, received us in a summer house in the courtyard flanked by two bodyguards in black fatigues carrying AK-47s modified for sniping. He strongly denied using the civilians in basements as human shields and accused the Macedonian authorities of effective ethnic cleansing. 'Our positions are outside the villages but the Macedonians are shelling people's homes. They are trying to use a scorched earth policy like the Russians in Afghanistan.'

Sokoli smiled when reminded by Douglas that Lord Robertson had that week called his men 'murderous thugs'. Lord Robertson was free to come and see the situation. 'The door is open to everyone except the Macedonian Army,' he said. 'None of the Albanian political leaders has had the courage to visit this area,' he added. 'They are just cowards who are pursuing their own interests.'

On the road back to Skopje, we mulled over our visit as Douglas filled the Land Rover with smoke from one of his Cuban cigars. At least one of the cellars appeared to have been packed with civilians at very short notice for our benefit. Some of the children had been playing football in the open air minutes before our visit. They did not seem unduly worried by the prospect of attack by the Macedonian Army. So far, Lipkovo had not been shelled because it was close to two reservoirs providing water for Kumanovo. A few days later, the rebels ratcheted up the crisis by turning off the water and demanding an end to shelling of the villages.

As we neared the sprawling town of Aracinovo, a few weeks later also to be seized by the NLA as it advanced ominously towards Skopje, we were stopped at a new Macedonian checkpoint that had not been there that morning. Special forces soldiers from the elite Wolves unit looked in the Land Rover and waved us on.

I felt uneasy at not accepting an offer to stay in the 'media centre' overnight together with the Hungarian photographer. Szandelszky was determined to press on to the main battlefront at Slupcane at first light, wanting to check reports that conditions in the cellars there were appalling, with heavy civilian casualties, shortages of food and medical supplies and dead animals littering the streets. It seemed pointless to expose the Land Rover to excessive curiosity from the Macedonians after Nick Wood's experience, however. We resolved to return soon to see Slupcane.

The plight of the civilians was undoubtedly exaggerated at times by the rebels but the reluctance of the ethnic Albanian village populations to leave their homes was worrying the International Committee of the Red Cross. François Stamm, a Balkan veteran who was the head of its Macedonian office, said he had never seen a crisis in which so many civilians turned down a chance of safety. 'It is a very, very sad and tragic situation,' said Stamm after a visit to the villages.

Efforts by British forces to prevent the NLA bringing weapons into Macedonia from Kosovo were also taking their toll. On 9 April, two RAF pilots, Captain Andrew Crous, 28, and Flight Lieutenant James Maguire, 31, died when the Puma helicopter they were flying crashed in bad weather on the border between Kosovo and Macedonia. The helicopter was carrying members of the Royal Tank Regiment on a bouncing patrol around the border area, aimed at intercepting ethnic Albanian guerrillas smuggling arms into Macedonia. None of the RTR men was seriously injured. Also in April, Adam Slater, a 20-year-old British soldier from Felsted, Essex, was killed when his armoured car struck a mine near Krivenik, where Kerem Lawton had died.

Back in Skopje, I visited a weapons fair in a cavernous exhibition hall where the region's arms dealers had flocked in readiness for the next Balkans war. The Macedonian Army's woes began in 1991 when the Yugoslav Army took everything transportable, even stripping the electric wiring out of its abandoned barracks.

A platoon of young sales reps in camouflaged mini-skirts showed off the latest sniper-rifles, grenade launchers and body armour.

'The Bulgarians gave us tanks, but we have to pay for the ammunition and spare parts,' Zlatko Samardzioski, a rep for the Macedonian arms manufacturer Eurokompozit said. He proudly displayed a Macedonian 120 mm rocket launcher. 'It's Yugoslav technology but we make it here now.'

In 1999, Bulgaria donated 150 T-55 battle tanks and 142 Soviet-made artillery pieces to Macedonia. Only about 100 are still in good working order, according to *Jane's Defence Weekly*. Germany, Italy and Greece sent Macedonia armoured cars, Britain promised body armour and mine detectors and the USA announced 13.6 million dollars in military aid for 2001.

Some of the US cash was to be spent paying the mercenary firm MPRI, set up by former US military officers, to train the army and help them adapt to the realities of modern warfare. *Jane's* cautioned that the army's 20,000 troops were still 'poorly equipped, badly trained and led'.

The arrival from Ukraine of four Mi-8 transport helicopters and two Mi-24 gunships gave the army a temporary psychological advantage, but its planners proved ill-prepared for a campaign of counter-insurgency.

By May 2001, western analysts estimated the NLA had 800 men under arms. NATO would put the figure at 2,000 by August. The NLA had no heavy weapons but proved adept at melting away from an assault and then reappearing to mount bloody ambushes. Some of the rebels claimed to have received training in guerrilla warfare from the SAS and other British special forces when NATO was Belgrade's enemy, though this was denied strongly in British defence circles.

The high point of the arms fair was a surreal ballet carried out by beautiful dancers of the Macedonian National Opera Company. Ordinary Macedonians were evidently more talented in the performing arts than in the art of war.

Near Kumanovo at the end of May, however, Richard Beeston discovered that some of the most haunting images of the ethnic cleansing in Balkans wars in Croatia, Bosnia and Kosovo had arrived in Macedonia, generated by both sides in the conflict.

A refugee convoy of tractors and ancient cars looked much like any other blocking the country's roads at the time. A bus in the convoy had ferried villagers out of the village of Matejce. Men and boys were being separated from their families aboard the bus and taken off by Macedonian police to an uncertain fate. 'It would have been easy to miss the tell-tale signs had the first policeman I approached not reacted so violently,' Richard recounted.[7] 'There was little fighting in this northern corner of the former Yugoslav Republic of Macedonia yesterday... yet the young officer was agitated. He swore and brandished his Kalashnikov, with a finger on the trigger to make sure I had got the point.'

'You bastards, this is all your fault,' the officer yelled.

The reason for his outburst became clear when Richard spotted a group of 40 men and boys, some as young as 12, sitting and standing aside from the rest of the refugees. Some looked at their relatives, who were being allowed to leave. Others stared down, avoiding eye contact with their captors. None spoke.

Details of how the men disappeared emerged when Salvete, 33, a mother from the group who was traced in hospital at Kumanovo, described the ordeal that her family had endured in the village of Matejce for most of the month. 'When the fighting started three weeks ago we went into the shelter of the house,' she said. 'At any one time there were up to 50 people down there – cousins, grandparents, lots of children. We rarely went out because of the fighting.'

The village became a front line between the government forces and the National Liberation Army guerrillas. A barrage by tanks, artillery and helicopter gunships pounded the village so hard that the minaret of the mosque collapsed.

'The village sheikh told us to leave this morning, so we got out as quickly as we could,' the mother said feebly as she recovered from exhaustion and dehydration. 'I do not know where my husband is or the other men in my family.'

Reporters had seen an old Yugoslav tourist bus escorted by paramilitary police in all terrain vehicles drive into Kumanovo's police station with the men, the first batch of scores of 'suspects' being taken in for questioning. Once in the cells, the men had their hands tested for paraffin, a discredited method of searching for traces of gunpowder, which can come up positive if the suspect has smoked a cigarette, handled fertilisers or been put in a military vehicle that has been used to transport ammunition.

Peter Bouckaert of Human Rights Watch, who had been monitoring the disturbing new trend in Macedonia, said that most would be roughed up during detention before being freed after a few days' questioning. Others would be held much longer and probably subjected to severe beatings before being forced to make a confession about links to the rebels. 'They are going to have a nasty time in there.'

The methods of the security forces contrasted starkly with the heroic efforts still being made by a significant number of ordinary Macedonians on both sides to try to stop the communities growing apart. In ethnically-mixed Kumanovo, the ethnic Slav Mayor, Slobodan Kovacevski, and Feriz Dervishi, the ethnic Albanian head of its inter-ethnic relations commission, both worked tirelessly to prevent the city being torn asunder. The two would confer daily and then visit their separate constituencies. Dervishi, 50, pleaded with ethnic Albanian patriarchs to be patient and prevent their children from enlisting in the guerrilla army. Kovacevski, 52, condemned the vigilante attacks in Bitola.

'Everyone thought Kumanovo would be a disaster,' said Dervishi. 'But the population itself still likes to live together.'[8] Both men attended a local school where ethnic Albanians and Slavs still share classes together. The two men met as they each climbed to the top local ranks of their respective, ethnically based political groupings.

Although a curfew was in force from 10 pm and industry was at a standstill because of key workers in factories moving to ethnically 'pure' towns for safety or leaving Macedonia, the two men soldiered on. They solved a heated local dispute over an ethnic Albanian graveyard and Kovacevski put pressure on the local police to try and curb frequent beatings of ethnic Albanian motorists by army reservists on checkpoints set up on roads in and out of the city.

The Mayor conceded that 'There are people saying "Let's finish with the Albanians, this is the time".' At a meeting with Slav city leaders at the former headquarters of the central committee of the Communist Party, 'People were concerned, they were worried, they were scared,' he said. 'I told them Albanians are their neighbours and in the future they will still live together. That is why Macedonians should be careful and responsible for their behaviour.'

In late May, government forces registered their first success with the recapture of Vaksince, which was visited by Ljube Boskovski, the Interior Minister. Government forces were supposed to resume their attack on the villages of Slupcane, Lipkovo and Matejce, but the offensive stalled when a special forces unit mutinied and had to be withdrawn from the front line.

A spokesman for the Interior Ministry confirmed that the commanding officer of the 'Tigers' police anti-terrorist unit, Major Mandarovsky, had been suspended together with his deputy after they complained of being sent into battle without adequate support, and refused to obey orders. The unit was confined to barracks.

Major Mandarovsky was apparently unhappy about the level of support his unit was receiving from badly trained army conscripts. 'The commander and the deputy have been suspended,' an Interior Ministry spokesman said. 'The interior minister issued the order for their suspension because they refused to follow orders and enter the villages.' Military sources said that, far from being a difference of opinion on tactics, the row had deteriorated into a mutiny.

The withdrawal of the Tigers from the action was a huge boost for the ethnic Albanian rebels. Similar problems were experienced at the time with the Wolves, the Macedonian Army's special forces unit, the other main frontline force against the rebels.

The Aracinovo Offensive

By the start of June, hundreds of NLA fighters had advanced, meeting virtually no opposition, to take the sprawling village of Aracinovo, just five miles from the capital. Now they threatened to shell Government buildings and the Parliament in the city and its international airport, which apparently were in their range.

'The message is that so far, this war has caused harm just to Albanians, now it is time to share it,' said the local NLA commander, Hoxha, a small, wiry man who we had met limping around Lipkovo on a wounded foot.

'So far they were bombing and shelling Albanian villages. But this position is a very strategic position. From here we can shell the airport, the refinery, the government, the parliament... this might be one of our strategies.'[9] Hoxha said his fighters had brought up 120 mm artillery. The Macedonian Interior Ministry said it doubted the rebels had guns capable of firing the eight miles to the centre but admitted the rebels might cause panic. The new threat to attack civilian targets was an escalation.

US government workers prepared to leave Macedonia after Washington ordered that non-essential staff should return home. The instruction followed increasing hostility to westerners and fears that the 2,000 Americans in the country were under threat. Britain and Germany ordered their citizens in Macedonia to take extra care.

Anti-Albanian rioting broke out in Bitola for a second time on 6 June. This time, some police officers actively participated in the violence. Dozens of Albanian homes and as many as 100 shops were burned by the mob. As in April, the spark for the ethnic cleansing was the killing of three policemen from Bitola, among five security force members who were killed on 5 June outside Tetovo. The homes set on fire appeared to have been carefully selected, including houses belonging to prominent ethnic Albanian politicians such as the Deputy Health Minister and the wealthiest ethnic Albanians.

The rioters also vandalised a village mosque in the Bitola area, breaking grave-markers and setting carpets inside the building alight. On the walls of the mosque, the assailants daubed swastikas and the slogan 'Death to the Shiptars', a derogatory term for Albanians. Human Rights Watch gathered chilling accounts of the events at Bitola from those who were attacked.[10]

Human Rights Watch acknowledged that not all the abuses during the conflict were perpetrated by Macedonian Slavs. On 7 June, the agency reported that the NLA had abused eight ethnic Serb civilians whom it had arbitrarily detained in the village of Matejce the previous week. Altogether, at least 21 ethnic Serb men, many of them elderly, were detained by the Albanian rebel group. NLA fighters had entered Matejce, which has a mixed Serbian and Albanian population, around 24 May and attacked its police station.

Sixty-year-old Krunislav Filipovic, an ethnic Serb, was taken from his home by NLA fighters on the evening of 24 May and taken to the village mosque together with three other elderly ethnic Serbs, he told Human Rights Watch. All four were fathers of Macedonian policemen. NLA fighters beat the four with their fists and gun butts and kicked them. On several occasions the men were subjected to mock executions and NLA fighters sharpened knives in front of them, threatening to behead them. The men were kept in detention, abused for four days, and then released in the village of Otla, where they were told to walk towards Macedonian positions. NLA soldiers fired above their heads as they fled.[11]

Later in the summer, the NLA allegedly kidnapped three road-workers, who were severely beaten and sexually abused for several hours. The apprehension of those responsible was to be a major obstacle to national reconciliation in the future.

On 12 June, the Macedonian Army Chief of Staff, General Jovan Andrevski, resigned in a surprise move that rocked the beleaguered Government as hundreds of civilians in Skopje demanded that the authorities give them weapons to fight the rebels on the outskirts of the capital.

General Andrevski quit because of 'bad morale of his troops' and because he felt personally responsible for the loss of 26 young army soldiers killed during the previous four months, an army spokesman said. The commander was replaced by his deputy, General Jovan Petkovski, but the abrupt resignation heightened the impression that Macedonian authorities were losing control of events. 'It's rather unusual in western terms for a commander to wear his heart on his feet,' a western military attaché commented.

British Airways and most other foreign airlines, mindful of the NLA threat to shell the airport at Skopje, abruptly cancelled their flights to Macedonia. I was virtually the only passenger on an Austrian Airlines flight to Macedonia from Vienna. From a nearby seat, Christian Jennings of the *Daily Telegraph* pointed down at columns of smoke billowing from NLA positions at Aracinovo, which was under heavy Macedonian fire.

The jetliner landed uneventfully and the next day I set out from a hot and oppressively humid Skopje to tour the grim, poverty-stricken suburb of Stajkovci, adjoining Aracinovo. According to the local newspaper, *Vest*, police had covertly distributed AK-47s to Stajkovci residents to defend themselves.

At least 200 Slavs had besieged the police station at Gazi Baba, marking the first time that Slav civilians from the capital had publicly asked for weapons. Few of the people of Stajkovci wanted to talk to foreigners. Spy fever was beginning to sweep Skopje.

'The worrying thing now is that whoever you speak to, Albanians or Macedonians, say that they are ready to take up arms,' a British diplomat said. Officially only reservists who had done national service received Kalashnikovs. In practice, we learned, the police were for the first time arming civilians who were not reservists.

8 An Outbreak of Peace?

The truth of the vanquished was quite different from the truth of the victorious.
Svetlana Velmar-Jankovic, Dungeon

As the conflict worsened, western diplomats led by Javier Solana, the European Union foreign policy chief, had sought to defuse the burgeoning civil war as early as April by sponsoring the creation of a Grand Coalition Government of National Unity, composed of both dominant Macedonian Slav political parties and the two main ethnic Albanian groupings. The coalition was eventually formed in May.

Solana brought to bear his previous experience as Secretary-General of NATO, where he took over on the day that the alliance led 60,000 troops from 30 nations into Bosnia to implement the Dayton peace agreement. He sought to guide NATO through a transition from Cold War thinking aimed mainly at protecting the West from a menacing Soviet Union to a more wide-ranging mission.

Initially, the suave Spaniard with a salt and pepper beard had disappointed some correspondents covering NATO. 'He specialises in soft talk,' one said, 'for a long time I wouldn't go to his press conferences. You would end up with nothing but nothing.' However, sources in the alliance soon convinced reporters that Solana was an extremely able negotiator. 'People at NATO said that behind the scenes Solana was a good consensus seeker. He wouldn't take no for an answer, a good diplomat,' one recalled.

Western diplomats in Skopje concurred that Solana's dedication to the peace process in Macedonia would turn out to be essential. 'He was kind of vital,' said one. Solana's achievements in the Balkans, in creating the Union of Serbia and Montenegro in 2003 out of the ashes of the old Yugoslavia, as well as in Macedonia, are cited by his supporters as qualifying him to realise his ambition to become a future European prime minister under the new EU constitution.

The peacemaking initiative reflected the extent to which foreign influence over the Macedonian state had remained extremely strong since its inception. James Pettifer noted during President Gligorov's stewardship that there was always a small committee of European Union and American ambassadors in Skopje, acting in a highly interventionist way over many policy and practical issues:

> As the FYROM government is wholly dependent on external funds from these countries for survival, it is usually possible for Skopje policy to be manipulated in any direction the foreign ambassadors see fit, including the reduction in Albanian influence over the government wherever possible.
>
> The EU diplomatic community has a function in Skopje akin to that of colonial governors in dependent territories, dispensers of largesse from the mother country, in this case the EU and the international financial institutions, and guardians and defenders of the local law and order authority, in Macedonia the ex-communist-dominated Interior Ministry.[1]

This theme was also explored by Tomlinson, the renegade SIS officer, in his book, *The Big Breach*. Tomlinson described the role of British and French officers in shoring up the Gligorov Government in the Albanian arms plot that landed many home-grown ethnic Albanian radicals in prison cells in Skopje in November 1993, opening the way for more radical leaders with Kosovar connections to dominate the Albanian spectrum. He implied that important planks of British Balkan policy were decided by secret and unaccountable elements in the state system, especially MI6 in alliance with the special forces in the military.

By the end of May, however, the coalition was in deep disarray, after the Albanian party leaders reached a putative secret peace deal with the NLA. The agreement was brokered mysteriously by the former American diplomat who had become a Balkan envoy for the Organisation for Security and Cooperation in Europe, Robert Frowick. The affair caused President Trajkovski much disquiet, and he warned that unless ethnic Albanian politicians renounced the deal the government would fall apart. 'If they don't do that, it will be impossible for us to work together.'

In a laconic statement issued on 18 May, Frowick disclosed:

> I have been engaged in intensive consultations this week with the DPA leader, Mr Xhaferi, leaders of the Party of Democratic Prosperity, Kosovar Albanian political leaders Rugova, Thaci and Haradinaj, as well as Gen. Ceku, and Albanian Prime Minister Meta aimed at persuading the ethnic Albanian armed groups that it is time to stop the armed struggle. All have told me that they agree with this objective.

Frowick did not disclose that the NLA political leader, Ali Ahmeti, had also participated in the secret talks at Prizren, Kosovo.

According to EU diplomats, the peace deal drawn up by Frowick and the editor of a leading Kosovo newspaper, *Veton Surroi*, called for the rebels to halt the fighting in exchange for amnesty guarantees provided by the ethnic Albanian coalition partners. The rebels would also gain the right to veto future political decisions about the scope of ethnic Albanian rights.

When the agreement became public, Frowick, who had been on the staff of the OSCE office in Skopje as the Personal Representative for FYROM of the organisation's chairman, left the country to avoid formal expulsion by the Macedonian Foreign Ministry, which said 'his services no longer are needed'. He was quickly disowned both by the US Embassy and the OSCE itself, which claimed the emissary had acted on his own initiative. Frowick flew to Bucharest to report on the situation to Romania's foreign minister, the OSCE chairman.

The US Embassy said that Washington 'rejects any kind of attempt to bring the so-called NLA into the negotiating process'. The European Union issued a similar denunciation, contending that the ethnic Albanian rebels 'who have planned and directed this terrorist campaign' should not be welcomed into the political process. 'If anyone has illusions that the so-called NLA has international support anywhere, they had better forget them,' the EU statement said.[2]

Frowick's work in Bosnia as OSCE head had received limited recognition from Richard Holbrooke, who described him in his memoirs only as 'the urbane American diplomat'.[3] A journalist in Skopje at the time recalls: 'Frowick was always at arm's length. One of the feelings was that he was there as an end run against any separate European diplomacy.'

After he left, one NATO official said Frowick was guilty of blabbing about the talks with the NLA:

Frowick misunderstood the critical issue, which is that it was impossible for the Macedonians to deal directly with the people they called terrorists. When he arranged the Prizren agreement which was signed by Ahmeti and Ihmeri and presented to the Macedonian Government as a fait accompli it was not the content that was a problem but that he told a sovereign nation 'this is the way it is,' and that he had negotiated with terrorists.

It was bound to fail. The Americans and British, everyone was bloody surprised. Once it was rejected a price had to be paid. The Macedonians wanted to throw him out and PNG him. The Americans said, 'Please don't do that, don't humiliate him like that.'

Not everyone was harsh on Frowick. 'He was right to try it but he got the public relations wrong,' said a western military attaché working in Prizren on the secret talks.

Some observers had preferred the style of Christopher Hill, the United States Ambassador to Macedonia in the late 1990s, who previously had been the US point man in Kosovo. 'Frowick was more of a smoothy, more of the silver-haired diplomat. There was more stagecraft and window dressing with the little Frowick operation,' one recalled. 'Frowick had a pompous flak [spokesman] who seemed to think he was working with the president of the United States. Chris Hill didn't need a flak. He was more down to earth and ready to speak, more off the peg.'

The negotiations underlined the extent to which the Albanian parties by this time shared common ground and demands with the NLA. 'I am not a militarist and, as such, I never accept fighting as an instrument to achieve political goals,' Xhaferi, the leader of the Democratic Party of Albanians, said. 'But it is very important to point out that the demands of the fighters are the same as ours.'[4]

Unsurprisingly, Xhaferi was supported by a large body of opinion in Albania. Tritan Shehi, a former Albanian foreign minister, commented at the time that: 'Macedonian authorities have hesitated during these last years to give due space to the realisation of the right changes, even constitutional ones, which could make possible the implementation of Albanian demands.'[5] Fortunately, the Socialist Government in Tirana made it clear it did not want the conflict to spread within its northern territories, effectively discouraging the NLA from opening up a southern front.

Only a few weeks on, NATO would effectively follow Frowick's example by seeking NLA approval for a last-ditch peace plan drawn up by President Trajkovski. Negotiations between the four main ethnic Macedonian and ethnic Albanian parties were held intermittently at the lakeside resort of Ohrid throughout June and July and the first two weeks of August, with ceasefires in the fighting being agreed periodically only to be broken again.

By now, Mr Trajkovski was receiving advice on public relations from Mark Laity, an ebullient NATO press officer and former BBC defence correspondent on secondment from Brussels answering directly to George Robertson, NATO's Secretary-General. Laity began writing many of the president's speeches and ghosting interviews attributed to Trajkovski, including one with the Albanian-language *Fakti* newspaper.

Laity was struck by the bizarre mood in Skopje when he arrived in May for his unusual assignment. 'Trajkovski was honest and he was decent but he had to face up to huge pressure without much support and his own team was far too small,' he recalled.[6]

> The atmosphere was very curious. One of the key problems that the Macedonian Government had was that you had a developing crisis but the number of people actually able and willing to do anything about it was very small. You had a very large bureaucracy but the number of people who mattered was extremely small. They not only had to make the decisions but to try and carry them out.
>
> On the one hand, you had the calmness of people who should have been busy and weren't, and on the other there was extreme jitteriness among a few people who were pulling all the levers, usually the right ones, but they weren't connecting.
>
> The President had created a big plan to end the conflict, a kind of road map that combined his instincts and ideas and International Community ideas. People said at the time that if there was a civil war in Macedonia it would be because the Macedonians were administratively incapable of stopping it.

President Trajkovski, in a speech to Parliament on 8 June, proposed a partial amnesty for ethnic Albanian fighters. We must give a chance to those who are ready to lay down their arms and integrate into the social life of the state,' he said; 'the plan for disarmament will be launched when conditions allow.' The offer was accompanied by the fiercest artillery barrage on rebel-held villages thus far. The speech was important because the Government had previously been unwilling to consider taking any concrete steps to induce guerrilla defections.

After capturing Aracinovo, leaders of the NLA had signalled their willingness to end their insurrection, provided the Government take certain steps toward establishing new rights for the ethnic Albanian minority. 'Now it looks hopeful,' Nikola Dimitrov, the national security advisor to President Trajkovski, said on 13 June during a lull. 'There is some sort of calmness,' even though low-level skirmishes continued.[7]

Dimitrov said the Macedonian Government had no objections if 'third parties' met with the rebels to secure their compliance. NATO's special representative to Macedonia, the German diplomat Hans-Joerg Eiff, met privately with Ahmeti in May to urge a halt to the fighting.

Trajkovski, who was spearheading the drafting of the plan within the Government, was willing to support a 'symbolic' presence of western troops in the country to 'reassure everybody', during the period in which the rebels disarmed, Dimitrov said. Western officials appeared increasingly open to some kind of deployment. The French President, Jacques Chirac, said at a meeting of NATO leaders in Brussels that 'we should rule out nothing in order to put a stop' to the rebellion, and the Greek Foreign Minister, George Papandreou, said that 'a presence of a peacekeeping force sooner or later... will be necessary'.

Muharem Nexhipi, an ethnic Albanian who was Macedonia's deputy health minister at the time, said he believed that Trajkovski was the only politician who could organise the constitutional change long desired by Albanians. Nexhipi, a native of Bitola whose house was burned to the ground by Slavic Macedonians in riots in the city, said as he was shopping for furniture in Skopje that 'there still is space for dialogue' that could end the conflict.

But he said he worried that Trajkovski might lack sufficient power to pull off a peace accord and that more nationalist politicians, including the Prime Minister, might still seek a military solution. 'The delay of the dialogue makes the (rebels) stronger every day,' Nexhipi said.

Western diplomats agreed that the mercurial moods of the powerful nationalist leader were indeed a barrier to a peace settlement. Georgievski, aged 36, personified the changes that had affected the mentality of the Slavonic political class since the NLA offensive started. An avowed Macedonian nationalist at the beginning of the 1990s, he pursued a policy of cooperating with the DPA, the largest Albanian party. The two parties started working together in 1996, during and after local elections that year. Georgievski came to power in 1998, bringing the DPA into a coalition government. The VMRO's relationship with the DPA was symbiotic, curiously allowing them to share power and its trappings though the two parties paid lip-service to contrasting and even mutually antagonistic ideals.

By June 2001, Georgievski's nationalist instincts had become inflamed by the casualties taken among the security forces and he pushed the state to declare a state of war. 'After two years of unprecedented partnership with the DPA, the last thing Georgievski expected was an Albanian rebellion,' Vladimir Jovanovski, an analyst with the Skopje bi-weekly *Forum*, commented then.[8] 'Now he believes the only way of resolving the crisis is by declaring war on Albanian militants. His public statements are inflaming tensions, just as the conflict seems set to escalate into a full-scale war.' A former close associate of Georgievski, Boris Zmejkovski, a member of a small party opposing the VMRO, said the insurrection had turned him into 'a crazy general'.

Georgievski's hand could be detected, the *Forum* analyst said, in the leaking to the press of a plan to divide Macedonia on ethnic lines by swapping territory with Albania or Kosovo. The plan was reportedly prepared by Georgi Efremov, a geneticist who is the chairman of the Macedonian Academy for Sciences and Arts, the country's reputed intellectual elite. Efremov consistently denied that he had prepared it. Political sources in Skopje believe it more likely that another academy member, Blaze Ristovski, had drawn up the plan. The Macedonian opposition parties had long claimed that the Prime Minister and VMRO-DPMNE were seeking both the partition of Macedonia and closer ties with Bulgaria.

Under the blueprint, cities with majority Albanian populations such as Tetovo, Gostivar and Debar, would be 'traded' for territory in eastern or south-eastern Albania, supposedly with a majority Slav population near the lakes of Ohrid and Prespa including the towns of Podgradec and Mala Prespa. The academics suggested that ethnic Albanians living in Kumanovo province should move to territory they propose to cede to Albania together with other Albanians from Skopje, Veles, Bitola and Kicevo. Equally, Macedonian Slavs would leave Tetovo and other areas to be ceded to Albania.

The exchange should be completed peacefully in three months, the Academy said in a statement quoted by the pro-government newspaper *Nova Makedonija*:

> This is the only solution that will endure because Macedonians and Albanians are so ethnically different they can't live together... Orthodox Christians and Muslims have different religions and customs. We have worked for years to create trust between them. But everything achieved has been destroyed in a few weeks of fighting that started in Tetovo.

The scholars said they had already contacted opposite numbers in the Albanian Academy of Sciences and that its president, Ylli Popa, had recently visited Skopje to discuss the proposal. However, Popa was quoted as rejecting the proposal. 'Inter ethnic problems cannot be solved by exchange of territories and populations,' he was quoted saying. 'The only solution to the Macedonian crisis is to respect the rights of Albanians living there.'

The *Nova Makedonija* newspaper quoted government sources as dismissing the suggestion as 'a fascist idea'. Whatever its origin, it prompted an angry statement from President Trajkovski's office. 'The only way to resolve these problems is through dialogue with the legitimately elected representatives of the Albanians and their parties and by developing life in common. What is important now is that groups of extremists and terrorists be isolated.'

Georgievski and the parliamentary speaker, Stojan Andov, a member of the Liberal Party, which was a junior partner in the coalition, were the only major politicians not to denounce the plan publicly. The opposition leader of the Social Democratic Party, Branko Crvenkovski, called the Macedonian Academy plan 'an incitement to civil war and suicide for Macedonia'.

But political feuding over the plan intensified after the daily *Vecer*, which is seen by western observers as an official tabloid voice of the VMRO, published a map of the planned exchange. Crvenkovski threatened to walk out of the grand coalition over the issue. Georgievski said he would not mind if the alliance did break up.

After it was rejected by the two Albanian parties as unacceptable and failed to find active support from the Macedonian groupings, Efremov was again quoted as backing off from the plan, saying it had been misinterpreted. Efremov now said that it was only one of 25 possible ways of solving the crisis and that it was not an official academy proposal, just the personal view of some of its members.

The plan heightened fears that the dialogue between Macedonians and ethnic Albanians might break down, that the peace process might be compromised irrevocably and that the EU might decide to review the validity of the Stabilisation and Association Agreement with Macedonia signed in Luxembourg on 9 April 2001.

'Whether it was a test of public opinion, an outright provocation or a serious project, the plan has certainly shifted attention away from the fighting in the north,' said Veton Latifi, a political analyst and assistant editor for the Institute for War and Peace Reporting in Macedonia.[9]

Aracinovo 'Recaptured'

Macedonian troops tried to recapture Aracinovo at the end of June, pounding the area with rocket and artillery fire for three days. The immediate threat to Skopje was removed when US troops, in one of the murkiest and most contested episodes of the conflict, escorted the NLA and their weapons out of the town, in part because there was concern that the Macedonian Army was unable to take it back from the rebels.

'I think that this is a very important step,' said Solana, who had flown in to mediate.' Everyone showed great responsibility... Skopje is no longer threatened.' But the two ethnic communities were growing further apart.

The Slav population would have liked the offensive against Aracinovo to continue until all the rebels surrendered or were killed. In the event, they were evacuated with all their weapons under a ceasefire agreement negotiated by the European Union and carried out by the Americans after talks with NLA commanders – a move that provoked violent anti-Government demonstrations.

'We tried very hard to persuade the Macedonians to let us get the Albanians out,' Laity recalled.

> By this time, Pieter Feith was in the country so we had already made contact with Ahmeti. Feith had a very restrictive mandate: 'You can talk to Ahmeti about a ceasefire without conditions and a laying down of arms but not about terms.' When the fighting at Aracinovo came up we were into a crisis big-time because the ethnic Albanian population was completely mobilised in support of the NLA. The more you shelled them, the more support. Xhaferi and Imeri were under pressure to leave the Government. At the same time, the Macedonian policies are getting nowhere. The NLA are threatening to escalate. At Aracinovo, we were looking at going from a low level insurgency to a major conflict with who knows what consequences.

> Initially, the Macedonians said they were winning. After two or three days this 'rapid conquest' of Aracinovo has got nowhere. Then they ask us through Trajkovski 'can you please get a ceasefire?' The Government is asking for help. Feith goes up to Ahmeti and Ahmeti offers a countrywide ceasefire and voluntary [NLA] withdrawal with weapons, not surrender.

Trajkovski initially rejected that proposal, insisting that the NLA surrender:

We say it is impossible. They've not lost. They then say they don't want a countryside surrender. We are having these talks at the president's residence on a Sunday morning, everyone was very tense with people walking in and out. In the end Trajkovski agrees that they can leave with their guns and only a local cease-fire. Solana says, 'What about the prime minister?'

We call the prime minister [Georgievski]. He says, 'This is nothing to do with me.' Solana and Feith say, 'You have to agree or we don't do it.' In the end he says, 'Yes.' We got the word out of him. Feith leads his team out [to Aracinovo] and the ceasefire is set for 2 pm.

Laity set up his headquarters in the seedy Bellevue hotel on the edge of Aracinovo working as 'a kind of combined liaison and operations officer but also acting as a relay to NATO'.

The diplomatic struggle to defuse Aracinovo was not yet over, however. KFOR had no mandate to take out the force of 300 NLA fighters so who was to remove them? 'In the end, the people who do it are the non-KFOR NATO people, a very small number of people and some military people who are doing information gathering but who were not armed and some people from the British Embassy,' Laity recalled.

We have to see Boskovski and Petrovski, the chief of staff, to arrange for Feith to go in. They try to reopen the negotiations. We say, 'Too bloody late.' By this stage, the OSCE and EU monitors have got involved. They only monitor in useful places. Feith leads a group in there and everything is fine. The NLA in Aracinovo agrees to leave. The Macedonian military and police were sorted out. Throughout this the military were very cooperative.

The problem was that there were no buses. We couldn't use KFOR buses. Later that day, we organised some buses for very, very early next morning. Feith and his team went in. We found that the bus company hadn't told the drivers what they have to do so the drivers wouldn't go out. The NLA also were thinking that they'll be shot up in civilian buses. This was when it started getting very tricky. Unless we could get people out we would be back to where we were before but worse. Fighting would restart and NATO would get the blame.

We then started ringing nations, who didn't really understand what's going on. It was time sensitive. But the Americans delivered. Everyone criticises the Americans, but on that day they helped us.

They sent from their base in Macedonia and from Camp Bondsteel. They managed to get a bunch of civilian Albanian buses from Tetovo that were available much earlier with the promise of NATO buses.

The first tranche went out on Albanian buses. The second on combined Albanian and American civilian buses, escorted by the 101st Airborne. They were taken to a place called Nikustak. At that stage we thought, 'We've done it,' we had the EU military monitors who had driven people in from Bosnia overnight. The ICRC also were very helpful. This was a NATO initiative but the number of people who did it were about ten.

We thought, 'Crisis over,' but of course it was just starting. And this was where we paid the price for not having got them out the night before because the Macedonian hardliners had all day to organise their demonstration. As the American convoy exited what should they meet but another 'spontaneous' demonstration that in fact had been manufactured. The hardliners saw an opportunity to crank up the pressure on the basis of saying this was a sell-out.

They were telling the public that they had victory snatched from their grasp because NATO leaned on Trajkovski. It was 4 am before the Americans found a way out.

In what was seen as a blow to Macedonian sovereignty, the safety of the villagers left behind was to be guaranteed by foreign observers from the OSCE and other international bodies.

'It is a sell-out,' grumbled an angry Macedonian father, who, like many residents of Skopje, spent much of the last week of April at a vantage point outside Aracinovo watching through binoculars.

The bystanders were not disappointed. The valley around Aracinovo echoed with the sound of heavy artillery and tank fire, pounding suspected rebel strongholds in the village. Every hour or so spectators looked up as the Ukrainian attack helicopters flew in, rocketing and strafing the village, where the only sign of life was the occasional stray dog. When army or police patrols drove past, they were greeted with cheers and applause by the onlookers.

However, the noisy barrage stopped suddenly in the afternoon and, as word spread of a ceasefire, mobs of ethnic Macedonians insulted and harassed foreign observers, journalists or any other westerners at hand.

Trajkovski triggered

On the night of 26 June, the office of Boris Trajkovski, the moderate President, was besieged by thousands of enraged nationalists, who demanded his resignation, stormed the presidential palace and fired shots in the air.

Chanting anti-Albanian slogans and attacking foreigners, the protesters held a long and noisy vigil in Skopje's main square. The crowd threw stones at police guarding the presidential palace, which also houses the country's parliament, then forced their way into the entrance hall, throwing the Macedonian flag to the floor and replacing it with the older more nationalist version scrapped to meet objections by Greece.

Richard Beeston watched from the throng as one protester armed with a Kalashnikov assault rifle appeared on a balcony and fired celebratory bursts into the air, to the cheers of the crowd below. Others began throwing computer equipment out of the windows and smashing official cars parked outside.

While security guards held back some of the protesters who tried to get inside, police outside the building appeared to do nothing to quieten the crowd. Later, police and army reservists fired protest shots in the air while the mob went on the rampage, smashing police cars and beating up two BBC journalists and a British aid worker, who were all taken to hospital.

One man screamed at Beeston: 'Get out of here you scum,' spitting at him and kicking a BBC colleague. 'This is all the fault of NATO and you foreign journalists.' Richard bewildered other assailants by jabbering at them in Russian before making his way back to the relative safety of the Holiday Inn to file his story. 'It did not pay to be British last night,' he wrote.

Marko Georgiev was also on the spot with his cameras, vulnerable as ever to his fellow ethnic Macedonians' hostility to the press:

> A journalist from *Dnevnik* newspaper got a stone in his head that had been thrown at me. After we witnessed a Danish photo reporter getting beaten up by the crowd, we decided to move some place safer. We went into an apartment just above the demonstrators, and were trying to take some photographs from above.

> But as soon as we started working from the balcony, someone with a gun started shooting in the air. Suddenly every person in the crowd who had a weapon decided to follow his example. The balcony was not safe any more. We got so upset we decided to stop working for the night and we went for a beer.

Many in the crowd, including armed police reservists and soldiers, demanded that the Government destroy the Albanian rebels by force rather than seek a settlement. 'I was surprised by what happened, and disappointed,' Trajkovski said.[10] 'I wanted to address the crowd, but you cannot speak to people firing rifles and throwing stones.' It is still unclear exactly what happened in Skopje that night. Some correspondents believe that a military putsch, probably inspired by Boskovski, was narrowly averted.

Despite the threat, the head of state was adamant that a political solution to meet the demands of the ethnic Albanian population was the only viable option. 'There are extremists in every country. My job is to lead the nation on the correct path, not follow the mob. The President has to do the right thing, and that is build peace and prosperity.'

In an address to the nation, the embattled president condemned the hardline nationalists as those who had 'chosen the path of evil'. The fiercely nationalistic agenda would break what was left of the 'unity of the country', he said. 'You gave me a mandate for peace and tranquillity, not war. That is what we are trying to achieve. It may be the long way, but it is the right way.'

The events of June 26 badly undermined the president's authority and there were fears that he might resign or be stripped of his rule by hardliners. 'Right now we have effectively lost our President,' commented Saso Ordanovski, the editor of the news magazine *Forum*. 'The question is, are we going to get him back?'

A western diplomat predicted that President Trajkovski would not go down without a fight. 'Either they will have to put a gun to his head and make him resign, or they will have to put a gun to his head and pull the trigger.' The USA urged Macedonians to pull back from 'mob action'. A State Department spokesman said: 'This is not the time for violent demonstrations.'

Mark Laity recalled the feeling among the international community at the time:

> Aracinovo had been a real crisis. If it had not been solved there would have been a civil war. But the people who wanted a military solution had been denied it. They tried to create a Government crisis. That's why they stormed the Parliament. We know that they were on the verge of ignominious defeat.

Laity insisted there never had been any question of trying to persuade the NLA to leave Aracinovo without their weapons:

They had not been defeated, they were not even surrounded and could still get supplies in. Their casualties were light. There were more Macedonians killed from friendly, Macedonian fire than Albanians. But what we had not anticipated or planned for was the fury of the hardliners.

People were talking about a coup. There was complete fury. This was the moment of truth for Trajkovski. The traditional policy in the Balkans is to talk to the people and put the blame on someone else. There were drafts of speeches that said that. Then there was debate and the alternative was to say: 'We were losing and we saved Skopje.' The debate raged for six hours. It wasn't just an intellectual debate. He felt that if he got this wrong he would be accused of letting Macedonia down and be forced to resign. In the end he opted to tell it like it was. As always happened eventually, Georgievski and Boskovski bottled out. Georgievski admitted that he had agreed to it and that was the end of the crisis.

The European Union also strengthened its mediating capacity on 25 June by appointing François Léotard, who once was seen as a future French president, or at least prime minister, as Europe's resident envoy in Macedonia. A full-time special envoy was felt to be necessary to carry out similar work to NATO's Pieter Feith in the southern Serbia crisis. Solana and Robertson had done a good job but Macedonia was not their only job.

In some ways, Léotard was a surprising choice. For ten years from the mid 1980s, Léotard was a rising star on the centre-right of French politics under his political mentor, Valery Giscard d'Estaing. His career as a frontline politician slipped after he chose to back Edouard Balladur, instead of Jacques Chirac, as the centre-right's candidate for the presidency in 1995. He faced accusations of financial wrongdoing, later dropped, such as the allegation that he used public money to build an extension to his villa when he was Mayor of Fréjus. In March 1998, he was accused in an investigative book of ordering the murder of a political colleague, Yann Piat, who was probing political corruption in his fiefdom, the Var.[11] Léotard sued and the book was withdrawn from circulation. He published a book of his own, entitled *I Gently Hate You All*. He resigned in September 1998 as president of the Union pour la Démocratie Française federation of centre-right parties but remained a member of parliament for the Var *département* on the French coast.

Léotard brought to bear considerable knowledge of military matters from his period as French Defence Minister from 1993 to 1995. He was to prove a solid negotiator in supporting President Trajkovski's efforts to promote peace, though some diplomats felt he was over-shadowed by James Pardew, the energetic American envoy who would be rewarded for his efforts by becoming US Ambassador in Sofia.

Pardew, like Christopher Hill, brought to bear experience of negotiating the run-up to the Dayton peace accords in Bosnia. Before working with Holbrooke, Pardew, a retired US army officer, had been director of the Pentagon's Balkan Task Force and closest aide on Bosnia to Joseph Kurzel, the Senior Deputy Assistant Secretary of Defense.[12] 'Léotard and Pardew played a soft cop, tough cop routine,' Laity recalled. 'It was a formidable double act.'

Yet the Macedonian President was a long way from re-establishing full control of the country. Nationalist mobs attacked the American and British embassies a few days later, accusing London and Washington of supporting the NLA. More BBC reporters were beaten up in the street. By and large, Skopje was a ghost town. Tourism by KFOR soldiers and international staff from Kosovo was in decline. Even the normally bustling Greek fish restaurant in the old Ottoman quarter of the Bit Pazar, famous for its catches 'flown directly from Montenegro', was empty.

The polarisation underway between ethnic Macedonians and ethnic Albanians was reflected in contradictory accounts in the Skopje press of what had happened in Aracinovo. In Macedonian press reporting, ethnic loyalties shaped distorting prisms through which both sides in the conflict viewed the crisis tearing their country apart.

Dnevnik, the most popular newspaper among Slavic Macedonians, offered its readers a novel version of the US-escorted withdrawal of ethnic Albanian guerrillas. It reported a former government official's claim that the operation was forced by foreign diplomats seeking to safeguard drug laboratories supplying narcotics to their children.

Fakti, Macedonia's principal ethnic Albanian newspaper, described the pull-out of fighters in unabashedly favourable but no less politicised terms. It was, the paper said, a joint effort by rebels and foreign diplomats to overwhelm 'slaves to blind war euphoria' in the Macedonian Government. No mention was made of the outrage felt by many ethnic Macedonians over the rebels being allowed to keep their weapons.

With the rebellion entering its sixth month, it seemed that there was little on which the polarised Macedonians and Albanians could agree. 'Newspapers don't want to be seen to be engaged in bridge-building work now,' commented Eran Fraenkel, who ran the the Skopje office of Search for Common Ground, a Washington-based organisation that promotes reconciliation.[13]

Fraenkel said the organisation's multi-ethnic kindergartens, school programmes, commercials and news-gathering efforts were under substantial strain. Media sources said that Slavic extremists had telephoned death threats to editors at *Dnevnik* and several television stations for taking positions on the rebellion not seen as sufficiently hardline.

Pressure for NATO to send troops into Macedonia was growing in Britain, where Paddy Ashdown, the former Liberal Democrat leader who would go on to be the international community's high representative in Bosnia, was one of the most vocal advocates of intervention. 'We fought the Kosovo war to protect Albanians and end the threat of greater Serbia but failed to address the threat posed by the concept of greater Albania,' he said.[14]

> So we end up with Macedonia and a crisis which looks more and more likely to slide from sporadic outbursts of conflict into civil war with the capacity to drag in a wider set of players, from Greece through to Bulgaria and Romania on one side and Albania and, God help us, Turkey on the other.

Lord Ashdown laid blame for the crisis on former Kosovo Liberation Army fighters. 'Flushed with success, they returned home to take up the cause of Albanians in their own country, where successive Slav governments have denied Albanians the rights they ought to have enjoyed in a country aspiring to join the EU.' The former Royal Marine rejected criticism of NATO for escorting the rebels out of Aracinovo. 'If it had not happened, the slide to full-scale civil war, with even wider consequences for the region, would have been unstoppable.' For the first time in the Balkans, the West was trying to act early and avoid conflict.

> If the West is to extract peace out of this witches' brew, it will only be by taking the initiative ourselves. I fear what we are looking at is a third NATO deployment in the Balkans which will be large, long-term and expensive. If we are lucky, this time we might just be able to do it before war happens, instead of having to fight a war to make it happen.

He acknowledged that western capitals were recoiling at the cost and danger. 'But now, as then, the cost of doing it will be far less than the cost of a civil war, with a potential to widen into a regional conflict involving two NATO nations, Greece and Turkey, on opposite sides.'

In early July, a shaky western-brokered truce was observed perfunctorily as negotiations on the peace plan went on behind the scenes.

New western casualties, the first since the death of Kerem Lawton of APTV, refocused international attention, nearly always low when only 'local' civilians are dying. Two EU monitors, a Slovak and a Norwegian, and a translator were killed on 19 July in a mine explosion. The NLA was using mines again and again with deadly effect.

Fierce fighting again engulfed Tetovo from 22 to 24 July. During this, a 12-year-old Albanian girl, Jehina Saliu, was mortally wounded in Poroj, the village on Tetovo's eastern outskirts where we had watched an army deserter join the NLA weeks before. The shelling of Poroj killed nine civilians on 23 July alone. Jeff Bieley found himself trapped in a basement in the village during the bombardment. 'It was held by the NLA in as much as police could not go there,' he recalled, 'but it was mainly a civilian target.'[15]

Against the background of combat, virtually all the international actors in Macedonia – NATO, the OSCE, the western media and non-governmental organisations – were still being accused by government officials of pro-Albanian bias.

Anti-western riots swept Skopje again on 24 July as furious mobs attacked the German Embassy and foreign businesses. Armed with metal rods and chanting nationalist slogans, about 200 young ethnic Macedonians smashed the windows of the embassy, a British Airways office and a McDonald's restaurant before storming the OSCE offices.

The riots had started after refugees who had fled Tetovo and neighbouring villages, gathered in the main square and tried to storm Parliament to demand that security forces regain control of their homes from the rebels. The Government accused the western envoys, Pardew and Léotard, of being responsible for restarting the fighting by siding with the rebels.

'NATO is not our enemy, but it is a great friend of our enemies who are attacking the future of this country,' Antonio Milososki, the Government's chief spokesperson, said on 24 July in a typical statement.[16] A new ceasefire was established the next day, however.

An opinion poll published by *Forum* magazine on 27 July showed that some 61 per cent of those interviewed – including ethnic Macedonians, Albanians and members of other minorities – wanted a peaceful solution to the crisis. A military solution had no support among ethnic Albanian respondents but some 30 per cent of ethnic Macedonian Slavs said that they preferred an armed conflict to a negotiated settlement. Asked 'Would you support any action against the terrorists?' 83 per cent of the Macedonians answered positively.

It was unclear to what extent the anti-western demonstrations were orchestrated by senior figures in the Macedonian nationalist party, the

VMRO. There was no shortage of historical precedent for such xenophobic agitation. In the run up to the Ilinden Uprising of 1903, for example, an anarchist faction of the IMRO, the Gemidzhii, blew up a French freighter, the *Guadalquivir*, in the port of Salonika, and derailed a train from Istanbul, in the hope of precipitating Great Power intervention. Salonika's gas piping was sabotaged, and the French-run Banque Ottomane was blown up, killing many German residents of the city.

This time, western intervention worked before such extreme measures were contemplated by hardline Macedonians. The first signs of real progress in the peace talks at Ohrid emerged on 1 August, when Léotard announced that the main ethnic Macedonian and Albanian parties had reached a compromise on the use of Albanian as an official language. This was a breakthrough but Léotard hurried to add that 'This accord is conditional on the continuation of the political discussions, notably on the issue of the police,' Léotard said. 'Therefore it is a conditional agreement.' James Pardew was not willing to show too much optimism either. 'This is a good deal for everyone, but I am not euphoric. There's a lot of tough work ahead.'

As late as 2 August, Georgievski and the President of Parliament, Stojan Andov, in speeches to mark the anniversary of the Second World War liberation of Yugoslavia and of the Ilinden Uprising, both said that the signing of the peace agreement while 'terrorists' still occupied part of the country would be a shameful act for Macedonia. Andov warned that Parliament would consider a political agreement only when 'the last terrorist [had been] disarmed'. Georgievski said:

> A document signed under occupation of Macedonian territories and with terrorists in our mountains will be disgraceful and humiliating for every Macedonian citizen. I would like to point out that the Republic of Macedonia possesses military equipment and competent soldiers and policemen to restore the constitutional order in the country. Territorial integrity must be re-established prior to the signing of any agreements, which have to be in the interest of the Republic of Macedonia.

Solana came to Macedonia once again on 5 August to bring his prestige to bear on the negotiations. After several meetings with the Macedonian and Albanian political leaders, he told a press conference that an agreement had been reached on the police issue. The accord called for 1,000 ethnic Albanian police officers, or about 20 per cent of the entire force, to be working by the end of 2003. At the time, Albanians constituted only six per cent of the police force.

The talks hit another snag on 6 August, however, when Georgievski's party demanded that the rebels disarm before the peace agreement was ratified by Parliament. NLA commanders had said they would only disarm after such ratification, but eventually backed down.

In Skopje, on 7 August, police raided a house in the district of Gazi Baba and killed five ethnic Albanians they said were NLA guerrillas. The Albanian daily in Macedonia, *Fakti*, said the men were killed while asleep and that as many as 300 policemen and members of special units had surrounded Gazi Baba at 5 am.[17]

'Blood, pieces of skull and brain are scattered all over the pillows and walls of the rooms,' *Fakti*'s reporter Lirim Dullovi wrote.

> The situation in this Skopje quarter, populated by a mainly ethnic Albanian population is very tense after this, latest provocation of the Macedonian police. Based on the arsenal used in this action, it is obvious that the Macedonian police came prepared for a wider confrontation with the local population.

Peter Bouckaert of Human Rights Watch inspected the house. 'There was no evidence at the scene to support the government version of events. There was no sign of an exchange of fire and victims appeared to have been shot as they were lying on the floor.'

The *Washington Post* reported that: 'The house looked more like the scene of a summary execution. A reporter saw no signs that the victims had fired a shot at the raiders. Windows were closed, and no bullet holes nicked the walls or ceiling. The front door had not been forced open.'

Kim Mehmeti, an ethnic Albanian journalist said, 'There is fear of ethnic cleansing – even Albanians who live here in Skopje think so. Things have gone so far.' Slobodan Casule, a centrist ethnic Macedonian politician, said 'the signs of disaster continue to build. We seem already like Humpty Dumpty.'

The peace agreement was finally accepted in principle, however, on 8 August by all the major Macedonian and ethnic Albanian parties after weeks of hard bargaining in the lakeside resort of Ohrid. It would be signed in Skopje on 13 August, with Solana attending. The accord provided for limited use of Albanian as an official language, police reforms in ethnic Albanian majority areas and the deployment of 3,500 NATO troops to disarm the NLA.

The ethnic Albanian negotiators generally succeeded in expanding minority rights. The Macedonian negotiators limited the erosion of their status as a constituent nationality. In general, both sides found the agreement unsatisfactory but workable, provided they could be persuaded that the other side would act in good faith.

According to the diplomats present, the mood at the simple signing ceremony at the presidential office was low-key and at times grim, with Georgievski making a sarcastic speech and the ethnic Macedonian politicians present wincing as Xhaferi addressed them in Albanian.

After the signing ceremony, Xhaferi again showed the sensitivity of the language question when he addressed reporters in Albanian and referred to his right to do so in the agreement. Prime Minister Georgievski walked out in protest and President Trajkovski called for Xhaferi to apologise.[18]

The International Crisis Group commented that:

> The strange context of the signing showed just how implausible it is that, without further extraordinary efforts, the agreement will actually provide a workable way to keep multiethnic Macedonia out of civil war. Details of the agreement had been hammered out by 8 August... Signature was delayed for five days while Macedonian government troops and ethnic rebels engaged in the deadliest series yet of tit-for-tat retaliations. Terms of the agreement were withheld from the public lest they provoke violent responses from hardliners on both sides... The ceremony, when it finally occurred, was carried out almost furtively, in a small room of the President's residence, without live television. [19]

The Crisis Group concluded, 'Although a political agreement has now been signed, and NATO is poised to enter Macedonia, the possibility of a full-blown civil war, with serious regional consequences, remains high.'

NATO and the NLA signed a technical agreement on 14 August on the weapons collection terms and modalities. Pieter Feith negotiated the agreement with Ali Ahmeti.

The revenge attacks in Bitola, meanwhile, had set a precedent for the increasingly ferocious blood-letting that was to plague Macedonia over the following months, in spite of the peace deal and partly in reaction to it. Extremists on both sides were determined to make the Ohrid accord a dead letter.

9 Warlords and Peacekeepers

There are things in this war that, I fear, will never be comprehensible to me. But perhaps this is also a blessing. If someone managed to understand everything about this inferno he would lose his mind.
Marko Vesovic, Chiedo Scusa se vi parlo di Sarajevo

AMONG THE MOST CHILLING episodes of the Macedonian conflict was the extrajudicial killing on 12 August 2001 of ten ethnic Albanians in the village of Ljuboten – evidently in revenge for the slaying of eight Macedonian commandos blown up by land mines and ten other soldiers killed in an NLA ambush.

The eight soldiers were killed, and eight others were wounded, on the morning of 10 August, when a Macedonian military truck ran over two anti-tank mines on a remote country road on the Skopska Crna Gorna mountain just north of Skopje.

The other group of ten government soldiers was slain in the ambush of a military convoy on the main Skopje to Tetovo highway two days earlier. The worst incident since the fighting began in February, the 8 August attack threw into jeopardy the peace agreement initialled at Ohrid hours later the same day.

'We will have peace on paper and war on the battlefield,' the Government spokesman, Antonio Milososki, said. 'What the rebels want is war, and they will get it.'[1]

The loss of 18 soldiers was an enormous blow for Macedonia's security forces. Most of the ten soldiers killed in the convoy attack on 8 August were from Prilep. Macedonian soldiers in Prilep solemnly carried the country's red and gold sunburst flag to the graveyard and stood behind Orthodox priests as the ten army reservists were buried. 'Albanians will rot in hell,' said one father as he crumpled atop his son's coffin.[2] Ethnic Macedonians in Prilep burned a mosque and Albanian homes in a night of rioting in reprisal for the ambush a short time before Ljuboten was attacked.

It has been argued by some that the number of ethnic Albanians and ethnic Macedonians dead in these incidents was still relatively small compared to the large-scale massacres of the Bosnian and Croatian wars. This may be true, but the loss of life had a tremendous psychological impact in a small nation of two million inhabitants. It is sufficient to imagine what the reaction would have been if 18 American or British soldiers had been killed in Macedonia or if ten French or German civilians had been dragged from their homes and killed in cold blood. Ljuboten also gave an international profile for the first time to Ljube Boskovski, the hardline Interior Minister who is a hero to many ordinary Macedonians but a simple-minded warlord in the eyes of many ethnic Albanians.

President Trajkovski dismissed the Macedonian Army Chief of Staff, General Pande Petrovski, on 9 August, following the attack on the convoy. Petrovski had told Macedonia's National Security Council that he 'would take responsibility' for the casualties. His deputy, General Metodij Stamboliski, replaced him. This was the fourth time that the armed forces command had changed hands in less than two months, another telling sign of the Macedonian Army's inability to cope with the rebellion.

The Macedonian Defence Minister, Vlado Buckovski, had appealed in vain for restraint after rioters attacked ethnic Albanian shops in retaliation for the rebel ambush of the army vehicles, several of which were set on fire:

> Let us give peace a chance. May this major tragedy mark the end of the war and not the beginning of a bloody civil war. It is very difficult in these moments to find words to demand from people that they show patience and think of peace. Believe me the situation will be even more difficult if war comes to our homes.

A few hours after he spoke, however, the NLA attacked the army barracks in the tinderbox city of Tetovo with machine guns and grenade launchers, killing an army soldier.

The road where the mine incident happened (a day after the defence minister's appeal) is above Ljuboten, a mainly ethnic Albanian village of some 3,000 people, and within its traditional grazing areas. Ljuboten is surrounded by the larger ethnic Macedonian villages of Ljubance, Rastak and Radisane. Two of the soldiers killed by the mines, Tome Batalevski, 33, a father of two, and his cousin, Goce Cankulovski, 39, were from Ljubance and most of the others from the Skopje area.

Boskovski is a former coffee shop entrepreneur in Croatia who went on to be deputy chief of Macedonian intelligence and took over the Interior Ministry in May. He was shown in a television newscast standing on the balcony of an empty house above Ljuboten looking down smugly into the village with other security officers. Ljuboten had been sealed off by security forces almost immediately after the mine attacks.

Houses could be seen burning in the newscast and there is constant noise of shelling and machine-gun fire. The newscast said Boskovski was part of a military operation to sweep the village of ethnic Albanian 'terrorists', who had planted the anti-tank mines. The taped television narrative says: 'Ljube Boskovski was present during the whole operation of the Macedonian security forces.'

The Macedonian police claimed that the operation was targeting an NLA stronghold, and that eight NLA members were killed and 12 were captured. Nearly a month later, however, no evidence had emerged that the seven ethnic Albanians or three others also killed in the village, were anything but civilians.

Human Rights Watch accused the Government forces of summary execution of civilians, arson and torture. The security forces' operation between 10 and 12 August, the report says, 'had no military justification and was carried out for purposes of revenge and reprisal'.

Boskovski is a hawk who was the most outspoken and visible proponent of a military solution to the Albanian insurgency and an avowed antagonist of NATO. He subsequently sought to distance himself from what had happened in Ljuboten, claiming that he arrived only at 4 pm that Sunday, after the operation had ended and that he did not direct it.

Boskovski also attacked Human Rights Watch, calling it an 'international mercenary organisation'. 'They accuse me of being present there and watching when civilians were murdered. That is a monstrous accusation,' he snorted. 'Who would bring a camera with him if he wanted to do something like that?'

Nevertheless, the UN War Crimes Tribunal in The Hague sent investigators to Macedonia to decide whether to open a full inquiry into what happened in Ljuboten and who might be responsible.

Boskovski shrugged off the prospect of an ICTY indictment. 'I fear only my people's tribunal, not the political one that was set up by America in The Hague,' *Newsweek* in September quoted him saying.

'It's important to understand that he [Boskovski] doesn't have to witness the people being killed to have some responsibility for what happened,' said Peter Bouckaert, a senior researcher for Human Rights Watch, who wrote the group's 23-page report on Ljuboten. 'It was done by troops under his authority in an action in which he was intimately involved.' The group's report noted that armed and uniformed rebels of the NLA had met foreign journalists in Ljuboten several times in June to escort them behind front lines.

Reacting to the report, Macedonian police unions said that Human Rights Watch was 'deaf and mute to claims of attacks against Macedonian authorities and civilians'.[3] 'This organisation persistently sees violation of human rights on one side and one side alone – that of the allegedly wronged Albanian minority.'

Human Rights Watch said the Macedonian security forces had shot dead six civilians in Ljuboten. Three more died in random shelling and another villager was shot dead as he tried to flee. At least 22 houses, sheds and stores were also burned.

> During a Sunday house-to-house attack, police forces shot dead six civilians. One man was killed by police as he tried to close the door to his home when police entered the yard. Two men were summarily executed by police after they were taken out of the basement in which they were hiding.

The evidence against the police was provided by named Albanians, who said that during the raid on 12 August, described as the worst day of the operation, police had hurled grenades inside their homes.[4]

The truth about Ljuboten has evidently been covered up in part because of international organisations' and western diplomats' determination not to embarrass the Macedonian Government over the affair. Nevertheless, still photographs of the television footage of Boskovski chortling on the terrace during the security forces' operation were picked up by newspapers around the world to become one of the defining images of the conflict, along with the shootings at the football stadium in Tetovo in March. The two incidents in which the 18 soldiers lost their lives happened far from the television crews.

Monitors from the OSCE were able to visit Ljuboten two days after that Sunday's attack and gathered significant information from the scene and villagers. 'However the OSCE chose to remain silent about the abuses in Ljuboten,' Human Rights Watch charged. 'By remaining silent, the OSCE has helped the Macedonian government maintain its version of events in Ljuboten and avoid any further investigation.'

The Spillover Monitoring Mission to Skopje is the OSCE's longest serving mission, set up in 1992 to prevent a spread of the conflict in the former Yugoslavia by monitoring the border between Yugoslavia and Macedonia. Boskovski sought to intimidate the OSCE over Ljuboten, even criticising its observers for trying to investigate events. 'OSCE representatives entered Ljuboten village during the day and through their information, they are trying to misinform the public that the Macedonian security forces did not kill five terrorists, but five citizens of Albanian nationality from Ljuboten,' he said.

Some OSCE representatives were 'carrying out a special propaganda war against the Macedonian security forces', he claimed.

> Certain OSCE representatives overstep their authorisations, usurping the legal and legitimate right of the Macedonian police and not the OSCE, to confirm legally relevant facts and circumstances for causes of death of persons on the territory of the Republic of Macedonia.

The OSCE's then Head of Mission, Ambassador Carlo Ungari, backed off from the reported comments of his monitors, who told journalists they had seen the bodies of five men apparently killed while running away. 'The misunderstandings occurred as a result of the intentional or unintentional misinterpretations of OSCE information [by] the foreign media,' he said. The Government spokesman, Antonio Milososki, said later that the OSCE had 'confirmed' that the people killed in Ljuboten were 'terrorists'.

The OSCE's stance at Ljuboten contrasted strangely with its role in the killing of ethnic Albanians by Serb forces at Racak in Kosovo, in which the forthright denunciation by William Walker of the OSCE of the incident precipitated NATO intervention.

The Government evidently also had Racak in mind when it attacked Ungari's team. The OSCE Skopje Mission, in a statement issued on 15 August, said that 'at no time has the OSCE Mission to Skopje made any comments about the nature of what happened in the village of Ljuboten'. The only confirmation to be obtained from this Mission was that 'a number of bodies have been found'.

> The OSCE Mission has never in the past commented on events before the facts were known with very high certainty and will continue to do so. Any allegations that the OSCE would 'want to stage a Macedonian Racak' are thus absurd and less than helpful for everybody.

After the killings, Human Rights Watch's report alleged, abuse continued for hundreds of ethnic Albanian civilians trying to flee Ljuboten.

> At least three men were beaten unconscious by ethnic Macedonian vigilantes in full view of the Macedonian police, and one was shot and wounded as he attempted to flee the beating. Over one hundred men were arrested and taken to police stations in Skopje, where they were subjected to severe beatings. Atulah Qaini, aged 35, was taken away alive from the village by police officers, and his badly beaten and mutilated corpse was later recovered by family members from the city morgue.

At least 24 men, including a 13-year-old boy, remained in police custody at the time of publication of the HRW report.

Carla del Ponte, the United Nations chief prosecutor, visited Skopje in November 2001 to announce two investigations – one into crimes allegedly committed by Macedonian soldiers against ethnic Albanian civilians, and the second related to crimes allegedly committed by ethnic Albanian militants.

Later in November, forensic experts reportedly found human remains at a site where Macedonian officials suspect ethnic Albanian rebels buried several people they killed during the insurgency. Investigators recovered 'parts of human bodies and bones' at a site between the village of Trebos and Dzepciste in the ethnically tense north-west, Aleksandra Zafirovska, a Macedonian investigative judge, said. She did not say how many bodies were found.

On 21 November, Macedonian forensic experts started digging at the site, 22 miles west of the capital, Skopje, and not far from Tetovo. The Government contended that 13 Macedonian civilians had been buried somewhere near Tetovo since April. Experts from the UN War Crimes Tribunal and EU representatives observed the excavation.

In addition to Human Rights Watch, at least two dozen eyewitness accounts of alleged killings, kidnappings, torture and the systematic destruction of mosques were gathered by the European Council of Humanity, Action and Cooperation (ECHAC), which carried out similar work in Kosovo and East Timor. The pan-European group asked The Hague tribunal to investigate Boskovski for 'grave violations of the Geneva convention, violations of the laws governing wars and crimes against humanity'.

The Council said that the police, army and paramilitary groups had been used during the war with the National Liberation Army as an excuse to launch a systematic campaign to force ethnic Albanians out of the country. 'An ample campaign was carried out aimed at varying the ethnic composition of the republic of Macedonia.' The campaign reached its peak when a 'majority of ethnic Albanian civilians were driven out of the southern town of Manastir (Bitola) and their homes and businesses damaged'.[5]

Other ethnic cleansing operations had reportedly spread as far as Rastan in the mountains near the central city of Veles, a long way from the fighting, where most inhabitants were ethnic Macedonians and only a few thousand Albanians lived in a handful of dirt-poor villages.

Masked gunmen came into the home of 13-year-old Tafil Veseli in Rastan, an ethnically-mixed village, on 8 August and opened fire without warning. Some of the gunmen were wearing police uniforms, according to his uncle, who witnessed the shooting. Within hours of Tafil's death, his family had packed up what possessions they could and left their house for good. As soon as they were gone the police sealed off access to the house where Tafil died. Tafil was buried in the nearby Albanian village of Slivnik, where the family had fled. A red and black Albanian flag was draped over his coffin. Old men wept as Tafil's father, Sabir, lowered his son into the grave, a bundle of white in his shroud.[6]

ECHAC has claimed that Boskovski was behind the ethnic cleansing campaigns, in collusion with senior Defence Ministry officials, but has provided little evidence of this. It appealed to the Hague Tribunal to demand documents about meetings and communications from the Interior Ministry that could show what was going on.

The sweep at Ljuboten coincided with heavy fighting on 11 August in the town of Raduša, where the rebels scored successes against security forces. Despite long-range rocket attacks and bombing by government Su-25 Frogfoot ground-attack warplanes, Boskovski acknowledged that police were forced to withdraw from the town after the insurgents set ablaze a police station and an adjacent watchtower.

Raduša saw the largest-scale use made of the ground-attack aircraft during the conflict. Macedonia had purchased them from the Ukraine – the four Sukhoi-25s (three Su-25 and one Su-25UB) flew from Odessa in Ukraine via Romania and Yugoslavia on 24 June before arriving at Petrovac. The first Su-25 took off from Petrovac the same day for a reconnaissance flight over Aracinovo in the midst of heavy fighting there.

The Su-25s were used for combat purposes at Raduša, 'this saving the lives of besieged policemen who were defending the village'. Igor Bozinovski, a journalist who follows Macedonian aviation, said that the Macedonian Air Force warplanes 'attacked Albanian terrorists in co-ordination with Mi-24V gunship helicopters using the proven tactics developed during the Soviet military intervention in Afghanistan'. According to the Macedonian Defence Ministry, quoted by Bozinovski, 'In these clashes Albanian terrorists were completely destroyed, retreating to Kosovo, leaving behind them more than 650 killed with no casualties on the Macedonian side.' The hyperbole was pure propaganda but it was as well that the peace agreement of 13 August put an end to the use of the Sukhois.

The Defence Ministry claimed that during Raduša the National Liberation Army 'captured one broken and abandoned T-55A tank from the Macedonia Army'. The Air Force 'reacted immediately with its Mi-24s (helicopters) and destroyed the tank', Bozinovski reported. This was strange, as the tank was later one of three the NLA captured that would be handed over during the disarmament.

Thousands of Albanian civilians fled the fighting for Serbia, which until only a short time before had been the last place they would have considered taking refuge. With no end to the crisis in sight, NATO-led peacekeepers in adjoining Kosovo were increasingly being sucked into the conflict.

'Operation Essential Harvest'

As part of the Ohrid peace agreement, a British-led NATO force of 4,000 soldiers was deployed in Macedonia on 12 August, in what was conceived officially as a limited mission to disarm the NLA as part of the peace plan brokered by the West. In actual fact, this would be a dramatic and highly unusual, if not unique, operation.

The 2nd Battalion of Britain's Parachute Regiment was responsible for collecting weapons from four handover points. Brigadier Barney White-Spunner, commanding Britain's 16th Air Assault Brigade, was in charge of the arms collection. The overall NATO commander in Macedonia was Major-General Gunnar Lange, from Denmark. The presence of the Paras would have a calming effect on the country. There were to be no attacks on the Paras and no real signs of hostility toward them.

2 Para, commanded by Lieutenant Colonel 'Chip' Chapman, included a company of Gurkhas and consisted of 680 men. Chapman had commanded a 2 Para platoon during the 1982 Falklands conflict and served in a senior post in Northern Ireland before assuming command of 2 Para in August 1999.

Other arms collection points were supervised by troops from France (530 troops of the 2nd Infantry Regiment of the Foreign Legion based at Nimes), Italy, Greece, Germany and Spain. The USA provided logistics troops and helicopters to transport the NATO soldiers. Turkey,

Spain, the Netherlands and the Czech Republic also sent troops but Britain provided 2,000 soldiers, about half of the total. Royal Scots Dragoon Guards with Scimitar armoured vehicles and later the Household Cavalry provided escorts for the truckloads of weapons handed over by the NLA. Royal Engineer squadrons included bomb-disposal experts. Special Air Service (SAS) units were engaged in reconnaissance missions.

'British defence sources agreed that the Balkans were awash with guns and that if the peace deal broke down, the rebels would have little difficulty acquiring more weapons,' a defence expert at the scene reported.[7] 'The rebels could rely on patrons among the Albanian diaspora in Switzerland, America, Ukraine, Turkey, and Spain. On the basis of the peace settlement, however, there was confidence that the rebels intended to stick to the ceasefire.'

Even before 'Operation Essential Harvest' reached its conclusion on 26 September, the Skopje Government had requested that some of the NATO peacekeepers remain, ostensibly to protect foreign observers from the OSCE being deployed to monitor the shaky ceasefire established under the plan. The number of NATO troops remaining initially after the bulk of the force had withdrawn from Macedonia by mid October was just over 1,000.

In London, some left-wing commentators poured scorn on the ex-pedition: 'Once again the television screens and the newspapers proudly show pictures of our crack Paras in their maroon berets – with the required quota of Gurkhas – flying off to sort out someone else's problems,' Richard Norton-Taylor wrote.[8] NATO apologists retorted that the operation was vital not only for the Macedonians but for the whole Balkan region. 'Macedonia is crucial,' Frederick Bonnart, editorial director of NATO's *Nations*, said. 'If the exercise fails because constitutional changes are not ratified or carried out, fighting is likely to resume with increased intensity and brutality. The economy would collapse, and elections... would return extremist parties to power.'[9]

> But if it succeeds and makes all groups feel confident in their ability to participate in national decisions affecting them, the country could achieve security and prosperity within a short period. Either way the repercussions would be felt not only in Kosovo and Bosnia, but in the whole of the Balkans.

Shooting resumed in villages outside Tetovo on 19 August. Rebels and security forces clashed for more than an hour and small arms exchanges quickly escalated into mortar fire. Western observers said it would not be enough to put off NATO. 'Fighting here always involves a lot of noise and activity,' a western diplomat in Skopje said. 'But the dynamic is... fewer people have died in six months of trouble here than in car accidents. It's not a bloodless war but almost. So NATO are unlikely to get put off deploying because of shooting at night.'

As British liaison officers met with the National Liberation Army commanders to prepare for disarmament, Macedonian officials became alarmed at the publicity the ethnic Albanian fighters were receiving from foreign television crews following the NATO troops.

By now the greying, urbane Ahmeti was evidently looking to start his mainstream political career, which would take off in Macedonia after the disarmament. He now became media friendly, telling the Skopje daily *Utrinski Vesnik* that ethnic Albanians in Macedonia 'were forced to go to war' and that before the armed conflict broke out 'no government official sat down with the Albanians in Macedonia to talk about meeting their demands and needs'.

Ahmeti said that the National Liberation Army could not be described as terrorist 'because it only shoots at people in uniform'. Ahmeti himself always looked ill at ease in military uniform with a silver pen tucked into his fatigues, surrounded by the guerrilla chic of his heavily bearded, bandanna-wearing rebels.

'Albanians are discriminated against and are denied even the basic rights to which any nation is entitled,' he told TV Kosova. Ahmeti took advantage of western media exposure to announce the appointment of 'diplomatic representatives' of the National Liberation Army to seven European countries. The arrival of NATO troops to oversee the disarmament of his rebels did not mean defeat for his movement but victory. His rebels would cooperate with NATO troops and willingly hand over their weapons because the peace deal is 'good for us'. 'The things we have not achieved we will take further by democratic means.'

Ahmeti was confident that the Macedonian side would not renege on the deal and attack them after disarmament. 'They will not betray us, not now we have NATO, the United States and the European Union here.' Asked if he would stand for election, Ahmeti said, 'I came back here to stay.' Red and black Albanian flags were everywhere in Sikpovica, the cars brandished homemade National Liberation Army licence plates and at one point a guerrilla rode down the main street on horseback like a medieval knight.

THE NATO DEPLOYMENT TO back up the peace agreement undoubtedly prevented an escalation of the fighting and killing on an intense scale (at least by Macedonian standards) that had raged throughout late July and early August.

The arrival of NATO troops was also a remarkable success story for a rebel force that a few weeks previously was being derided in the West as a group of terrorists and thugs. The overriding aims of the NLA had been to get foreign countries involved in its fight with the Skopje Government and to earn international respect.

The transformation of the guerrillas' image had been achieved in less than six months. When the NLA started firing from the hills above Tetovo, Lord Robertson denounced them and indicated that NATO would help to stifle the violence. When Macedonians responded with artillery fire aimed at Albanian hill villages, NATO said that the Skopje Government was retaliating with reasonable restraint. The NLA's strategy had followed classic phases. The initial gunfire had been aimed to attract a disproportionate response from the Government. Once that was achieved, the aim was to provoke the sympathy of foreign powers and to force western envoys to arrange a peace deal that met their demands.

In spite of diplomatic optimism, a series of incidents ruptured the ceasefire and marred the run-up to the disarmament.

In late August, international media reported that a fourteenth-century Orthodox church, once the pride of the village of Lesok, had been blown up. The destruction of the copper-domed St. Atansius church, which was actually rebuilt in 1926 on the foundations of a fourteenth-century church destroyed by the Turks, and some of the houses near an adjoining monastery gates, led to an exodus by Macedonian inhabitants. Of the 380 villagers in Lesok, 40 remained. Major businesses, including a nearby Macedonian-owned textile factory in the rebel-held village of Tearce, were razed to the ground.

Macedonian media played up the incident. One worshipper, Slobodan Markovski, after lighting a candle at the shattered entrance to the church, was quoted as saying, 'The Turks were here for 500 years and they never did anything like this. These are pure Albanian bandits.' This was bogus, since the Turks had destroyed the original church, but similar comments were widely picked up by western media.

Next to the church is the grave of Kyril Pejcinovik, the father of the modern Macedonian language, adding symbolism to the site. The Minister for Culture, Ganka Samoilova-Cvetanovska, compared the act to the destruction of statues of the Buddha by the Taleban in Afghanistan.

The destruction of religious sites had not been a feature of the Macedonian conflict as it had been during the war in Kosovo, when dozens of Serb Orthodox churches were targeted. Diplomats in Skopje questioned whether the attack might have been the work of a Macedonian nationalist dirty-tricks squad. But a senior NLA officer and other NLA sources said that Albanians blew up the church in retaliation for the shelling of a mosque in the neighbouring village of Neproshteno. The church was blown up using the same technique as in Kosovo, leaving the façade still standing, almost exactly like the church destroyed in the centre of Djakovica.

At Celopek, a village motel was blown up on 26 August, killing two Macedonian employees. The two had reportedly been tied to a pillar before they died. Vele Ristoski, the owner of the motel, condemned those responsible for failing to allow his two members of staff to leave before blowing up the building. 'I have no guns here, no weapons, why has this happened? I could have been here sleeping myself.'

Right up until the start of the planned NATO operation, the Macedonian Government continued to receive huge planeloads of arms from Ukraine and Russia delivered secretly. Giant Antonov transport planes were seen landing at night at Petrovac airport in spite of EU pressure on Ukraine, which had officially agreed to consider suspending arms shipments to Macedonia, western sources said.

The Russian Government complained later that NATO had not consulted Moscow sufficiently over 'Operation Essential Harvest'. The continuous flow of arms to Skopje was evidently one way for Russia to express its displeasure, while maintaining influence in Macedonia and the Balkans. After the disarmament operation the Slav population of Macedonia would be among the most heavily armed in the region.

The NLA also was continuing with its arms-smuggling routes to ensure that if the peace deal broke down, it would have its own supply of weapons. The NATO-led Kosovo force (KFOR) had significant success, however, in catching smugglers using mountain trails to ferry weapons for the NLA from the province into Macedonia. From June to August, KFOR soldiers had seized more than 600 rifles, 49,000 small arms rounds, about 1,000 anti-tank weapons, 650 mortar rounds and 1,400 grenades and mines. It was estimated that there were still 600,000 weapons in Albania available for sale on the black market, stolen when the country slid into chaos in 1997.[10] (In September, Macedonia would receive about 30 T-72 battle tanks from Ukraine, stiffening the resolve of nationalists who resented western intervention.)[11]

The arms collection force suffered its first casualty hours after the attack on the motel, raising doubts in Britain once again about the purpose of the mission. Sapper Ian Collins, 22, with two operational tours behind him in Bosnia and Northern Ireland, had barely started his third mission when a group of Macedonian Slav teenagers threw a large chunk of concrete from a flyover bridge at his Land Rover, smashing through the windscreen and striking him on the head.

The youths, aged between 14 and 17, ambushed his vehicle as he drove under the bridge crossing the main Skopje to Kumanovo dual carriageway. When the Land Rover skidded and overturned, they surrounded the vehicle and 'further threatened' the fatally injured driver and the young officer from his regiment sitting next to him. Captain Matt Wilkinson, 28, from Hereford, was assisted by American soldiers who stopped at the scene. He managed to give his young driver first aid to try to keep him alive and contacted medical authorities on his radio.

Medical personnel with the US Army's 407 Ground Ambulance Company described how the hostile crowd surrounded them as they were trying to save Sapper Collins' life. Staff Sergeant Edna Flores described her 20-yard sprint with the stretcher to escape the mob as the longest moment of her life.

The Americans thought that they were heading for a traffic accident when they answered a call for help. Sergeant First Class Joseph Kaiser, 39, started to work on Sapper Collins, while the others radioed details of his condition to a hospital. Sgt. Flores noticed people coming from the shadows. She and her colleague, Sergeant Dencil Vargas, 28, estimated that there were about 30 of them. Some were making obscene gestures, shouting, waving their hands and yelling. Nervous, the Americans picked up Collins on a stretcher and headed back for the car. The run seemed to go on forever.

The youths appeared to have been motivated by the Government's political denunciations of NATO's role in planning to disarm the ethnic Albanian rebels of 'only' 3,300 weapons. Sima Stojic, an 18-year-old Macedonian Slav mechanic living in a house in the hamlet of Madjari, where the ambush took place on the evening of 26 August, saw the murder of the young soldier from 9 Parachute Squadron Royal Engineers, based in Aldershot. 'There were about ten of them on the bridge and another five at the side of the road,' he said.

> Five of them on the bridge were on one side looking out for a military vehicle, the other five were standing ready with a piece of concrete about 1 ft long and 9 in wide. I saw one of them lift this concrete slab high over his head and then throw it down when the vehicle went under the bridge. It went through the windscreen and another piece went through the window.

> The vehicle skidded violently from side to side for about 15 metres and then turned over. It was a dreadful sound. Some of the boys

then ran down to where the vehicle was and started to throw stones at it. But soldiers came from other vehicles and they ran off. I know the youths, I know their names.

As soon as Stojic described what he had seen, a Macedonian policeman approached from the bridge and spoke to him. Within minutes a police car had arrived and he was taken for questioning. He was released about six hours later. He said that even though it was known where the ambush had taken place – the British Army had the precise grid reference – no police officer had interviewed him or anyone else in Madjari.

A NATO spokesman, Major Barry Johnson, admitted that no one could describe the environment in Macedonia as 'friendly' after six months of war and that 'emotions were running high', particularly among the young, whose actions appeared to be based 'on the rhetoric they hear'.

THE DEATH OF SAPPER Collins nearly overshadowed the first day of NATO's arms collection operation, in which the NLA handed over about 400 weapons near the village of Otlja, about ten miles from Kumanovo. In what NATO described as a 'formal' ceremony, the NLA placed the weapons in a warehouse before they were counted by alliance troops, identified and packaged for eventual destruction. The weapons included 300 assault rifles, 60–80 light machine guns, 10 heavy machine guns, up to 15 rocket launchers and 50 mines.

In London, there were claims that the Government had not made clear the role of NATO in Macedonia. The future Conservative leader, Iain Duncan Smith, complained that no senior minister had explained the basis of the British deployment. 'The death of Sapper Collins is a tragic reminder that however meticulous the planning, deploying soldiers to a country divided by ethnic hatred involves a high degree of risk however limited their brief,' said *The Times*.

> The most valuable lesson of the British Army's previous Balkan experience – in Bosnia, Croatia and Kosovo – was that armour... not only provided crucial protection for soldiers but deterred potential armed troublemakers. However from when the arms-collection mission was discussed there was no intention to send an armoured NATO force.

The aim was to send a lightly armed force, rapidly deployed as soon as the peace settlement was signed, without giving the impression of imposing an occupying presence on the Macedonian people. The only country that had initially seemed keen to bring armoured personnel carriers was Germany, but the German contribution had not yet arrived.

Had the intervention been deemed peacekeeping rather than mere arms collection, the British Army's Warrior armoured infantry vehicle would have been deployed. The only concession after the incident was to send eight armoured Scimitar reconnaissance vehicles from Kosovo to Macedonia to escort the trucks of weapons handed over by the NLA as they were taken to Krivolak to be destroyed. A defence correspondent at the scene wrote:

> Boskovski, the Interior Minister, has in particular been accused by Western diplomats of inciting ethnic hatred between the Slavs and ethnic Albanians. Sapper Collins was a victim of this hatred, because Slav extremists consider that NATO is backing the Albanian rebels, even though its troops are helping to disarm them.[12]

The dead Royal Engineer's father, Kevin Collins, 44, from Sheffield, said: 'I don't think that our soldiers should be there. Kosovo was different. A lot of innocent people were getting hurt. This is a civil conflict with two factions fighting amongst themselves.'

Eight of the youths were arrested after the death of Sapper Collins, but charges against them were dropped by a local court in Skopje in January 2002 because of insufficient evidence. Prosecutors objected that NATO had started its own investigation before the Macedonian authorities, and considered this tantamount to interference. The Royal Engineer's parents, Sue and Kevin, subsequently launched a private campaign to try and bring to justice those responsible for his death. They travelled to Skopje from Sheffield in July 2002, offering a reward of £20,000 for information that could help identify the perpetrators.

Rudolf Scharping, the German Defence Minister, said that his country's troops heading for Macedonia would be given special training and new equipment after Sapper Collins' death. The first party of what would eventually be about 500 German troops, equipped with Leopard tanks, arrived in Skopje at the end of August after a vote in the German Parliament to approve the mission. Gerhard Schröder, the Chancellor, fought off a backbench challenge and almost 500 out of 637 deputies of the Bundestag approved the mission.

Inspecting surrendered weapons, Lord Robertson said that the alliance's mission would 'take out the guns from politics' in Macedonia. Flying by helicopter to the weapons storage at the town of Krivolak,

Lord Robertson hammered home NATO's theme that the number and quality of weapons surrendered was not crucial:

> It's not just the number of weapons that matter, it is the fact that the so-called NLA is handing over these weapons and disbanding as an organisation. I hope the people of Macedonia will see these weapons coming out of Macedonian politics and will draw the right lesson.

British defence officials said the hundred of weapons handed in included some sophisticated ordnance including surface to air missiles. But not all the weapons were the latest models.

The director of Skopje's museum, Gjorgji Colakovski, asked NATO not to destroy arms that could be of historical value.[13] Lord Robertson played down criticism that many arms dated back as far as the Second World War. 'Some of the weapons may be old but you can kill with old weapons as you can with new weapons.' NATO commanders had told him that about 70 per cent of the weapons handed over so far were serviceable and therefore capable of killing.

By 29 August, the disarmament programme was in full swing. Michael Evans reported from Brodec, about six miles north-west of Tetovo in the heart of NLA territory, which was occupied by about 300 members of 2 Para and 100 Dutch paratroopers from King's Company, 11 Netherlands Battalion. Most of the Paras were hidden in the thickly wooded mountains across from the River Pena, looking down at a line of uniformed NLA members. Evans wrote:

> In true British style, soldiers from the 2nd Battalion The Parachute Regiment had ordered the male and female members of the National Liberation Army to form an orderly queue and to wait their turn before handing in their AK47 Kalashnikov assault rifles. The queue had begun to form at 8 am when the British paratroopers opened for business and by the time that a Chinook helicopter appeared and landed on a patch of grass next to a narrow, nearby stream, bringing with it the huge sea container that was being used to store the arms, the line of rebels was 50-strong.

Already, three Sam 7 surface-to-air missiles 'in operational order' had been handed over to the soldiers – the first handover of six Sam 7s that the NLA admitted it had in its weapons stockpile. There was no sense of imminent danger as the Paras received the disbanded weapons, wrapped them in hessian bundles and took them to be deposited inside the container.

The NLA members, some dressed all in black and others in combat clothes and orange-red berets, stood silently, holding on to their Kalashnikovs. A lone Macedonian parliamentarian, Mirko Ivanov, from the Social Democratic Union Party, watched as each NLA man and woman was steered by the British paratroopers into a half-built, three-storey house serving as the weapons handover reception centre. Ivanov was encouraged by the sight of the rebels disarming.

Lieutenant Colonel Chapman said that about 100 weapons including assault rifles, anti-tank rocket launchers, light machine guns and the three Sam 7s had been handed in over about five and a half hours. 'We have to be impartial,' Chapman said, 'so we don't want to fraternise with the NLA and they haven't told us how many weapons they are going to hand over. But it's going well and it includes new weapons as well as old ones, the whole panoply of infantry weapons.'

In September, the Parachute Regiment disclosed that it was using snipers to ensure the safety of troops involved in collecting arms from the NLA. The team of 12 snipers from the 2nd Battalion of the Parachute Regiment was armed with a specialist .338 rifle that has a shoot-to-kill range of about 1,000 yards. They spent several days and nights using their optical sights to watch every movement in the area chosen for a weapons handover to ensure that there was no risk of gunmen opposed to the rebels setting up a sniper position to target them as they came forward with their rifles.

The snipers kept watch as British liaison teams, some of them from the SAS, met NLA commanders in the villages above Tetovo. 'Both sides know we are serious and if they should mistakenly choose to do something, then we're ready and they would regret it,' Lance Corporal Paul Fryer, 27, from Andover, said. Fryer said that he had seen Sten guns that probably dated back to the days of the Special Operations Executive (SOE), the organisation of British agents that operated behind enemy lines in the Balkan countries during World War II. The Para snipers also noticed that when the NLA fighters handed over their own sniper rifles, the telescopic sights had been removed.

As part of the deal agreed between NATO commanders and both sides in the six month conflict, a total ground and air exclusion zone was set up around the designated arms-collection points in west and north-west Macedonia. This was to ensure that rebels felt secure when they came down from the hills to hand over their weapons. Macedonian helicopter gunships and Su-25 ground attack aircraft were banned from approaching the locations.

The weaponry handed over to NATO troops by the NLA included three Russian T-55 tanks, two captured from the Macedonian forces at Raduša in July and the third at Nikustak. Commander Msusi, the leader of the National Liberation Army's 115 Brigade, whose post was dug into the hills near Raduša just south of the Macedonian-Kosovan border, proudly displayed to reporters one of the tanks captured from 'the enemy'.

The men of 115 Brigade said that their tank had seen action and that they were sorry to see it go. Eight shells were left in the ammunition box. Commander Msusi, 45, a teacher by profession who was to go back to his classroom once disarmament was complete, promised to hand over everything from his brigade, from the T-55 to a trench-full of rocket-propelled grenades at his unit's main training area outside the village.

It was difficult to envisage those tough-looking men voluntarily swapping their Kalashnikovs for a broom and a pitchfork. Well-concealed British soldiers, believed to be SAS men engaging in its traditional role of deep reconnaissance, arrived in advance of the arms collection and won the respect of Commander Msusi as they made sure his arsenal was gathered together and placed in the collection point nearby.

By the end of 'Essential Harvest', most pundits, who had been sceptical at the outset, declared it a success. Because almost exclusively European forces took part in the NATO-led operation, some saw it as the EU's proposed Rapid Reaction Force coming into being without almost anybody noticing and little blood being shed. There had been fears of far higher casualties being sustained by British or other NATO troops in Macedonia. 'More by accident than by design, Macedonia has become a key testing ground for an independent, post-NATO European security policy.'

In early September, anti-Albanian and anti-NATO feeling was still visible in Skopje. Angry protesters surrounded the Macedonian Parliament on 1 September. Chanting 'Macedonia's name will never die', they blocked off entrances to try to stop MPs voting on a series of reforms granting the Albanian minority more rights.

An Albanian MP, Zehir Bekteshi, was attacked. He had to run for cover as he was punched in the face and kicked from behind. Television cameramen were pelted with eggs and kicked. Most of the crowd were refugees who fled from areas occupied by the NLA. Some of the refugees carried placards reading 'NATO intruders', or 'NATO and the USA leave Macedonia within 24 hours'. Leaflets were handed out condemning the West's 'efforts to destroy the Macedonian nation'.

'How would you feel if you were forced out of your home in England and had nowhere to go?' asked a woman from Lesok. 'The Albanians want to take away Macedonian land and NATO is helping them,' another woman said.

Vladimir Stefanovski, a lawyer who was watching the demonstrations, said:

> It is American policy to support a Greater Albania. The Americans want to destabilise the Balkans, because that gives them an excuse to keep NATO here. We feel that we are being forced to negotiate at the point of a gun. I feel like my country is being invaded.

Stefanovski echoed the long-standing ethnic Macedonian fear of being demographically undermined:

> When I opened my office in Skopje 25 years ago, there were only a few Albanians in that part of town. Now they are 95 per cent in that area. These Albanians all have ten children each. People compare here to Northern Ireland, but the Irish and the British share the same culture. The Albanians are Muslims, they are completely different from us.[14]

The refugees twice managed to force delays in the debate on the reforms. The extent that anti-NATO demonstrations could cause public order problems had diminished, however. Hundreds of people attended the protest in September compared with the thousands who had stormed the presidential palace in June.

The ethnic Macedonian nationalists were still deeply disaffected. Boskovski expressed the view of many Macedonians that NATO's weapons target was too low and also hinted at the kind of security crackdown that NATO feared would trigger a new wave of fighting after it left. 'When NATO leaves,' he said, 'the Macedonian authorities will still have to re-establish the rule of law on every millimetre of Macedonian soil, including Sipkovica and other current logistical centres for these terrorist groups.'[15]

On another occasion he scoffed at a visit by the EU foreign policy chief, Javier Solana, and the Commissioner for Foreign Affairs, Chris Patten, during which they told the Government there would be no reconstruction aid for Macedonia until constitutional reforms were enacted. 'Macedonia cannot wait for some missionaries to say whether this condition or that condition is fulfilled,' Boskovski said. 'Macedonia is a sovereign country and we have our red line.'[16]

On 15 November, Boskovski quit a panel of state and western officials implementing the peace deal. The Interior Minister dealt a blow to the August peace pact by announcing that his security forces saw no point in adhering to plans agreed by 'this unserious co-ordinating committee' for a step-by-step reintegration of guerrilla areas. 'The interior ministry is the institution most competent to genuinely handle the crisis,' he said, in evident code language hinting that he might follow through on threats to unleash police special forces on villages that were home to demobilised rebels.

The Crisis-Handling Coordinative Body consists of senior government and NATO, EU and OSCE officials overseeing steps to implement the western-brokered peace deal. Boskovski flouted the panel's guidelines on 11 November by ordering his elite special force units to charge past unguarded truce lines into old guerrilla territory to secure an alleged mass grave. The 'Lions' arrested one of the most radical NLA commanders in Trebos, after his NLA comrades betrayed him to the police. The incursion provoked fighting with nervous former guerrillas, the first serious ethnic clash since the peace accord was signed. Three police troopers were killed.

Boskovski massed armoured units of 'Lion' and 'Tiger' commandos at entrances to the Tetovo Valley, vowing to sweep it in search of the killers. In reaction, ethnic Albanian villagers retrieved automatic weapons withheld as a precaution from the NATO disarmament scheme and set up checkpoints, vowing to resist Boskovski's forces. Albanians seized a bus containing dozens of Macedonians and held them hostage.

A purported extremist offshoot of the disbanded NLA said it was mobilising to beat back any advance by Boskovski's forces. 'We declare all territories with majority Albanian populations... a forbidden zone for the forces of repressive Macedonian machinery. If they enter, they will be deemed legitimate targets and get hit without warning,' the Albanian National Army (ANA) said in an e-mail sent to a western news agency. NATO peacekeepers intervened, technically going beyond their mandate to separate the two sides and defuse the incident.

Boskovski said the swift reappearance of ethnic Albanian gunmen vindicated his view that disarmament was a farce and that the rebels' true agenda was territorial, not better minority rights.

The Peace Accord Ratified

The incident was not serious enough to derail the peace process, however. On 16 November, the Macedonian Parliament ratified the Ohrid peace accord designed to end the conflict by giving the Albanian minority greater civil rights including greater representation in the police and civil service and for Albanian to be used as an official language in districts where ethnic Albanians were a majority. It passed

15 amendments to the constitution in just under 20 minutes. Barely a word was uttered by MPs from the ethnic majority who had spent so much time trying to block the reforms.

Shortly afterwards, President Trajkovski announced that all former ethnic Albanian guerrillas would be amnestied, including about 120 detainees and convicts. Only those indictable by the UN war crimes tribunal were exempted. The support of the VMRO-DMPNE, previously vocal opponents of the deal, gave the amendments the required two-thirds majority.

Filip Petrovski, a senior MP, said, 'Now we will see how the other side will behave, whether they really want human rights or a Greater Albania.' Imer Imeri, the leader of the Party of Democratic Prosperity (PDP), said international pressure would be needed to see the changes properly implemented. 'Our reaction is positive, and it gives us hope. But in practice we are far away from what's being promised on paper.'

Paramilitary Build-up

The continuing pacification notwithstanding, the build-up by Boskovski of the paramilitary-style Slav Macedonian forces caused increasing alarm among western diplomats in Skopje. The 'Tigers' are an aggressively promoted and feared official police unit technically under the control of Risto Galevski, the Macedonian police commander. The 'Lions' then were an unauthorised body of former police and military reservists sponsored unofficially by Boskovski. Only in the autumn, after the conflict, did the Lions become an official police unit.

A huge video monitor in the centre of Skopje urges young men to join the Tigers. 'It's these groups we're worried about not dissident Albanian rebels,' one western diplomatic source said. The Tigers reportedly took part in the heavy-handed attack on the village of Tanusevci in February 2001, the first major engagement of the conflict.

Boskovski was the real commander of the Tigers, diplomatic sources say, and he also nurtured the Lions, referring to them as 'noble' citizens carrying out their duty for the country. He said in late August 2001 that the Lions would have to deal with the aftermath of NATO's withdrawal and denied it was a paramilitary group.

The Lions were believed to have about 2,000 armed members. Slogans promoting their cause began appearing in the Albanian quarters of Skopje in March. Some sources linked the unit to Paramilitary 2000, which was active in using the threat of ethnic cleansing against Albanian businesses in Skopje. The Lions were also blamed in some quarters for violence in Bitola when Albanian families were driven out of the city in actual ethnic cleansing, the sources said.

Radical nationalists in the Macedonian police structure also controlled another paramilitary group, the Red Berets. The paramilitary groups continued to intimidate and harass ethnic Albanian civilians even after the peace agreement. Five Red Berets abducted Muharem Ibrahimi, a Tetovo-based activist with an ethnic Albanian humanitarian organisation, on 15 September and tried to kill him by throwing him in the Vardar river.

The Lions were lionised as recently as 9 January 2002, when Georgievski appeared at a controversial ceremony where the head of the Macedonian Orthodox Church, Archbishop Stefan, gave medallions of Christ to the paramilitaries. 'God is with us,' the inscription on the medallion said. Meto Jovanovski, of the human rights watchdog the Macedonian Helsinki Committee, said it was still unclear whether the Lions were even a legal body. The event 'is obviously in opposition to the spirit of the Ohrid Agreement'. The Lions' Commander, Goran Stojkov, was promoted at the ceremony to the grandiose rank of major general, despite having been sacked as President Trajkovski's bodyguard for what a local report called 'misconduct in last year's pre-election campaign'.[17] 'Macedonia is a holy country but also a country of heroes,' the Archbishop said during the solemn proceedings at a police base north of Skopje. 'Prepare to protect Macedonia.'

The independent magazine *Forum* said in late January 2002 that the Lions included 'members with renowned criminal history' and that it was created:

> not to defeat the Albanian extremists but to help in achieving other political goals: escalation of military clashes, inciting disorder and provocations based on the need of one faction in the VMRO which includes pressures and liquidation of political opponents in the country... who are not in line with the aggressive military plans of Boskovski and his superior.[18]

Forum charged that Boskovski:

> is rather an unsuccessful figure in the government in the field of security, politics and reforms... the Macedonian police under his leadership has mainly been defeated during last year's security crisis and in most cases the killing and wounding of Macedonian policemen was a direct consequence of the unprofessional, amateur, violent and arrogant conduct of the leading personnel at the Ministry of Interior.

Boskovski had failed to deliver on promises to arrest members of the previous Social Democratic government allegedly embroiled in corruption, *Forum*'s Saso Ordanoski said, and graft and crime had soared in Macedonia and within the VMRO to beyond the levels experienced under the previous government.

Forum also accused Boskovski of trying to intimidate independent journalists in Skopje:

> The author of this text accompanied by a well-known colleague had the honour to meet Mr Boskovski and his wife shopping in Yucan, in the centre of Skopje that for that occasion was packed with police. On that occasion the first words directed to me by the always cordial Boskovski in the presence of about 20 witnesses were 'If I were not a minister you would be beaten up for each of the stories you write.'

> The minister recently told another colleague, Editor in Chief of a Macedonian medium, that 'he would be liquidated' 10 days after Boskovski leaves his ministerial position.

Perhaps more seriously, *Forum* charged that 'the political damage that Boskovski has inflicted on Macedonia on an international level is something that will require "smoothing out" for many years after he leaves this function'.

In May 2002, Georgievski came under renewed media pressure to dismiss Boskovski after he accidentally wounded four people while firing from a grenade launcher during a public exercise of the Lions in Leunovo, western Macedonia. The wounded were a journalist, a French Embassy interpreter, the Skopje police chief, Marinko Kocovski, and another policeman. They were standing near Boskovski when he test-fired the grenade launcher and were wounded by shrapnel that ricocheted off a target wall.

A Lions commander, Colonel Boban Utkovski, said that the people who had been wounded had disregarded police warnings to stay at a distance from the firing. Boskovski is an experienced handler of grenade launchers and 'is very fond of such kind of weapons', Utkovski told state radio.[19]

'I am deeply sorry for the incident,' Boskovski said. 'Such things happen.' While that is a remark that would be unlikely to elicit much sympathy at The Hague, there are indications that the investigation into Ljuboten is no closer to reaching a successful conclusion than the eight-year hunt for Radovan Karadzic and Ratko Mladic.

After the nationalists' defeat in the September 2002 elections, the Lions were finally disbanded in early 2003 with about half their members absorbed into the police and half discharged to fend for themselves. This has only partially deprived Boskovski of his power base, however.

10 What Options for Macedonia?

There are unknown heroes who are modest, with none of the historical glamour of a Napoleon. If you analysed their character you would find that it eclipsed even the glory of Alexander the Great.
Jaroslav Hasek, The Good Soldier Svejk

By August 2001, a decade after the international community first intervened to mediate in the Yugoslav conflict, Macedonia was teetering on the brink of a full-scale war. In six months of tragic internecine fighting between the security forces and ethnic Albanian guerrillas, between 150 and 250 people were killed and at least 650 others wounded. Total casualties can be estimated at up to 1,000 people.[1]

About 140,000 people left their homes either through forced displacement or voluntary flight. Many had not returned a year later and of these a large number never will. The security forces lost control of 20 per cent of the country to the insurgent National Liberation Army and have yet to recover all of it.

The Macedonian Army and paramilitary police suffered a series of defeats by the rebels in Tetovo and the Kumanovo region, at Aracinovo on the outskirts of Skopje and in the renewed fighting that raged near both Tetovo and Kosovo in August. Ethnic Albanians bore the brunt of civilian casualties while many of the security forces' losses were barely-trained Macedonian reservists thrown into the front line by inexperienced commanders. An unknown number of ethnic Macedonian soldiers were killed by friendly fire.

The nationalist-led Government and the successive 'grand coalition' administration failed to contain the crisis. Bolstering the army with sophisticated helicopters and warplanes bought from Ukraine failed to defeat the National Liberation Army. Mobilising reservists and making a series of command changes within the armed forces failed.

As the casualties mounted among the Macedonian forces, a nationalist rebellion against President Trajkovski by Slav paramilitaries and street thugs simmered. Ethnic cleansing ravaged the cities of southern Macedonia and Skopje. There were revenge attacks of the kind that led to the killing of 10 Albanian civilians at Ljuboten in August. The security forces' heavy-handed tactics radicalised the ethnic Albanian population. Soon a majority of the ethnic Albanian community supported the National Liberation Army.

It was clear that the Macedonian political class that seceded from Yugoslavia in 1991 had not been entirely ready for independence. Despite, or perhaps because, the ruling Slavonic class received substantial foreign assistance in what verged on a post-colonial relationship, within ten years it had proved incapable of governing in the face of the growing tensions between ethnic Macedonians and ethnic Albanians.

The Macedonians wanted independence largely to avoid domination by the Serbs and Montenegrins in the Yugoslav federation after the withdrawal of Croatia, Slovenia and Bosnia. And Macedonians feared further involvement in Belgrade's wars. Thus Macedonian independence was at least as much the result of the implosion of Yugoslavia as of a real wish to create a separate state and realise the old dream of Delchev and the Ilinden committee men, who had died bravely in 1903 fighting for a free and independent Macedonian nation.

Macedonia's turbulent first five years of independence were overshadowed by the problems of UN sanctions against Yugoslavia and the vicious dispute with an incandescent Greece conniving with Milosevic that threatened Macedonia's very existence.

President Gligorov by 1996 had rather miraculously normalised relations with the four potentially unpleasant predators on Macedonian borders: Albania, Bulgaria and Serbia as well as Greece. But his party, the Social Democrats, was unable to solve the severe economic problems that followed from no longer being able to rely on federal funding. They lost public confidence through their corruption, although this would turn out to be small-scale graft by comparison with most of the nationalists' tremendous capacity for bribery in office. The Social Democrats' moderate Albanian allies, the Party of Democratic Prosperity (PDP), were given little real power and failed to meet their constituents' concerns over human rights.

The new government coalition that took power at the end of 1998, dominated by the Internal Macedonian Revolutionary Organisation

(VMRO), promised to reform and improve the economy. Members of the radical ethnic Albanian DPA led by Arben Xhaferi were given important posts in government and some of the main human rights grievances of the Albanian minority were addressed, for instance through the release of political prisoners such as the ethnic Albanian mayors of Gostivar and Tetovo. The Government allowed greater representation of ethnic Albanians in the police and civil service. It also passed long overdue economic reforms, introducing legislation to privatise the land and abolish the old state planning system.

But the Kosovo crisis severely hurt the new coalition. Macedonia's good reputation suffered when large groups of ethnic Albanian refugees were initially refused entry and forced to live between border fences without water, food or sanitation. The Government's support of NATO was highly unpopular with demonstrators from the Serb minority attacking the US Embassy in Skopje as Christopher Hill sought to defuse the situation from inside his beleaguered mission.

The biblical influx of hundreds of thousands of Kosovar refugees further radicalised the ethnic Albanian population. They felt frustrated at what by then was seen as the slow pace of reform. Inside Kosovo after the NATO victory the leaders of the former Kosovo Liberation Army found the independence process blocked. They sought another outlet for Albanian nationalism after NATO negotiated an end to the fighting between ethnic Albanian guerrillas and Yugoslav forces in southern Serbia. Skopje's agreement with Belgrade to cede Macedonia a chunk of territory from Kosovo provided the pretext for the first clashes between Macedonian special forces and the National Liberation Army at Tanusevci. The main rebellion erupted around Tetovo and spread to the Kumanovo area and the outskirts of Skopje.

The international community moved relatively quickly. It supported the Ohrid peace plan that President Trajkovski drew up, by banging heads on both sides to get the blueprint accepted by the warring parties and by overseeing its slow but so far steady implementation. This western reaction was far swifter and more effective than it was in the other former Yugoslav republics of Croatia and Bosnia.

European policymakers preserved Macedonia's fragile identity and protected it for the time being from possibly explosive exploitation of the crisis by the 'four wolves' Albania, Bulgaria, Greece and Serbia.[2]

The NATO disarmament operation in Macedonia, as we have seen, was initially greeted with considerable scepticism in some circles in the West.[3] In the event, 'Essential Harvest', brilliantly planned and carried out, was generally deemed a success by everyone except the Macedonians themselves, who objected that the disarmament was in many ways cosmetic since just 4,000 weapons – only a small part of the Albanian arsenal – were collected, and the democratic Serbian authorities were still trying to cope with Albanian agitation in southern Serbia. However, as a recent paper for the Conflict Studies Research Centre at Sandhurst notes: 'This may well be justified at one level, although the proliferation of small arms supplies in the region generally probably makes the whole issue largely symbolic.'[4]

The disarmament did underline that the NLA was giving up the armed struggle, at least for the time being. Casualties were negligible during 'Essential Harvest' and Macedonia had come to be seen as an important testing area for an independent post-NATO security policy.

Nevertheless, there were disconcerting signs that Macedonia was already in the process of becoming a 'European Colombia', with rival Slavonic and Albanian paramilitary groups linked to the main political parties vying for control of extortion, smuggling and other organised crime rackets so as to leave the state virtually powerless.

The 'four wolves' had been kept at bay from a scramble to dismember Macedonia. But after the Ohrid peace agreement, Macedonian territorial integrity still was at risk from destabilisation by the Kosovo Albanians.

The underlying causes of the internecine fighting were Albanian and Macedonian nationalism and a weak, corrupt central Government controlled by cynical politicians using anti-Albanian rhetoric. These were still strong even after the two chauvinist movements were obliged to cooperate with President Trajkovski and the international community in signing the peace plan. Considerable potential persisted for the conflict to flare up again and spread to Kosovo and other areas of the southern Balkans such as Bulgaria, Greece and Serbia. It will take years before Macedonia may be considered a stable country.

Macedonian Nationalism

Unfairly demonised in the past by countries like Greece and Bulgaria, the Macedonians have deservedly received western support for their struggle to preserve their identity. Understandably, perhaps, some of them shrink from the Albanian reference to them as 'Slavs,' which, they feel, following the demonisation of Serbs in Yugoslavia, became to an extent a dirty word in the West. Macedonians also feel their ethnicity is distinct from the vast swathe of Slav countries stretching from Russia and Poland to Croatia and Slovenia as well as Serbia.

But while the leaders of the ethnic Macedonian political class enjoy western sympathy on one level, by no standards can they be considered to be angels. Like their counterparts in Serbia before the fall of Slobodan

Milosevic, they proved incapable of managing conflict and polarisation without violence controlled by warlords.

Ljubco Georgievski, in particular, in many ways personifies the chronic instability of Macedonia. The nationalist leader was a literary figure popular for his dark erotic poetry. The Prime Minister was regarded as 'occasionally erratic' in Skopje's diplomatic circles because of his rampant nationalist views and what is seen as a cynical pursuit of power. Some would even go so far as to compare him privately, and of course highly unfairly, with that other Balkan poet turned politician, Radovan Karadzic, the former Bosnian Serb president wanted by the International Criminal Tribunal for War Crimes in the former Yugoslavia.

Georgievski's firebrand rhetoric and espousal of the war option contrasted with the statesmanlike stance of President Trajkovksi, a moderate who hoped to transform the VMRO into a responsible party dedicated to national reconciliation. 'Trajkovski says conciliatory things but doesn't inspire people,' a western intelligence source in Skopje said. 'They don't take him seriously. Georgievski is taken seriously. He's mad but clever and fascinating, one of the darkest politicians you can imagine, rather like Tiberius, with total cynicism. You have to watch *I Claudius*, to understand him.'[5]

Throughout the crisis, the Prime Minister skilfully used the ethnic Macedonian community's resolute refusal to grant greater civil rights to the ethnic Albanian community and the intransigent, trigger-happy attitude of the Macedonian Army with the strong Serb diaspora element in its officer corps to promote his own popularity and strengthen his power base, Macedonia watchers say. This goes back to the start of the fighting at Tanusevci, when the Interior Ministry special forces, or possibly the Army's Wolves, were used by the nationalist Government to precipitate clashes on the border with Kosovo.

The nationalists were not the only party to exploit the ethnic divisions in the country. All the Macedonian coalition governments of the 1990s learned that the best way to preserve their power base while exploiting international concerns was to demonstrate that they were able to keep the tensions under control at a price of continued western support, including tolerance of corrupt and heavy-handed government. But Georgievski and his party pushed this policy to unprecedented levels of cynicism.

At the time of writing, it is evident that Georgievski and his cronies might well be tempted to exploit anti-Albanian feeling again and set off another round of fighting, even though there is no guarantee that the West would intervene a second time to prevent a humiliating defeat of the Macedonian Army by the NLA or its offshoot, ANA.

Although Ohrid was seen by the ethnic Slav Macedonians as making major concessions on civil society and in the cultural fields to the ethnic Albanians, it probably tilted the military balance in favour of the ethnic Macedonians as, until 2003, there was no attempt by NATO or the West to disarm the paramilitary groups or members of the ethnic Macedonian population, who had obtained weapons from the police or elsewhere during the conflict. The collection operation organised by the Government in liaison with EU forces during autumn 2003 was voluntary and met with a limited response. The authorities were criticised by some observers for offering Macedonians who handed in firearms tickets for lotteries in which they could win prizes such as new cars. This was seen by critics as potentially rewarding killers for using weapons.

As we have seen, the nationalists in office in 2001 were different men to Gligorov, the Fox of the Balkans, and even before the fighting started they were trying to govern under different pressures after the NATO invasion of Kosovo changed the region's political landscape. By then, Macedonia was showing all the characteristics of the area that the Russian historians Nina Smirnova and Alla Yaskova called the 'instability arc' on the territory of the former Yugoslavia and southern regions of the former Soviet Union as a result of acute inter-ethnic conflicts.[6]

Macedonia and Kosovo

As long as the future of Kosovo remains undecided Macedonia continues to be vulnerable to the risk of further subversive military activities being sponsored by the former Kosovo Liberation Army (KLA) commanders who helped to mastermind the creation of the NLA from the province.

In its public statements, the NLA always claimed it was an entirely home-grown force and insisted that it had had no intention whatsoever of changing Macedonia's borders. This claim was repeated by the inter-national media, though it was clear that one immediate cause of the conflict had been the accord between Serbia and Macedonia that gave Skopje a small chunk of sensitive territory from what had been Kosovo in an area where Albanian and other crime gangs previously had carried out large-scale smuggling of arms, drugs and people with impunity.

Throughout the ethnic Albanian uprising, Macedonian super-hardliners such as Boskovski and his political master, Georgievski, insisted that the crisis was entirely imported. There is no doubt in the western intelligence community that strategists from the Kosovo Protection Force, the former KLA, played a key role in fostering the

Albanian uprising in Macedonia. The demise of Slobodan Milosevic encouraged them to undertake the adventure in the knowledge that there was likely to be little Serb reaction. If Milosevic had still been in power, the Yugoslav Army might have quickly joined the Macedonians to crush the rebellion, possibly with a view to re-assimilating Macedonia into Yugoslavia.

In July 2001, the international authorities running Kosovo suspended five top commanders in the Kosovo Protection Corps after they appeared on a US blacklist because, as the White House put it in an executive order signed by US President George W. Bush, they were trying to destabilise the Balkans by promoting ethnic Albanian insurgency in Macedonia. Two of those suspended were Kosovo Protection Corps regional commanders while the other three occupied senior positions in the corps hierarchy.[7] No further action was taken against them, however. The unwillingness of the USA to take tougher measures against the KPC over Macedonia fuelled the nationalist suspicion of NATO, which had always been seen by Macedonians as pro-Albanian because of the bombing of Yugoslavia during the Kosovo crisis.

One of the most insidious effects of ethnic Albanian propaganda during the conflict was to present Macedonia's future as an entirely two-sided battle. 'This is a country with seven or eight ethnic groups including Gorans, Turks, Greeks, Serbs and Roma as well as Macedonians and Albanians,' a veteran observer in Skopje commented. 'It used to be a properly multi-ethnic country. The Albanians are in favour of simplifying things.'

Macedonians pointed out that they had never had a serious problem with other ethnic groups in the country (some of whom, such as the Turks, received privileges during the Gligorov era in order to make them a counterweight to the Albanians). Nor do Albanians have a good record of treatment of non-Albanians living in their territorial bases. This is evident from the plight of the Serb minority in Kosovo. A lot of Macedonian Turks and Bosniaks in western Macedonia, dominated by ethnic Albanians, feel unfairly treated by Albanians there.

Apologists for the ethnic Albanians stress that they too made concessions during Ohrid, not only by undertaking the only disarmament that took place, but also by not insisting on protection from the international community for ethnic Albanians and Muslims in cities like Prilep and Bitola, where they were subject to ethnic cleansing and their historic mosques were damaged or burned down.

Nevertheless, it is hard to escape from the conclusion that the radical ethnic Albanian leaders in Macedonia want more than equality with ethnic Macedonians. They want preferential treatment, probably as a prelude to carving up a slice of western and northern Macedonia and attaching it to Kosovo if they can get away with that. To what extent they have the general support of the ethnic Albanian population for that goal is unclear. Probably it is more widely subscribed to now than before the conflict, even allowing for a measure of disillusionment among many ordinary ethnic Albanians over disruption of lives, loss of homes and civilian casualties during the fighting.

When our host in Germo pointed to the floor of his shepherd's hut and said 'This is Kosovo', he was expressing a sentiment commonly felt in and around Tetovo. Many ethnic Albanians feel that because of their higher birth rate compared to that of the ethnic Macedonian Slavs it is only a matter of time, perhaps as little as ten years, before they become a numerical majority within Macedonia, after which some form of union with Kosovo would be much more easily achievable.

As Christopher Hill noted, 'The conflict in Macedonia is organically linked to the unresolved issues in Kosovo. One certainly wishes that the ethnic Albanians would focus on completing the task in Kosovo that NATO and the U.N. have provided conditions for.'[8] Many of the NLA, he said, had been:

> simply engaged in... trying to create Albanian state structures on top of what they believe to be Albanian lands, defined by some ethnographic map in their minds from the 19th century. In short there's nothing to be particularly inspired by in these people. This is not about 20th or 21st century human rights. This is about 19th century ethnic carve outs... this problem of a continued desire to put state structures over land that is defined in ethnic terms has driven the crisis there for over 100 years.

The challenge, Hill added, is:

> to create a sense of belonging to the state. In the Balkans, state structures are seen as the executive arm of a nationalist agenda. And until that is broken and until state structures are seen as existing to protect civic society, not ethnic society, we will continue to have problems... Clearly [as well] the Balkans have got to be integrated into the European mainstream... One cannot talk about a Europe that is whole and free and at peace if the Balkans are left out of it, and are left in conflict.

The border agreement reached between Macedonia and Yugoslavia in February 2001 subsequently continued to be a major source of tension between Skopje and the newly elected Kosovo Government. In March 2002, the newly elected Kosovo Prime Minister, Bajram Rexhepi, said, 'Kosovo institutions do not recognise the border demarcation agreement signed by Skopje and Belgrade, based on which some 2,500 hectares were taken away from Kosovo and added to Macedonia.' Rexhepi said the issue could not be ignored 'as long as people cannot work their lands because of the presence of a border'. The Macedonian Foreign Minister, Slobodan Casule, called Kosovo's failure to recognise the border 'extremely dangerous. Unilaterally revising borders without the necessary mechanisms of agreement is a declaration of war which shakes Europe's very foundations.' Rexhepi later backed off threats to take the issue to the UN Security Council, saying that this would not happen until Kosovo was independent.

In May 2002, the issue resurfaced when the Kosovo Parliament again claimed that the frontiers agreed were invalid because representatives of ethnic Albanians in Kosovo had not been consulted and that they 'endanger the territorial wholeness of Kosovo'. The UN administration cancelled the resolution and censured the Parliament, but the rumpus caused considerable alarm in Skopje.

There is a consensus among Albanians in Kosovo, including moderates, that any long-term settlement that does not provide for the separation of Kosovo from Serbia is unacceptable. The NLA insurgency was highly popular in Kosovo, drawing support from Rugova's LDK as well as the ex-KLA parties of Hashim Thaci (PDK, Democratic Party of Kosovo) and Ramush Haradinaj (AAK, Alliance for the Future of Kosovo). The conflict in Macedonia relieved pressure on the ex-KLA leaders from KFOR and Kosovo public opinion saw the NLA as in many ways an improvement on the KLA that avoided its military errors and used the media more deftly to present its case.

The conflict was a serious setback for Serbia, since it allowed the Kosovo Albanian leaders to move forward on the path to independence. As James Pettifer noted, 'Within Kosovo, the conflict showed the basic residual strength of the ex-KLA political tradition, and the increasingly polycentric nature of contemporary Albanian nationalism.'[9]

Some Kosovars want more than independence. The long-term aim of some Kosovar politicians such as Rexhep Qosja, a nationalist writer and grandee of Kosovo politics, is a Union of Kosovo and Albania. However, the experience of the 500,000 Albanian Kosovars who sheltered in Albania during the Kosovo war militated against them adopting the goal of the unification of all the lands inhabited by Albanians into a Greater Albania. Only a tiny handful of Kosovars had been to Albania before the war.

The experience of the Kosovar refugees exploded myths about 'Mother Albania'. Kosovars appreciated the welcome they received but were shocked by the poverty and the corruption of the country they had grown up idealising. There was bitterness as well when many of the refugees were robbed. Increasingly, independence is seen as an end in itself rather than an interim stop on the way to uniting all Albanians in one state.

Before the conflict, western perceptions of Kosovo, particularly in Britain, were based on the assumption that ex-KLA parties could be diverted from pressing on with the drive for independence by peacekeeping efforts including 'psyops' to prevent military adventures by the Kosovo Protection Corps. The West cautiously supported Rugova's LDK and it was believed that talks could be opened with Serbia with a view to planning the return of Kosovo to a moderate, democratic Yugoslavia. The international community now realises that such an option is probably not realistic.

More British commentators have now begun joining American policymakers, who have long argued for Kosovo independence. Churcher, for example, concludes that Albanian nationalism is unstoppable in the province:

> The break up of the Ottoman and Austro-Hungarian empires, followed by that of Yugoslavia, has resulted in what Albanians in the southern Balkans (and perhaps the Russians) see as a proliferation of Slavic states. The Albanians whilst carefully avoiding the phrases 'Greater Albania' or 'Greater Kosovo' have started talking about a proliferation of Albanian states (the United States of Albania perhaps).
>
> An effective answer is a fast track solution to the problem of Kosovo's status, and conditional independence, in return for an agreement that will keep present borders unchanged, and a Kosovar Albanian government responsible for keeping the peace and suppressing organised crime under threat of failing to gain a final status of independence.[10]

For practical reasons, officials of the UN Mission in Kosovo (UNMIK) have been giving the province many of the attributes of statehood since Serb forces withdrew. With all Yugoslav authority gone, the UN had established customs on the borders of Macedonia and Albania and was using the revenue to fund its administration of Kosovo. The Yugoslav dinar was abolished and replaced with the mark and then the euro because there were no Serbian banks left. The UN started issuing identity cards and travel documents along with car number plates. On the other hand, British and EU policy remains strongly against the founding of any more mini-states in the Balkans.

As Tim Judah says in his study of the province: 'At the turn of the millennium, Kosovo seemed set fair for independence but there was no telling how long this process would take or how it would come about.'[11] In the long run, he adds, Kosovo might remain a unique and expensive protectorate in which its guarantors, NATO and the UN, just hope that they do not become the eventual targets of Albanian rage.

The US military for its part appears to be planning to remain in the region for generations to come. Close to the Kosovar town of Urosevac it has built Camp Bondsteel, the largest US base to be built since the Vietnam war, with a helicopter port and solid housing for 5,000 soldiers.

Against this background, destabilising Macedonia as a way of putting pressure on the international community to speed up the independence process in Kosovo is an option that Albanian leaders in the province may be tempted to use again. As Bernd Fischer wrote:

> It is for the postcommunist democratic forces in Albania to determine whether the nationalism built on [Albanian King] Zog's foundation and further inspired by Hoxha – as a direct result of Albania's wartime experience – will become a positive or a negative force in the Balkan region.[12]

Macedonia, the EU and the West

Would the West have moved even earlier to prevent the blood-letting in Macedonia if there had been fewer preconceived ideas among policymakers about Albanian human rights, or if Macedonia's turbulent history had been better known to western politicians or public?

The international community's recognition of the sensitivity of Macedonia goes back to 1993, when the USA sent peacekeeping troops to the Balkans, not to the conflict zones in which civilians were being rounded up and killed, but deployed on the northern borders of Macedonia. At that stage, the USA seemed in many ways more concerned that the Yugoslav conflict might spread to Macedonia or Kosovo than with the impact of fighting in landlocked Bosnia. Susan Woodward noted:

> There was still no cause to defend Bosnia's borders with military force, but if war occurred in Kosovo or Macedonia, it would have

international implications. A war in those areas could threaten to involve Albania, Bulgaria, Greece, and perhaps Turkey and oblige a NATO response, including intervention between the two NATO members.[13]

The limited policy toward Macedonia leading to the deployment of the monitors did not 'address the increasing internal instability of Macedonia, exacerbated by pressures from all four neighbours, especially Greece'.

By 9 December 1992, the UN Secretary-General had recommended – on the basis of the request made on 11 November by the Government of Macedonia and the report of an assessment team sent on 28 November – authorisation of a United Nations Preventive Deployment Force (UNPREDEP) presence along the Macedonian border with Serbia and Albania to monitor conditions and report any threatening movements. Seven hundred troops were sent and were joined by 300 Americans in June 1993.

These fears of the ramifications of war in Macedonia have prevailed to the present, as we have seen.

The UN deployment was ended in 1999 after Skopje recognised Taiwan and China broke off diplomatic relations with Macedonia and vetoed the extension of the Force mandate in the UN Security Council. By then, NATO already was deploying in Macedonia prior to the Kosovo war and the UN troops, mainly from obscure and minor nations, had become ineffective, with many border posts unmanned. The UN deployment represented a serious international commitment to the stability of Macedonia in the early 1990s. But by leading to neglect of Macedonia's defence capacity in the end it probably contributed to the crisis and the Macedonia Army's inability to defeat the National Liberation Army.

By the end of the millennium, however, Montenegro, with only 600,000 inhabitants compared to two million Macedonian citizens, had seemed to many observers a more immediate risk to the fragile peace in the Balkans than Macedonia. 'The present author would have staked his reputation... on the outbreak of a diversionary war in Montenegro in the autumn of 2000,' Brendan Simms commented, 'and in the light of recent events it is possible he was too optimistic about Macedonia.'[14]

The effectiveness of western policy in persuading the Montenegrin President, Milo Djukanovic, to back away from independence from Belgrade was acclaimed in Brussels as another policy success for the EU in the Balkans that reinforced the peace process in Macedonia.

Macedonia and Montenegro's strategic regional importance are intertwined. Had Djukanovic pressed on with his previous policies of creating a totally independent country from Serbia, it would greatly have encouraged Kosovar Albanians to do likewise and thus rekindled the ambitions of the KPC in Macedonia. Instead, Djukanovic agreed to remain in federation with the Serbs in a new Union of Serbia and Montenegro that has consigned the name Yugoslavia to history. It was far from clear that Montenegrin separatism was dead as a political force, but events in Macedonia helped to constrain Djukanovic to curtail his ambitions.

Concern about Montenegro probably prevented policymakers focusing more clearly on Macedonia but, once the EU and NATO had given their support to President Trajkovski's peace plan, western mediation efforts proceeded at breakneck speed. Since Georgievski and other nationalist leaders continued to challenge the Ohrid peace plan until early August 2001, it is difficult to imagine how peacekeepers could have been deployed more rapidly.

Amid continued uncertainty about the future of the Balkans, Macedonians were keenly aware that only a near miracle would prevent their shot at forming an independent state from being deemed a failure on a far bigger scale than the end of Montenegrin aspirations for a return to independence.

'You can't talk about the crisis here in the past tense,' a diplomat says. 'Fundamental problems have not been solved.' The Macedonians cannot believe how far they have fallen in the league for applications for joining NATO and Europe, he says.[15]

> They were particularly insulted that they were bracketed with Albania as applicants for NATO while a country like Bulgaria that they regard as uncivilised is ahead of them. Now Bulgarians can get into Schengen countries without visas. That hurts them a lot because they regard Bulgarians as primitive savages. It's like the Lebanese and Syrians and Egyptians realising they are having to work for the Saudis who they regard as a lower form of life.

> They keep harking back to when, as Yugoslavs, they could travel around the world and had money to spend doing so. They can't believe how badly things have gone.

> Nobody's seriously proposing that they can do anything except putting themselves in the queue. Either they join EU institutions or there is just the gangster solution in which you fester in your own

filth. No politician is going to stand up and suggest that but it may be what ends up happening.

Macedonia has been overtaken by most of Eastern Europe. The Government says that they are moving toward NATO and Europe but in fact they have moved away.

NATO's Image in Macedonia

Popular hostility to NATO is another barrier to avoiding further ethnic violence in the future. The diplomat notes:

> The politicians are saying they want to move toward NATO membership but the electorate hates NATO, as Georgievski has said. As Macedonians see it, they were attacked from a NATO protectorate and were pressured into a disastrous peace agreement that rewarded ethnic violence. Most Macedonians believe there is nothing to stop the Albanians coming back and asking for more. Unless they see one serious piece of action by the international community against Albanians such as Albanians going to The Hague tribunal for trial for war crimes or being put in prison they won't believe the West is on their side.

As remains the case in the fledgling democracy of Serbia, one of the ethnic Macedonians' biggest heroes is Ratko Mladic, the former Bosnian Serb commander indicted for the 1995 killing of 8,000 Muslim men and boys at Srebrenica, Europe's biggest post-war massacre. A number of Macedonians fought alongside Serbs in Vukovar during the Croatian war. They also believe that Mladic was instrumental in ensuring that the JNA withdrew smoothly from Macedonia during independence. Boskovski's rhetoric when he rails against the ICTY recalls that of the hardline Serb nationalists who hero-worship Mladic and Karadzic.

Europe's latest war was fought in a Balkan backwater that today is largely unknown territory for even the most well-informed West Europeans. A century ago, by contrast, the British educated public was well informed on events in Macedonia, Bulgaria and Serbia. Newspapers enjoyed the services of a breed of dashing, totally dedicated journalists such as Bourchier, who was a personal friend of Bulgarian Prince Ferdinand.

Recent work by the Serbian historian Markovic has cast light on the immense influence of men such as Bourchier as the First World War approached.[16] 'A century on there is still a tendency to divide up the Balkan populations into good guys and bad guys,' he says. 'We Serbs until recently were the bad guys and the Albanians were the good guys. Now it seems as though that may be reversed.'

Whatever the case, there is little doubt that the latent sympathy for the ethnic Albanian cause in Macedonia that initially existed among the international community and press corps was eroded by indiscriminate Albanian guerrilla artillery fire on Albanian civilians and journalists. Albanian fighters stopped short of the apparent excesses carried out by the Macedonian security forces in Ljuboten and elsewhere, but reports that Macedonian soldiers and policemen were mutilated by the NLA are widely believed and deserve investigation.

Macedonian authorities for their part condemned what they saw as the use by 'terrorists' of Albanian civilians as human shields, a charge partially confirmed by the scenes in the cellars at Selce and in the Kumanovo area. But, as we have seen, their army gunners had also fired on civilians during supposed ceasefires. Potential good guys in Macedonia are in short supply. The EU and NATO consciously decided to avert the collapse of the Skopje Government, but in so doing turned a virtual blind eye to many of the more unattractive aspects of its politicians and their security forces.

In contrast to the experience of the Bosnian war, when British officers serving with the United Nations were often pro-Serb, however, many of the Parachute Regiment soldiers involved in the disarmament operation seemed to sympathise with the NLA rather than the Macedonian security forces, confiding privately that the ethnic Albanian fighters were the 'sharper outfit' or the 'more disciplined army'.

In spite of insistent denials by the Defence Ministry in Skopje, there are strong grounds for presuming, as we have seen, that the Macedonian Army was responsible for the death of Kerem Lawton, the British APTV journalist killed in Kosovo. What amounted, wittingly or unwittingly, to very direct and effective intimidation of the foreign media continued with the blowing up of the BBC Land Rover near Kumanovo, shots being fired at an Agence France Press reporter, the arrest of London *Times* and other journalists and other deplorable incidents.

The exact role of Boskovski in the killing of ethnic Albanian civilians at Ljuboten remains unexplained. In April 2002, the International Tribunal for War Crimes in the former Yugoslavia (ICTY) supervised exhumation of the bodies at Ljuboten so that they could be examined by forensic experts.

The anti-NATO rhetoric of Boskovski and Georgievski also set the scene for the murder of Sapper Collins. It would have been hypocritical of the West to support these politicians in general elections in Macedonia.

Paramilitary Threat?

Boskovski was also the main sponsor of the Lions and their associates in Paramilitary 2000, which encouraged ethnic cleansing at Bitola and in Skopje. Efforts by NATO to have the Lions disbanded initially came to nothing. Indeed they were lauded, as we have seen, by the Macedonian Orthodox Church. However, the new Social Democrat Government finally dissolved the unit in early 2003, and this was a major achievement in consolidating the peace process.

In April 2002, Boskovski backed efforts by the Lions to take over an army barracks. President Trajkovski resisted the plan, but observers believed the Lions and other forces under Boskovski's command were becoming increasingly confrontational towards the Army, possibly as part of preparations Boskovski was making to run for president.

A senior aide to President Trajkovski believed the Lions posed a threat to Macedonian democracy. He told me:

> I am firm in my belief that the structure called Lions was the worst thing that happened in Macedonia in the last 10 years. More than 1,500 people were recruited last June on one criterion alone – membership of the VMRO. Many of them were people with crime dossiers before entering the police force. With no training, they all became majors, colonels or even a general within two and a half months.
>
> They were not engaged in any real battle, they were only shooting randomly, they were intimidating villagers, completely corrupted, asking for bribes. They were simply a shame for our country. Now part of that unit is legitimised and formally employed in the Ministry of the Interior.
>
> It's a cause of concern for anyone who wants democracy instead of a European Colombia.

This book has sought to explain what went wrong in the former Yugoslav republic, whose sophisticated Slav political class seemed to have combined the best of their Serbian and Bulgarian roots to secede peacefully from Belgrade and avoid the bloody conflicts experienced by Croatia, Bosnia and Kosovo.

By mid 2001, the threat of civil war made ethnic partition, as embodied in the plan proposed by the Macedonian Academy of Arts and Sciences, appear attractive to nationalists in both the Macedonian and ethnic Albanian camps. Some such partition already happened informally, as is evident from the slow rate of return of Macedonian refugees to western Macedonia compared with the rapid return of ethnic Albanians in that area. The reverse side of this is that while the UNHCR has concentrated considerable efforts on trying to encourage the Slavs to return to the Tetovo area, the same priority has not been applied to helping Albanians to return to towns like Prilep and Bitola, where they were driven from their homes by Slav paramilitaries.

'There has been very modest progress indeed in reversing the ethnic cleansing of the 2001 conflict period,' Pettifer noted. As elsewhere in the former Yugoslavia, from Sarajevo to Slavonia, populations have continued to shift from where they are minorities through voluntary house exchanges or other property arrangements without necessarily entailing coercion. The Albanian population in the east and the number of the Slavonic Macedonian inhabitants in the west have been declining steadily. This has led some commentators to argue that Macedonia's future might best be secured by cantonisation on the Swiss model.

Of course, it cannot be denied that there have also been impressive achievements in the peacemaking process begun at Ohrid. The first 11 guerrillas to be pardoned by President Trajkovski under the amnesty agreement were released from Skopje's grim Sutka detention centre on 5 December 2002. In February 2003, Macedonia's Parliament finally ratified the amnesty promised in return for the NLA's surrender of its weapons. But tension was still high in the country on the ground and at the official level, as nationalists such as Boskovski and Georgievski predicted the NLA would eventually take up their remaining arms. In fact, radical ethnic Albanian nationalism was seriously discouraged by the terrorist attacks in the USA on 11 September 2001, as NLA leaders realised that they could expect little sympathy from their traditional US allies for further military adventures. But clashes were still going on intermittently in the volatile Tetovo region throughout 2002 and the first half of 2003.

Former insurgents refused to give up control of the north-western villages they hold even after legislators enacted the amnesty for them. The rebels want police checkpoints removed and more ethnic Albanian officers recruited into the police forces.

Splinter groups emerged after the NLA was officially disbanded. One is the Albanian National Army (or Armada), which claimed responsibility for several recent attacks on Macedonian security forces. Another was the Real National Liberation Army, led by a man who calls himself Laraska, Albanian for 'raven'.

'Our initial mission is not completed,' he said, 'we are not satisfied with the implementation of the peace agreement and constitutional amendments; the peace deal has undergone enormous changes.' He claims his faction has the support of most former NLA commanders and fighters, who share his belief that the NLA political leader, Ali Ahmeti, abandoned the cause and 'stopped fighting too soon'.

Macedonia remained riven by frustration and anger. Hundreds of people marched through the south-western resort town of Struga on 16 February 2002, demanding that the Government release six men accused of helping the rebels the previous year. The men had been jailed without charge for months.

Xhaferi, formerly one of the most respected ethnic Albanian leaders but increasingly under pressure because of his failing health, said the Macedonian Government's action – or inaction – would determine the rebel factions' next move. 'The non-existence of state authority and lack of law and order, in regions formerly controlled by the rebels could spell trouble in the spring,' Xhaferi said.[17]

In February 2002, Albanian rebels were reported to be buying millions of pounds worth of weapons with the proceeds of heroin smuggling from Afghanistan.[18] In March 2002, five people were killed when the Albanian National Army attacked the former NLA headquarters on the outskirts of Tetovo, the most serious rupture of the peace agreement since the killing of three police commandoes in November 2001. But apart from these incidents, the dire predictions by the nationalists of a new round of spring fighting in 2002 proved groundless.

Whether Macedonia turned its back on bitter internecine fighting depended in large part on the outcome of the parliamentary elections later in 2002, in which the Government could not appear to be too soft on the ethnic Albanian minority or too subservient to NATO. In the event, to the relief of western observers, it lost heavily in the polls in another proof of the Macedonians' impressive capacity to step back from the brink of confrontation.

The Together for Macedonia coalition, led by the opposition Social Democratic Alliance (SDSM), took some 40 per cent of the vote, well ahead of the 24 per cent won by Georgievski's VMRO. The Democratic Union for Integration (DUI), the political reincarnation of the National Liberation Army, won 12 per cent of the national vote by attracting well over half of the ethnic Albanian voters support. Electors responded to the SDSM campaign, accusing Georgievski's Government of widespread corruption, mismanaging the economy and exacerbating the 2001 crisis.

Macedonia and Bulgaria

Bulgarian influence surged in Macedonia during the heavy fighting in 2001, with Sofia supplying the hard-pressed Macedonian Army with ammunition and small arms. Georgievski's party traditionally has a close connection with Bulgaria, and his opponents charge that Bulgaria would like to see Macedonia split, with the Slav population coming under loose control from Sofia, perhaps on the model of the relationship between the Serb-run half of Bosnia, Republika Srpska, and Belgrade.

Bulgaria is also unique among East European Slav countries in the region in having a good relationship with ethnic Albanian leaders in western Macedonia and trade between Bulgaria and Kosovo in food and other goods has flourished. The Bulgarians have also worked hard at modernising road and rail links with Skopje, spreading the Bulgarian media's influence in Macedonia and bolstering military ties with the Macedonian security establishment.

Also in February 2002, Sofia reached a landmark agreement with Skopje on the delicate language issue and agreed that Macedonian police should be trained in Bulgaria. Relations between Macedonia and Bulgaria are now closer than for many years. Increased influence in Skopje is useful for the Bulgarian former king, Simeon II, as he seeks to keep the election promises that catapulted him to fame in 2001 as Bulgaria's Prime Minister and as the first former monarch to achieve power in East Europe.

Most Macedonians do not relish the prospect of becoming a Bulgarian puppet state as nationalists and a wide spectrum of the elite in Sofia would privately like, but some experts argue that the death knell may have been sounded for the more extreme aspects of the post-war separate Macedonian Slav culture. 'Sofia intellectuals have every reason to expect that as the artificial Titoist period "Macedonian" identity and totalitarian language reforms dictated by communism wither away, elements of traditional Bulgarian culture will reassert themselves in Macedonia.'[19]

Macedonia and Serbia

Serbian regional foreign policy after the demise of Milosevic was predicated on the need to restore domination of the Balkans together with Greece. The resolution of the Presevo conflict with the UCPMB in January 2001 and the reoccupation of the buffer zone with Kosovo by the Yugoslav Army were encouraging signs for the Belgrade Government of the late Zoran Djindjic, the Prime Minister, who called events in southern Serbia 'our first victory for ten years'. Djindjic was assassinated in March 2003 by members of the Serbian elite 'Red Berets' police special force unit, whose commanding officers were at the very least involved in training the Lions in Macedonia in 2001 if not active in operations during the conflict.

Belgrade had also obtained an agreement with Britain to share intelligence with Yugoslavia and Macedonia on ethnic Albanian insurgency and the recognition of the border between Macedonia and Serbia was another important diplomatic achievement. Macedonia was seen as an important link in the chain with Greece and relations were warm between Macedonian President Trajkovski and his then Yugoslav counterpart, Vojislav Kostunica, for whom the Macedonian head of state had once worked.

Albanians in Kosovo and Macedonia see Serbia and Greece as traditional enemies and one additional strategic motive for the former KLA leaders' decision to sponsor ethnic Albanian agitation in Macedonia was to keep the two apart. Serbia was weakened by the conflict because of the destabilisation of its southern border and any residual hopes of recovering control of Kosovo were dashed by the rise of Albanian influence.

Belgrade provided Skopje with limited military assistance during the crisis but Macedonia received more from Bulgaria, which increased its influence at the expense of Serbia, and from Ukraine.

The loss of influence meant that the Democratic Opposition of Serbia (DOS) reformers in office in Belgrade were unable to wield much influence in the Ohrid peace process to protect the rights of the 40,000 Serbs in Macedonia. Serbs by and large did not become involved in the fighting in the area of Kumanovo, where they are most concentrated, but Belgrade lost a chance to raise their problems, particularly those of the Serb Orthodox Church in Macedonia, in the Ohrid negotiations.

Serbian influence in Macedonia is likely to revive following the VMRO's defeat in the September 2002 general election by the Social Democratic party that has traditionally been linked to Belgrade. The Social Democratic victory may revive the power struggle between pro-Serb and pro-Bulgarian military and intelligence officials in the Defence and Interior ministries.

Macedonia and Albania

The political fall-out from the Macedonian crisis in Albania showed the extent to which the political establishment in Tirana was out of tune with the growing nationalist influences in Macedonia and the southern Balkans.

The Socialist Government of Ilir Meta assumed that the NLA would be crushed rapidly by Macedonian security forces and cooperated fully with NATO to contain the conflict. The start of the fighting in Tetovo coincided with the Albanian national election campaign and the right-wing Union for Victory coalition led by Sali Berisha received an immediate boost in the opinion polls, though not enough to win.

The Meta Government was criticised for not foreseeing the conflict, for not doing more to help refugees and for not preventing what was seen as the ethnic cleansing of Albanians in Bitola and areas near the Albanian border in late April 2001. The Government even allowed NATO to carry out some counter-insurgency activities against the NLA within Albania.

The anti-communist Albanians in Macedonia had few contacts with Tirana political circles while some Socialist politicians such as the Albanian Foreign Minister, Pascal Milo, had closer links to former communists in the Skopje Government.

Albanian Government policy, probably wisely, was to prevent getting involved in the crisis lest it spread into Albania itself. Tirana has traditionally seen a Slav-Albanian conflict in Macedonia as more potentially destabilising than conflict in Kosovo. For this reason, among others (such as the unsuitability of the terrain in the south compared with the mountains around Tetovo), the NLA decided against opening up a second front in southern Macedonia in May 2001, judging correctly that it would need the support of Tirana.

Some nationalists in Tirana urged the Government to send troops to Macedonia to protect the Albanians in the Bitola area against revenge attacks by paramilitaries but the Socialists judged that this would widen the crisis uncontrollably.

Criticism of inactivity in the Macedonian crisis led to Meta losing his position as Prime Minister in a Socialist power struggle after the election and to Milo being removed as Foreign Minister.

Macedonia and Greece

Macedonia's sensitivity for regional stability was highlighted in May 2002 when plans for the European Union to take over 'Operation Amber Fox' from NATO were thrown into doubt by a Greek-Turkish dispute over the terms of the mission. The takeover was supposed to go ahead in the autumn on the basis of the 'Berlin Plus' arrangements that spell out how the EU has assured access to NATO's planning, assets and capabilities.

Greece held up agreement on the Berlin plan by insisting it should also include a general code of conduct. Greece sought the same terms that the European Union gave Turkey, which lifted its objections to Berlin Plus after receiving assurances that the European Union would not use alliance assets to undermine Turkey's national, security or geographic interests.

The issue was picked up by the Greek opposition ahead of November 2002's municipal elections and made it difficult for Constantin Simitis, the Greek Prime Minister, to compromise with the EU. 'We are not against the European Security and Defence Policy,' the Greek Foreign Minister, George Panadreou, said, 'but given historical problems in the region, it would be good to have a code of conduct.'[20] Greece argued that Turkey, a member of NATO but not of the EU, should not have a say in the 15-nation bloc's defence policy.

The Macedonian crisis shocked Greek public opinion and disrupted important Greek trade routes north to Serbia as well as tourist routes south to Greece. The fighting meant that the Greek Government was unable to maintain its promise to public opinion that Greek influence in traditional alliance with Serbia in the southern Balkans would be restored after the fall of Milosevic to the level that was enjoyed before 1990.

Greece had been heavily involved with Britain in preparing the overthrow of Milosevic and gave strong support to President Vojislav Kostunica in Belgrade. Previous Greek policy of blockading Macedonia was seen to have been short-sighted in that it destabilised the Slav majority and prevented it dealing with the ethnic Albanian problem earlier.

Greek economic interests in Macedonia are strong. After 1995, Greece became the biggest foreign investor in Macedonia, owning the country's oil refinery north of Skopje, a brewery, cement plants and chains of supermarkets. Macedonia is dependent on oil from Thessaloniki and a new Greek plan for power station reconstruction proposed in 2002 would involve building new power stations fuelled exclusively with Greek lignite.

However, there still is considerable popular anti-Greek feeling in Macedonia and the crisis fuelled anti-Albanian feeling in Greece. Greece cooperated with the Macedonian Defence Ministry in permitting tanks and heavy weapons to be supplied to Macedonia through Greece, but this created fears that Athens was becoming over-committed to supporting an oppressive nationalist regime in Skopje.

The Greek military has had to relocate resources to the northern border and the Government has been obliged to cope with fears of an influx of refugees, a wider spillover of the conflict. Public opinion in Athens has questioned whether Greece over-committed itself in Macedonia economically and to what extent those economic interests are in jeopardy.

Superpower Interests in Macedonia

Mediation in the conflict, led by the EU, reinforced the position of Brussels as the main power broker in Macedonia. The USA continues to supply substantial military aid to Skopje, for instance by paying for training of the Macedonian Army by Military Professional Resources International. But Macedonian nationalists continue to view Washington with distrust because of what the VMRO perceives as the continued American sponsorship of Albanian nationalism in Kosovo.

Future relations between Macedonia and the USA are likely to be influenced significantly by the extent Washington makes progress in fostering its project for a trans-Balkan pipeline through Macedonia to secure the passage of oil from the Caspian sea. The project's manager, Edward Ferguson, the President and CEO of the Albanian, Macedonian and Bulgarian Oil Corporation (AMBO), which manages the project, said on 15 February 2002 that the concern is in 'regular discussions' with Chevron Texaco Corporation and ExxonMobil Corporation about building the 1.13 billion-dollar pipeline. AMBO, registered in the USA, has letters of acceptance from the governments of the three Balkan countries for the 898-kilometre (560-mile) underground pipeline. The main consumers of the oil carried through the trans-Balkan pipeline would be north-western Europe and the USA rather than the Mediterranean region.

'America's own crude resources are declining rapidly and it already imports over 50 per cent of its annual needs. Europe enters in a similar situation – reserves in the north are declining and it will start running out of oil supplies around 2010.'[21] AMBO was confident that another planned 607 million-dollar pipeline sending crude from Russia to Greece via Bulgaria would not threaten its own project as the two had targeted different investors and consumers.

Russia established its influence in Macedonia in May 1992 by becoming one of the first countries to grant full diplomatic recognition to Skopje. Moscow has closely watched the rise of western influence in Macedonia and is likely to increase its contacts with Skopje through Ukraine, the Government's main arms supplier, which played host to President Trajkovski in late September 2001 in Kiev at celebrations to mark the tenth birthday of an independent Ukraine, ceremonies also attended by the Russian President, Vladimir Putin. Russia complained that it should have been consulted at an earlier stage about NATO intervention in Macedonia.

Few observers expect Russia to try to restore the influence it enjoyed in the Balkans in the nineteenth century. However, Moscow is likely to provide a major stumbling block to any real attempt to create an independent Kosovo. Such a state would have to be approved by the UN Security Council, where Russia would be likely to use its veto to avoid setting a precedent for an independent Chechnya and would almost certainly be supported by a further veto from China for fear of encouraging Tibetan independence.

After Ohrid

Western mediation (in the form of repeated visits by Javier Solana and Lord Robertson and the work of the special envoys for the EU and the USA, François Léotard and James Pardew), together with the disarmament operation, brought a halt to the Macedonian conflict. Léotard's successor, Alain Le Roy, has won praise for his work in implementing Ohrid, although, as we shall see, this has been uneven.

In late December 2001, Macedonia's political problems no longer seemed to be the country's main concern, as the former Yugoslav republic battled the bitterest winter for decades. Some 500 policemen from the elite Lions and Tigers units were deployed in towns throughout the country to clear streets blocked by nearly a yard of snow. 'Our weapons now are shovels,' said one Lions officer busy removing snow from clogged lanes that lead to a boulevard in Skopje. 'I'm not trained for this, but it's a job too.'[22]

But Macedonian democratic processes remain extremely vulnerable. Macedonia is still a long way from being an open society. Much of the media is state controlled, and independent journalists are subject to harassment and threats from the authorities. Additionally, communist-era habits of surveillance of opposition politicians have not died out in Macedonia. A telephone conversation between Crvenkovski and Xhaferi, the leaders of the opposition Social Democratic Union (SDSM) and the Party of Democratic Albanians (DPA), was leaked after the peace agreement to a television station that accused them of conspiring against national interests.

In January 2001, the Social Democrats presented evidence of the unlawful tapping of 150 telephone conversations involving prominent politicians, journalists and foreign embassies between September and November 2000. The Interior Minister, Dosta Dimovska, resigned after a parliamentary investigation stopped short of allocating responsibility for the bugging. The bugging scandal resurfaced in 2003, with President Trajkovski coming under heavy media fire for supporting Mrs Dimovska.

A tremendous weakness in the philosophy behind Ohrid was that it was based on the hypothesis that there is an efficient state that can be resuscitated as a democratic framework for everyday life. 'Most important of all, Ohrid does not fully address and question the survival of communist-period *modus operandi* in the Defence and Interior ministries. The power base of Slav-Macedonian extremism remains completely intact.'[23]

As legislative elections approached, Boskovski and Georgievski showed no sign of intending to disband the paramilitaries, who were generally expected to intimidate the VMRO's political opponents. The presidential aide explained:

> The political mentor of the Lions unit is the Prime Minister. Boskovski is only his operational hand. They are using patriotic rhetoric and whipping up anti-Albanian feeling even though they are in power with the DPA. Every possible move taken by Boskovski is approved by Georgievski. He is a kind of despotic leader. He's changed the composition of the Government frequently. Anyone who seems like a serious contender for the party leadership is simply removed. It's probably the most corrupted Government in Europe.

By the summer of 2002, Macedonia's biggest and most influential businessmen were already being pressed by the VRMO to make campaign contributions or face intimidation. In the end, however, the nationalists underwent a massive defeat in the polls.

President Trajkovski sought to increase public awareness of the threat to democracy, for example making a major speech in March 2002 denouncing corruption and organised crime. Government officials responded by ordering criminal proceedings against Anatol Taci, a presidential advisor, for articles he had written that were published in the newspaper *Dnevnik*. 'That was a clear and direct message to the president,' the presidential aide said.

International Assistance

In December 2001, UN agencies in Macedonia appealed to donors for contributions of 41 million dollars for contributions to its 2002 conflict relief operations in the tiny Balkan republic. Amin Awad, the UN humanitarian coordinator for Macedonia, said the money would mostly be used to assist an estimated 100,000 displaced people and others affected by the conflict.

The agencies said in a report that besides the displaced people, some 260,000 people in Macedonia would benefit indirectly from activities to stabilise and build confidence between communities. Funding needs included 400,000 dollars for food, 8.4 million dollars for agriculture, 4.86 million for health, 3.85 million for family shelter and 3.5 million for education.

The Macedonian Government estimated that Gross Domestic Product fell by 18 per cent in 2001 as part of severe losses by the economy because of the conflict.

The international community skilfully used its control over finance to curb nationalist excesses, for example cancelling a donors' conference for Macedonia initially scheduled for autumn 2001 until after Parliament had agreed to ratify Ohrid. In practice, this has meant that Macedonia has more than ever become a de facto protectorate held together by NATO and foreign financial assistance.

The requested cash was only pledged at an EU donors' conference that in the end was held in March 2002. International donors exceeded Skopje's expectations, pledging 515 million dollars (592 million euro). The funding agreed by the World Bank, the European Commission and 40 countries included 241 million dollars for general economic development and 247 million dollars to finance the budget and reconstruction.[24]

To what extent the aid is playing a role in healing the scars of the conflict through reconstruction and kick-starting the war-torn economy, which was already strained severely by the embargoes imposed by Greece and by the West on Serbia, remains to be seen, however. A weary western diplomat in Skopje commented:

> A lot of it's just filling in holes rather than building anything new. Much of it will be used to pay for gaps in the budget for last year's defence expenditure. They need people to come here and open factories. But what foreign investment there is tends to be asset stripping, not long term.

Security assistance is essential for Macedonia. NATO will continue to reinforce controls on the Kosovo border but seems to be powerless to prevent a considerable flow of weapons, drugs, arms and people being smuggled in from the province. The USA has pledged to support Macedonian police reform, training of ethnic Albanian police officers, the return of refugees and the new Southeast European University set up in Tetovo to provide higher education in the Albanian language.

But whether these measures and the activities of the OSCE and European Union's 180 peace monitors will be sufficient to overcome the tension between the two communities is highly doubtful. Indeed, the presence of the monitors in western Macedonia, where Macedonian refugees have been slow to return, has to some extent led to a de facto separation between the two communities on a scale unknown before the conflict.

The likely lifespan of the Ohrid peace agreement was highly questionable. The small German-led NATO force in place since the end of the weapons collection operation was heavily overstretched and quintessentially represented a continuation of a German operation that had been based at Tetovo for some years dating back to the Kosovo war. The Germans handed over leadership to a Dutch contingent of 350 in June and the total strength of Task Force Fox was cut from 1,000 to 700. NATO subsequently handed over these duties to a small European Union force.

This lack of strength raises the question of whether NATO and the international community would be able to enforce the peace if community relations deteriorated rapidly or unexpectedly. The experience of Srebrenica in Bosnia, where Dutch peacekeepers were unable to prevent the massacre of 8,000 Muslim men and boys by Bosnian Serb forces, has shown the risk of inadequate force in peacekeeping in the Balkans.

Ohrid left the ethnic Macedonian Slavs as one of the most heavily armed civilian populations in the Balkans. In June 2002, Ali Ahmeti, the National Liberation Army leader, launched a new political party, the Democratic Union for Integration, intent on winning the support of those who had supported the two existing ethnic Albanian parties. The enthusiastic reception given to his political debut reflects ethnic Albanian concerns that only Ahmeti may be able to organise the self-defence of the community if Ohrid collapses.

The West cannot afford to be smug about Macedonia.

11 Implementation of Ohrid

There's no other profit, nor loss, be it from a defeat or a victory. For whoever remained sane after a victory? And who ever gained any experience from a defeat?
Mesa Selimovic, The Fortress

IN APRIL 2002, I returned to Macedonia to report on the implementation of the Ohrid peace settlement.

From a tour of Tetovo and surrounding villages it was clear that the 'former' NLA ethnic Albanian gunmen had partially rearmed, controlling a swathe of territory in the area and, diplomatic sources said, others around Gostivar and Kumanovo. The pursuit of a plan for ethnically mixed Macedonian and Albanian police units to re-enter those areas had been plagued by setbacks but was making progress.

Hundreds of ethnic Albanians threw up roadblocks in villages around Tetovo in April to prevent police patrolling in protest at the refusal by Macedonian authorities to release two former NLA men accused of abducting and sexually abusing a group of Macedonian road-workers at the height of the fighting. Such protests are organised by the Coordinating Council of Arrested Ex-NLA Men, which argues that there should be no exceptions to the amnesty law, although this does not in fact apply to prisoners accused of war crimes.

'We've stopped police deployment in all villages today,' said the Council's president, Xevad Abdullaqin, an old-style Marxist militant, who claimed:

> They arrested two of our men, Fadir Faraji and Shkodren Driei, and held them for six months without charging them. The ICTY is not interested in these two guys but the court is very interested in

Ljuboten, in Boskovski. We have called on the whole population to stop the deployment. We will continue the protest until the two are released or it is explained why they are in jail. Without European standards of justice there can be no democratic progress. No money from abroad can substitute for freedom. Such violations of the Ohrid agreement could bring us to a new war.

In Semsevo, a farming village 15 miles north-east of Tetovo, inhabitants drinking Turkish coffee in the local bar refused to answer reporters' questions about why the planned police redeployment has not taken place. The villagers' eyes were blank with fear as small boys led mules along the dirt track outside where a black and red Albanian flag fluttered on a telephone pole.

Monitors for the OSCE explained that Albanian gunmen in Semsevo had kidnapped a Macedonian reserve policeman, Dusko Simovski, and badly beaten him up. 'They tried to make him sign a statement that he was planning to approach the house of a former NLA battalion commander, Isar Samyu, that he was going to kill him,' said Aytekin Aktas, the OSCE Tetovo station chief, a calm and efficient Turk. 'The police want to go into the village to arrest these people. The Albanians oppose it. We are trying to speak to the population to explain that the police should go in to investigate it.' The incident was typical of problems implementing the Ohrid accord, he said. 'Sometimes you talk to the Albanians' leaders for four or five hours to let the police into villages. At the end they say no.'

The situation was improving but remained very fragile, he added. The Albanian population know they control the territory and are always making new demands, for example that the police should wear Albanian-language shirts. The Macedonian population is 'really disturbed' and in case of a potential conflict would leave the area, he argued. 'There are many weapons here. It seems that disarmament was not successful or that there is a need for a second round.'

In December 2001, police killed an Albanian farmer near Semsevo. The Lions were the main suspects for the killing, the OSCE officer said. 'The Lions were removed from that point. But on Friday I saw two APCs full of Lions moving around. The police still need time to believe that there is not going to be a renewed conflict.'

Craig Jenness, ambassador to the OSCE mission in Skopje, acknowledges that there is a general lack of confidence between the two communities. 'The Albanian community sees them [the police] as the instrument they fought against during the war. So it's going to take a lot of time before they treat them as their own.'[1]

Jenness said that Ahmeti's move toward mainstream politics left a vacuum in the leadership of the National Liberation Army into which more hardline commanders have stepped. But Jenness also said that such groups do not appear strong enough to overturn the peace process. The vast majority of people are tired of fighting and want to get on with their lives.

The effect of population displacement during the conflict is another major obstacle to a return to normal living. The current population trends raise the question of whether Macedonia might soon need a Cyprus-type, 'Green Line' peacekeeping framework. Some 70,000 Macedonian civilians fled Tetovo and other ethnically mixed regions for Skopje. The UNHCR is trying to persuade them to return by rebuilding homes, repairing schools and providing bus services. A further 70,000 ethnic Albanian civilians fled, most of them to Kosovo. All but 7,000 ethnic Albanians had returned but at least 19,000 Macedonians had not, a UNHCR official in Tetovo, Senni Bulbul, also a Turk, explained.

'It is unrealistic to expect everyone to return,' he concludes. 'Some of them will never come back. For some of them there is nothing to come back for.' The Jugocrom aluminium factory at the town of Juginovice, for example, was closed after privatisation and thousands of people were dismissed. Many Macedonians felt better off in refugee centres set up in Skopje where they receive three meals a day. Others with children at school in the capital would not consider moving back until the end of the academic year in June.

We visited Neproshteno, an ethnically mixed village of 1,200 people, 15 miles north of Tetovo. Some villagers, in a play on words, call it *neprosteno*, meaning 'unforgiving' in Macedonian. About 200 Macedonian families left during the conflict but only 40 had returned. 'There was fighting here, 28 Macedonian houses were destroyed by shelling,' said an elderly Macedonian, who refused to give his name, in a dilapidated village shop empty except for chocolate and plum brandy.

> We lost 58 cars, all our tractors and our television sets. I came back here on 5 January. From August, I was in Skopje. In the autumn we came back here in convoys to collect some possessions. We only stayed here during the day. Most of the people in Skopje only come back here at the weekend.

> The Albanians have too many weapons. Even underage kids can kill you for fun. NATO moves too slowly. Perhaps it will be all right in 15 years.

Is the Government doing enough to help them? 'We curse them,' another Macedonian said, his friends nodding agreement. 'If it depended on the Government nothing would happen. We know that we are dependent on European help.'
Would they vote in the elections?

We are going to think about it because nobody from Skopje helped us here. The politicians never came to see us. During the last elections I wasn't called to vote. I went to the polling station and they said there was no need to vote because it already was fixed for the VMRO. Nobody's interested in the poor people. The Government and the MPs only think about themselves.

The previous summer, NLA gunmen kidnapped three Macedonian men from the village who still were missing, the villagers said. A fourth man was found shot dead in his backyard. The three, Kirsto Gorgovski, 68, and Cvetko and Vasko Mihailovski, aged 54 and 35, were among 12 Macedonians who disappeared and were believed to have been kidnapped by the NLA in a case that set off a nationwide furore similar to that over the raped road-workers. The fourth man found dead was Stojan Mihailovski, a cousin of Vasko.

Macedonian special police had set up sandbagged positions in the fields surrounding Neproshteno. On the Albanian side of the village, which is divided into ethnic areas by a small stream, farmers such as Veb Zulbehar, 48, complained that the police presence meant they could not sow this year's crop of corn, potatoes and tobacco. 'We worked the fields last year but the police took one of us,' he said. 'We blocked the roads and they released him.' Many of the police in the fields were Macedonian farmers from the village called up as reservists. Others were members of the Lions, OSCE sources say.

A Swedish reporter, Hans-Henrik Ronnow, and I drove up the winding mountainous road above Tetovo to Sipkovica, the former NLA headquarters where Ali Ahmeti was preparing to launch his political career as a war hero in the general elections set for September. The drive brought back some poignant memories of the battle for Tetovo the previous year. Since covering the conflict, I had become deeply depressed. For weeks, I was unable to string a written sentence together. The previous year's adventures had been intense, but Macedonia had disappeared from western media attention, eclipsed by September 11th and Afghanistan.

My state of mind was not unique. Even journalists who survived numerous risky assignments physically were prone to battle fatigue while trying to cope with the reality of peace. Juan Carlos Gumucio, a close friend from Rome and Lebanon, became deeply disillusioned with what he saw as modern journalism's ignoble tendencies after he was fired by his daily newspaper for 'insubordination'; he shot himself in his native Bolivia. Bill Frost, another friend who worked in Vukovar, Croatia and Bosnia, died 18 months earlier when he lost a battle against cocaine and heroin.

In Sipkovica, my gloom began to lift, blown away by the cheerful camaraderie of Hans-Henrik and his driver Deny, a fearless ethnic Macedonian. We met two German liaison officers from Task Force Fox (TFF), the 900-strong NATO peacekeeping force in Macedonia, who had been deployed in an Albanian house in the village to try to prevent further clashes such as the fighting between the ANA and former NLA gunmen with heavy machine guns and rocket-propelled grenades that left four people dead in nearby Mala Recica. One of the two, Frank Ohden, admitted the NLA veterans were heavily armed in Sipkovica. 'The ANA would grab into a hornets' nest if they started anything here.'

Another 'harvest' arms collection was being discussed for before the election, but it would be a mistake to limit it to the Albanian community, he added. 'It might backfire but it would be a good idea if the weapons were not used as part of the electoral process. A harvest is needed for the Macedonian community. They handed out arms to everyone and his dog.'

His comrade was in Skopje in 1999. Anti-NATO feeling had diminished by comparison with the level of animosity during the Kosovo crisis, he opined. 'In '99, they were throwing stones at NATO vehicles. There's none of that now.'

> The peace process is going slowly but it's getting there. There have been teething problems with the amnesty law. Many people have been amnestied and some have not and if the reasoning is a bit obscure you will always have problems. People want to know why their brother has not been amnestied.

The police re-entered Sipkovica on 1 April. 'It has worked since then. There were some minor grudges but they have been sorted out. The villagers were a bit suspicious at first. What they don't need is people running around with semi-automatic weapons.'

The Macedonian Army was deployed on Cale Mountain, formerly another NLA stronghold. The army garrisoned at Popova Shapka, formerly Macedonia's most important ski resort. 'People with holiday homes are upset.' An Italian army captain who was part of a TFF demining unit, Stefano Rugge, was killed a month later when the vehicle he was in ran over an anti-tank mine near Popova Shapka. The death of Rugge, 28, was front-page news in Italy. The captain was a native of Lecce, the beautiful city known as the 'Florence of the south'. A majority of Italy's peacekeepers still come from the relatively impoverished *mezzogiorno*. Rugge, a member of the 10th regiment of Genio guastatori (engineers) based at Cremona, one of 160 Italian soldiers in the TFF force, was due to be married to his fiancée, Lucia, on 25 May.

A German officer in the vehicle was wounded. The incident happened as a TFF convoy made up of three German Wolf vehicles and an ambulance carried out a reconnaissance mission in the area, which was where two European observers – a Slovak and a Norwegian – were killed in another mine blast in 2001. Rugge was navigating in the lead vehicle with the German soldier at the wheel. He was treated by a Greek army doctor travelling in the ambulance who managed to reach him in spite of the possibility of other mines going off, but it proved impossible to save him. Because of the terrain and declining visibility, Rugge's body could only be recovered 16 hours after the explosion.

Il Messaggero of Rome noted that Macedonia 'is a country that is still living through a difficult situation. The Government of Skopje wants to join NATO but at the same time its army is acquiring massive quantities of arms from ex-Warsaw Pact countries to use in clashes with Albanian guerrillas.' Rugge, a career officer, had been on his second tour of duty in the Balkans, previously serving in Bosnia. He was the 17th Italian soldier to die in Balkan peacekeeping.

On the road back to Tetovo, we passed a mixed police patrol on its way out of Sipkovica, its vehicle escorted by a TFF Land Rover with another carrying OSCE observers. Their presence was perhaps symbolic but still reassuring. In the event of a serious flare-up of violence, it is unclear what the rules of engagement would be for such patrols and their escorts, however.

Shooting breaks out regularly in Tetovo, where a curfew was lifted in March. Macedonian police remain hunkered inside their barracks. The feeling that Macedonians have become observers of fighting in their own cities has deeply dented public morale. The latest incident took place at the Dora Café, the headquarters of Menduh Thaci, the deputy leader of the DPA with a reputation for brutal racketeering and control of much of the smuggling trade from Kosovo.

Thaci is known to hope to obtain parliamentary immunity for his business interests and much of the intra-Albanian shooting is linked to his efforts to maintain hegemony over illegal trafficking. Ahmeti opposed Thaci gaining power on the ground that the Albanians need fresh faces. 'It's a harsh battle in which machine guns and rocket launchers are going to be used again,' a senior Macedonian official said.

Also active in Tetovo was Castriot Hadji Reja, the leader of an extreme ethnic Albanian political party who argues Macedonia ought to be transformed into a bi-national state through federalisation.

On the motorway back to Skopje, we passed what was left of the motel at Celopek, blown up in August with its two Macedonian employees inside, tied to pillars. The concrete ruins are a stark reminder of that summer's violence.

Carla del Ponte was expected in the capital, which was abuzz with speculation that she would issue indictments for the killings at Ljuboten, where exhumations of the dead Albanians were under way under the auspices of the ICTY.

The main political parties had begun gearing up for the general election in September. The VMRO party of the then Prime Minister, Ljubco Georgievski, had already begun campaigning on an aggressive nationalist plank. Opinion polls correctly predicted an easy victory by the opposition Social Democratic Party (SDMS), largely because of popular disenchantment with corruption.

To find out more about the political situation, I visited Zoran Jachev, the Executive Director of the influential NGO Forum, which is sponsored by the Soros Foundation, together with the newspaper also called *Forum*. Zoran expressed the fear that the VMRO may use the fresh intra-Albanian violence as an excuse for widespread intimidation of electors by the paramilitaries. He said:

> The ANA can be an ace in the sleeves of Georgievski and Boskovski to start the conflict up again and activate the crazy Lions. I'm afraid that we will have a Lebanisation of Macedonia. In a worst case scenario we'll have a state on paper but real power will be in the hands of the paramilitaries.

Zoran was convinced that only a Macedonian version of Serbia's OTPOR, the popular student opposition movement that was instrumental in the overthrow of Milosevic, can save the country.

Eight months after Ohrid, Macedonians remained deeply suspicious of NATO's intentions. The part of the peace agreement that was most painful for Macedonians was the amnesty for NLA guerrillas, a Skopje-based western envoy said. 'They can't see why they were forced to grant it.' VMRO patriotic propaganda claims that only the Lions, not

NATO troops, prevented the NLA from destroying the country. At the time, it seemed, ironically, that the nationalists' best hope of winning the election would be for Mr Boskovski to be indicted by the ICTY.

'If only one Macedonian is indicted and goes to The Hague but no Albanians are prosecuted it would confirm every fear that the Macedonians have that the international community is trying to destroy them,' the diplomat said.

Concern in the diplomatic community about Boskovski's tactics was heightened in March 2002. The police said they had shot and killed seven men described by the Macedonian Government as members of a terrorist cell that was planning to attack the US, German and British embassies in Skopje. Police said that at least five of the dead were Pakistani or Middle Eastern. Authorities had been following the men since detaining two Jordanians and Bosnians in February and seizing computer disks with information on embassies and government installations in Macedonia, officials claimed. Boskovski said that 'they planned attacks on important buildings, foreign diplomats most probably from the US, Germany and the UK – those that were involved in the fight against global terrorism'.[2]

Authorities said that the men were killed on the northern outskirts of Skopje after the police attempted to detain them. When the police fired warning shots, the men returned fire, leading to a shoot-out, officials said.

It was the second time since September 11th that authorities said they had prevented an attack on a US facility in the Balkans, where thousands of American troops are peacekeepers. US forces and Bosnian police arrested a number of North African and Middle Eastern men in Sarajevo who were allegedly targeting the US Embassy in Bosnia and may also have planned attacks on the US military, officials said.

In the weeks after the shooting of the seven in Skopje, however, serious doubts surfaced over whether the dead men really had been terrorists. The police said that they had seized automatic weapons, pistols, Chinese hand grenades and a rocket-propelled grenade launcher with ammunition. They said that they had also found more than a dozen new uniforms bearing the insignia of the ethnic Albanian National Liberation Army. Officials said the men killed had been wearing civilian clothes.

Diplomats suspect that the men at worst may have been involved in arms smuggling. The uniforms appeared to have been planted in the truck. The NLA denied any connection to the men. Evidence emerged that at least one was a Pakistani immigrant on his way to Greece, where he had hoped to join a brother and find work.

The official version of the incident bewildered other observers such
as Hugh Poulton, who commented: 'The evidence produced by
Macedonian authorities was highly suspect and human rights groups
like Amnesty International suspect this was an extra-judicial execution
(as do foreign diplomats).'[3]

Repeated requests we made to Boskovski for an interview were refused
by his office, confirming his international image as a man unfriendly or
indifferent to the media. Instead, I was warmly received by Stevo
Pendarovski, then President Trajkovski's national security advisor.

Other heads of state in the Balkans occupy grandiose buildings.
President Tudjman surrounded his sprawling palace in Zagreb with a
splendid Lilliputian-style guard in colourful uniforms, for example.
But President Trajkovski and his Cabinet operated from a nondescript
floor of offices at the back of the Macedonian Parliament building,
modest surrounds that some would say reflected his lack of real power.

Pendarovski estimates that during the conflict 17 per cent of
Macedonian territory, some 120 villages in total, was in NLA hands.
Patrolling had begun in 100 villages, so far only for two hours at a
time, but this would gradually be increased under the re-entry plan.
'The presence of the police force is not enough to control the territory,'
he conceded.

> Their task is quite different – community policy, making contact
> with the villagers, asking about their problems and dealing with
> local crime. If we wanted to control that territory, anti-terrorist units
> would have to be used. Until now we haven't used any anti-terrorist
> police because the situation is very fragile.

In some areas, police deployment was blocked because villagers wanted
more local Albanians in the police force.

> So far we have 500 Albanians in the police. Next year it will be
> 1,000. We are aware it's not meaningful control. But ten months
> ago we were not able to feel secure in the outskirts of Skopje let
> alone Sipkovica.

> Everyone is aware that there is a long healing process ahead of us.
> We can't just cover up the wounds and say nothing happened.

In spite of the intra-Albanian fighting, he was optimistic that no
major conflagration was imminent. Most Albanians were waiting for
Parliament to approve eight or nine laws foreseen under Ohrid on

issues such as Albanian language rights, minority rights in identity documents and citizenship rights. 'They are in the middle of procedures to improve their rights so they have no reason to start fighting.'

Because of the election campaign, the Government had dragged its feet on implementing the legislation envisaged by Ohrid. The president's office expected that only pressure from NATO, the EU and the OSCE would lead to the laws being passed. If they were not passed, Macedonia risked forfeiting IMF and World Bank assistance. The 309 million euro earmarked by the EU were also conditional on implementing Ohrid.

Foreign aid is badly needed to kick-start the ailing economy. Unemployment currently runs at 30 per cent and most young Macedonians are trying to emigrate, many to new destinations such as New Zealand or Manitoba in northern Canada, in spite of its harsh climate.

In June 2002, the pressure to obtain access to the aid bore fruit when Macedonia's Parliament approved nine new laws to make Albanian an official language as envisaged under Ohrid. The laws make it possible to use the language in all government matters. Deputies voted on each law separately, but the central law in the package, which dealt with the use of Albanian in government settings, was passed by 88 votes to 3, with the remaining deputies abstaining.[4]

The 120-seat Parliament had debated the package for weeks. The laws also include a separate regulation calling for the use of both languages in a census in November.

The kind of bitterness still affecting the country was underlined when a workshop to curb the problem of football violence in Macedonia held in June 2002 ended with a punch-up, guns being fired and 30 of the participants being arrested.

Everything had gone well at the government-sponsored initiative, which was timed to coincide with the World Cup. Dozens of fans of the country's six main teams had gathered at a lakeside hotel in Ohrid for a grand finale dinner. Organisers of the event, called Stop Violence, were about to declare it had been a resounding success. The next thing anyone knew, fists were flying and gunshots rang out. Fortunately nobody was seriously injured. The fight apparently broke out over which team had the better players.

In March, a policeman had been shot and seriously wounded in Skopje after a day of fighting between rival fans. But the violence was about ethnicity as much as about football. The fighting was between rival groups of ethnic Macedonian and ethnic Albanian fans. The match was between two local teams: Vardar, which is mainly supported by ethnic Macedonians, and Sloga, which is mainly supported by ethnic Albanians.

Unlike Jachev and his fellow idealists at *Forum*, the embattled President's staff nourished little hope of an OTPOR-like third force emerging in Macedonia. 'We don't have enough uncorrupted people. You would need thousands and thousands of people. We have more than 50 parties here but we don't have enough able people.'

Macedonians have looked enviously at the situation in Bulgaria, where the exiled king, Simeon II, returned home and set up a new party that transformed the political landscape. 'We don't have enough good human material for a meteor to come down like that in Macedonia,' Pendarovski said. 'The exit from the Gordian knot could be to change the existing elite in the two main parties. We need to have a good executive, a good administration and good penal law. That will be enough if it is applied properly.' Pendarovski argues convincingly that time is running out for Macedonia. 'We are becoming a country without prospects,' he said. 'Some people say this election is the last chance for the democratic process in Macedonia.'

At *Forum*, I met Saso Ordanoski, the magazine's Editor-in-Chief. In spite of spats with Boskovski and the Government, he was optimistic about Macedonian democracy, or at least more so than his analyst colleague Zoran. 'I don't consider what Boskovski says to be a specific intimidation of the press,' he chortled.

> He's not intimidating me as a journalist – it's just his style. As a journalist, I consider it my duty to report Boskovski's threats without deciding whether he's a lunatic or just unbalanced. Overall, they are not able to intimidate the press and 80 per cent of the press is against the Government.

The treatment of the press is only part of a wider problem, he argued. 'It's not just the press, it is the public who they are trying to manipulate. They are afraid of the public, running the country like a company.' The then prime minister's bizarre style was a root cause of the modern Macedonian malaise, he added.

> In three out of five press conferences that he gives, Georgievski has a very tough quarrel with the journalists. He is frustrated, he doesn't know how to communicate. Basically, he and Boskovski have considered us at *Forum* as being part of the CIA. That's a metaphor: They think that we are an arm of the West. It's fear of something that they can't control. They are not afraid of the opposition media because when they cut a deal with the opposition they can cut a deal with its press too.

Unlike Zoran, the editor was opposed to disbanding the Lions, arguing it would only make them less accountable.

> What we did with the Albanians was to rehabilitate KLA criminals. Now if we dissolve the Lions we are going to do the opposite, we are going to have 500 to 800 armed men who will be a party militia of the VMRO. At least now they wear uniforms and have some kind of chain of command and can be held responsible. If they shoot someone in a restaurant now, we know they are Lions.

The Lions were a necessary evil, he argued, and it was better to use criminal thugs as a deterrent against future ethnic Albanian adventures than innocent conscripts. 'Why send 19-year-old recruits to fight criminals on the border when we have our own criminals?'

Like so many observers, he concurs that what happens in Kosovo is the great unknown in the future of Macedonia. 'We do have some democratic achievements here. If the situation regionally becomes better we are on the right track. We are pretty much on the way out if there is no destabilisation from Kosovo, southern Serbia or Albania.'

The President of the Skopje branch of the Helskinki committee on human rights, Mirjana Naycheska, who Boskovski had denounced as 'the No. 1 enemy of the state', had a more pessimistic point of view.

> The main abuse now is the abuse of the right of life because there are plenty of people who have no possibility to survive. There are 450,000 unemployed in a population of 2 million. There is a possibility for huge manipulation. People don't believe in democracy or a state of law because they never saw democracy or state of law. There is still a lot of hate speaking. There are still abuses by the Macedonian police reservists.

She had been working on a case of two Macedonian Muslims (not ethnic Albanians) who were very severely beaten in the village of Oktisi near Struga 'just because they were Muslims'.

> This is a very strange case, because Macedonian Muslims are very quiet people. They were afraid to go to court. There are many cases like that. The communities remain apart. It's almost impossible now not to have effective ethnic cleansing in many parts of Macedonia. It's a pity. For centuries it was a multi-cultural society. People were living together and now it is almost impossible.

In spite of such pessimism, President Trajkovski over the following two years presided patiently over the implementation of the Ohrid agreement's concessions to the ethnic Albanians. But the untimely death of the liberal statesman in an air crash in Bosnia as he and his aides travelled to an international conference in the city of Mostar on 26 February 2004 seemed likely to revive instability in Macedonia. At this time, a recent nationalist resurgence in Serbia had raised fears that ethnic Albanian militants in Kosovo might again stir up discontent in Macedonia as a way to put pressure on the international community to give Kosovo independence from Belgrade.

These fears were heightened when the worst ethnic violence in four years broke out in Kosovo in March 2004, leaving at least 31 ethnic Albanians and Serbs dead as fierce fighting raged in the divided city of Kosovska Mitrovica, Serb churches were torched by ethnic Albanians across the province and Serbian demonstrators in Serbia proper reacted by attacking mosques in Belgrade and Nis. Thousands of extra peacekeeping troops were deployed in the province, and Macedonia closed its borders with Kosovo.

President Trajkovski's last official act before boarding the flight to Mostar had been to sign Macedonia's application to join the European Union. Even before his state funeral was held in Skopje, hardline nationalist ethnic Macedonians in the media began pouring scorn on western appreciations of the dead president, arguing that he had received western support mainly because he was a 'vassal' of the United States of America.

The dramatic circumstances of the crash, in which Trajkovski's fate remained unknown for two days as Bosnian rescue teams and NATO peacekeepers struggled to breach uncleared minefields to reach the rugged area where the small, 26-year-old presidential aircraft went down, seemed to symbolise the difficulties afflicting true peacemakers in the Balkans even when death touches them on the shoulder.

Western observers were acutely aware that in 2001 Trajkovski, by his courage and sheer force of character, could be said to have headed off a fifth Balkan war virtually single-handed. Now the maturity of ordinary Macedonians would be tested again as they were called on to elect a successor capable of defending the country from warlords and rebels on the path to stability and economic prosperity.

Chronology

1995	Greece lifts embargo, Macedonia admitted to OSCE, Council of Europe.
1996	Federal Republic of Yugoslavia recognises FYROM. Mandate of UNPREDEP peacekeepers on Macedonian borders extended. Military cooperation agreement with NATO signed.
1998	Nationalist VMRO-DPMNE wins elections, forms coalition Government.
1999 January–February	New Government authorises pre-deployment of NATO troops to enforce Kosovo agreement.
February	Macedonia recognises Taiwan, China breaks diplomatic relations with Skopje, vetoes extension of UNPREDEP mandate. Macedonia and Bulgaria sign normalisation agreement.
March	UNPREDEP mandate ends.
March–May	Massive influx of Kosovo refugees as NATO launches airstrikes against FRY.
March	US Army border patrol captured by Serb forces.
June	Macedonia agrees to deployment of additional 14,000 NATO troops. KFOR troops deployed to Macedonia.
November	US President Bill Clinton visits Macedonia.
December	Macedonia and Greece sign defence and aid agreements.
2000 February–June	Macedonian Army goes on heightened alert on border with Kosovo.
October	Association and Stabilisation agreement concluded with EU.
2001 January 22	One policeman killed in a grenade attack on a Macedonian police station in the predominantly ethnic Albanian village of Tearce.
February 17	First clashes between government forces and ethnic Albanian rebels of the self-styled National Liberation Army near Tanusevci.
February 23	Macedonia and FRY sign border agreement.

March 4	Three Macedonian soldiers killed in fighting near northern border.
March 8	Rebels attack government convoy, killing driver. NATO allows return of Yugoslav forces into part of buffer zone around Kosovo.
March 14	Rebels attack police in Tetovo; 10 civilians are wounded.
March 15	Rebels move to within 12 miles of capital, Skopje.
March 20	Rebels issue ultimatum demanding talks to transform state into a confederation.
March 21	Rebels announce they will hold fire following a government ultimatum.
March 22	The President, Boris Trajkovski, announces tough action against rebels. Security forces launch offensive near Tetovo with little success.
April 28	Eight soldiers and police are killed in rebel ambush.
May 3	Government offensive in Kumanovo area also fails.
May 13	Government of national unity is formed, including two major ethnic Albanian parties; political feuds start.
June 8	Rebels take control of Aracinovo just outside Skopje.
June 15–20	Negotiations between Macedonian and Albanian Government parties fail.
June 24	After more fighting, the EU Security Chief, Javier Solana, wins a cease-fire. NATO evacuates rebels from Aracinovo without disarming them.
June 28	The EU appoints François Léotard as Macedonian envoy; he joins US envoy James Pardew at peace talks.
July 5	Another ceasefire under UN auspices, but fighting persists around Tetovo.
July 19	Albanian parties suspend negotiations. Two EU monitors and a translator killed in mine explosion.
July 22–24	Fierce fighting around Tetovo.

	Government accuses NATO of pro-rebel bias; foreign embassies attacked in Skopje.
July 28	Peace talks resume in Ohrid.
August 5	After agreement on Albanian as second official language in ethnic Albanian-dominated areas, rival factions also agree on police reform. Rebels control more territory, road links.
August 7	Macedonian police kill five ethnic Albanians accused of planning 'terrorist actions' in Skopje.
August 8	Ten Macedonian soldiers killed in an ambush just outside Skopje. Parties agree to sign deal in formal ceremony.
August 10	Army truck hits land mine north of Skopje, killing eight soldiers.
August 11–12	Scattered clashes between rebels and government forces.
August 13	Rival sides sign peace accord.
August 15	NATO authorises partial deployment of task force.
August 17	First French and British NATO advance troops arrive in Macedonia.
August 22	NATO authorises full deployment of 3,500-troop force to collect and destroy rebel arms.
December	Parliament approves Ohrid reforms. Newly formed multi-ethnic police begin to deploy in regions previously or still in rebel control.
2002 January	Macedonian Government requests NATO prolong until October its mission, now codenamed 'Amber Fox', which had been due to expire March 26. NATO agreed in the light of threats by Albanian underground movements. Macedonia's armed forces continued reform programme worth US 152 million dollars.
March	Macedonia signs free trade agreement with Albania, completes accession negotiations with World Trade Organisation.

September	Nationalist VMRO party suffers heavy defeat in general election to Social Democrats, who form new Government.
2003 March	'Operation Amber Fox' is transferred from NATO to EU command in first such test of the Unions defence arm, and renamed 'Operation Concordia'. Macedonia gives USA overflight rights for its Iraq campaign and use of the Petrovac airbase near Skopje as well as training facilities.
May	NATO invites Macedonia to join Albania and Croatia in new Adriatic Pact, intended to promote the three countries prospective NATO membership.
October	Macedonia agrees to exempt US citizens from prosecution by the International Criminal Court, removing danger of Skopje losing US military aid.
November 10	Defence ministers of Albania, Greece and Macedonia meet in north-western Greek city of Kastoria and pledge to step up military cooperation to address common threats, including cross-border terrorism during the Athens 2004 Summer Olympics.
November 15	Voluntary weapons collection operation sponsored by Macedonian government begins, aimed at estimated 170,000 citizens holding unregistered firearms.
2004 February 26	The Macedonian President, Boris Trajkovski, is killed when an aeroplane carrying him to an investment conference in Mostar, Bosnia, crashes in Bosnian mountains.
April	New presidential elections scheduled to be held.

Glossary of Abbreviations

ANA	Albanian National Army
DOS	Democratic Opposition of Serbia
DPA	Democratic Party of Albanians
FRY	Federal Republic of Yugoslavia
FYROM	Former Yugoslav Republic of Macedonia
GPS	Ground Positioning System
ICTY	International War Crimes Tribunal for Former Yugoslavia
KLA	Kosovo Liberation Army
KFOR	UN-led multinational peacekeeping force in Kosovo
KPC	Kosovo Protection Corps
LDK	Kosovo Democratic League
LPCK	National Movement for the Liberation of Kosovo
LPK	People's Movement for Kosovo
MUP	Ministry of Internal Affairs
NLA	National Liberation Army
PDK	Democratic Party of Kosovo
PDP	Party of Democratic Prosperity
SDSM	Social Democratic Party of Macedonia
SPS	Socialist Party of Serbia
UCPMB	Liberation Army of Presevo-Medvedja-Bujanovac
UNMIK	United Nations Mission in Kosovo
UNPREDEP	United Nations Preventive Deployment Force
VJ	Yugoslav Army
VMRO/IMRO	Internal Macedonian Revolutionary Organisation

Notes

Chapter 1

1. Visar Salihu.
2. Peter Beaumont, Ed Vulliamy and Paul Beaver, 'CIA's bastard army ran riot in Balkans', *The Observer*, 11 March 2001.

   The report quoted 'senior European officers who served with the international peace-keeping force in Kosovo' as well as 'leading Macedonian and US sources' saying: 'The CIA encouraged former Kosovo Liberation Army fighters to launch a rebellion in southern Serbia in an effort to undermine the then Yugoslav President Slobodan Milosevic'.

   One European KFOR battalion commander said: 'The CIA has been allowed to run riot in Kosovo with a private army designed to overthrow Milosevic. Now he's gone the US State Department seems incapable of reining in its bastard army... US policy was and still is out of step with the other NATO allies.' A senior Macedonian official was quoted as saying: 'What has been happening with the National Liberation Army and the UCPMB is very similar to what happened when the KLA was launched in 1995–1996... US intelligence agencies have not been honest here.' A US State Department official blamed the last administration. There had now been 'a shift of emphasis'.
3. See Anthony Loyd, 'A Very Dirty Little War', *The Times*, 14 May 2002, *Times 2*, p. 4. Ejupi was one of four Albanians arrested on charges of blowing up an express bus from Nis, Serbia, to Kosovo, in which 11 Serbs, including Danilo Cokic, a two-year-old boy, were killed. The investigation into the bombing was blocked at every stage and all four suspects are now free. UNMIK officers claimed Ejupi had been a source for US intelligence. 'They believe that Ejupi was released from Camp Bondsteel either because US intelligence agencies did not wish to be implicated by association in the bombing of Nis Express, or because they wanted to establish the identities of the men who authorised the bomb attack to use for their own ends,'

Loyd said. One senior UNMIK official said, 'We really don't know what happened with Ejupi. It is possible that he was released, but if that was the case then it was the act of an agency acting without State Department or Pentagon approval.'

4. Bob Churcher, *Kosovo Lindore/Preshevo 1999–2002 and the FYROM Conflict*, Conflict Studies Research Centre, Ministry of Defence, UK, March 2002, p. 6.
5. Tim Judah, *Kosovo: War and Revenge* (Yale University Press, 2000), p. 168.
6. Ibid. p. 103.
7. Abaz Zhuka's identity as Ali Ahmeti was revealed in the first volume of the Kosovo politician Ramush Hardinaj's war memoirs.
8. Meeting and other biographical details described in a profile of Ahmeti by Belgrade's independent Beta agency, 2 August 2001.
9. Medvedja is now majority Serb.
10. In his article, Churcher said that the Macedonian elite 'Wolves' special forces were used in the attack at Tanusevci but subsequently described them as interior ministry forces. Interview with the author, November 2002.
11. Churcher, *Kosovo Lindore/Preshevo 1999–2002 and the FYROM Conflict*, pp. 18, 21.
12. Milcho Manchevski, 'NATO gave us this ethnic cleansing', *The Guardian*, 15 August 2001.

Chapter 2
1. Stefan Troebst, 'IMRO + 100 = FYROM? The Politics of Macedonian Historiography', in James Pettifer (ed.), *The New Macedonian Question* (Palgrave, 2001). Troebst characterised the nationalist Macedonian view as a formula, IMRO + 100 = FYROM (Former Yugoslav Republic of Macedonia).
2. For the Albanians, Bitola is Monastir.
3. RJ Crampton, *The Balkans Since the Second World War* (Pearson Education, 2002), p. 293.
4. Kyril Drezov, 'Macedonian Identity: An Overview of the Major Claims', in Pettifer (ed.), *The New Macedonian Question*, p. 49.
5. Recounted in Elisabeth Barker, 'Macedonia: Its Place in Balkan Power Politics' (London: Royal Institute of International Affairs, 1950); reproduced in Pettifer (ed.), *The New Macedonian Question*.
6. LS Stavrianos, *The Balkans Since 1453* (New York University Press, 2001), p. 157.
7. Stevan K Pavlowitch, *A History of the Balkans, 1804–1945* (Longman, 1999), p. 196.
8. Mark Mazower, *The Balkans* (Weidenfeld and Nicolson, 2001), p. 93.

9. Noel Malcolm, *Kosovo: A Short History* (Papermac, 1998), p. 231.
10. Robert D Kaplan, *Balkan Ghosts* (Vintage Books, 1996), p. 56.
11. Hugh Poulton, *Who Are the Macedonians?* (Indiana University Press, 2000), p. 54.
12. Misha Glenny, *The Balkans, 1804–1999: Nationalism, War and the Great Powers* (Granta Books, 1999), p. 172.
13. According to official Bulgarian figures, there were 785 Bulgarian schools in Macedonia in 1900. The Serbs arrived later but, by 1899, there were 178 Serbian schools in the vilayets of Uskub, Monastir and Salonica. The Greeks had 927 Greek Schools in the vilayets of Salonica and Monastir in 1901. 'Obviously the main struggle for cultural and educational influence in Macedonia at the beginning of the 20th century was fought between the Bulgarians and the Greeks,' Slobodan Markovic wrote; figures given in Slobodan Markovic, *British Perceptions of Serbia and the Balkans, 1903–1906* (Dialogue, 2000).
14. 'Some were highly disciplined, courageous and ascetic men, who often came from good families in the freed Slav countries, who harried the Turkish troops, particularly those sent to punish Christian villages, and who held unofficial courts to correct the collapse of the legal system in the Turkish provinces. Others were fanatics who were happy in massacring Turks but even happier when they were purging the movement of suspected traitors.' Rebecca West, *Black Lamb and Grey Falcon: A Journey Through Yugoslavia* (Penguin, 1994), p. 641.
15. Glenny, *The Balkans*, p. 190.
16. There are good reasons for questioning to what extent this interpretation was largely a myth, albeit one that would be potent after a separate Macedonian republic was set up as part of Yugoslavia at the end of the Second World War. Stefan Troebst argues convincingly that at the time 'the term "autonomy" was seen as an unfortunate but necessary preliminary stage for unification with Bulgaria by pro-Bulgarian groups in the Macedonian spectrum'. Troebst, 'IMRO + 100 = FYROM?', p. 68.
17. Quoted in Kaplan, *Balkan Ghosts*, p. 59.
18. Markovic, *British Perceptions of Serbia and the Balkans*, p. 53.
19. Pavlowitch, *A History of the Balkans*, p. 199.
20. 'There is no doubt that they are southern Slavs; they have a language, or a group of varying dialects, that is grammatically akin to Bulgarian but phonetically in some respects akin to Serbian, and which has certain quite distinctive characteristics of its own. The Slav Macedonians are said to have retained one custom which is usually regarded as typically Serbian – the Slava, or family celebration of the day their family ancestor was converted to Christianity... it can

safely be said that during the last 80 years many more Slav
Macedonians seem to have considered themselves Bulgarian, or
closely linked with Bulgaria, than have considered themselves
Serbian, or closely linked with Serbia (or Yugoslavia). Only the
people of the Skopje region... have ever shown themselves much
tendency to regard themselves as Serbs. The feeling of being
Macedonians, and nothing but Macedonians, seems to be a sentiment
of fairly recent growth, and even today it is not very deep rooted.'
Barker, 'Macedonia', p. 8.

21. John R Lampe, *Yugoslavia as History: Twice There Was a Country* (Cambridge University Press, 2000), p. 117.
22. John Gunther, *Inside Europe* (New York: Harper and Brothers, 1938).
23. Stavrianos, *The Balkans Since 1453*, p. 768.

Chapter 3
1. Poulton, *Who Are the Macedonians?*, p. 95.
2. Ibid. p. 98.
3. Cited in JA Cuddon, *The Companion Guide to Jugoslavia* (London: Collins, 1986), p. 227.
4. Milovan Djilas, *Wartime* (Harcourt Brace Jovanovich, 1977).
5. Quoted in Josip Krulic, *Histoire de la Yougoslavie de 1945 a nos jours*, Italian edition (Milan: Bompiani, 1997), p. 35.
6. Quoted in Crampton, *The Balkans Since the Second World War*, p. 35.
7. See Susan L Woodward, *Balkan Tragedy* (Brookings Institution, 1995), p. 240.
8. Djilas, *Wartime*, p. 283.
9. *Daily Telegraph*, obituaries, 11 October 2002, p. 29.
10. Poulton, *Who Are the Macedonians?*, p. 116.
11. Ibid. p. 108.
12. Information in this and the following paragraph, ibid. pp. 116–7.
13. Drezov, 'Macedonian Identity', p. 51.
14. Trevor Beeson, *Discretion and Valour: Religious Conditions in Russia and Eastern Europe* (Collins, 1982), p. 308.
15. Ibid.
16. Ibid.
17. Information on Bogdanovski and in following paragraph from Poulton, *Who Are the Macedonians?*, p. 121.
18. See Pettifer, 'The Albanians in Western Macedonia', in *The New Macedonian Question*.
19. West, *Black Lamb and Grey Falcon*, p. 634.
20. Figures quoted in Poulton, *Who Are the Macedonians?*, p. 125.
21. Ibid. p. 128.
22. Ibid. p. 133.

Chapter 4

1. Both songs cited in Troebst, 'IMRO + 100 = FYROM?', p. 71.
2. Quoted in Takis Michas, *Unholy Alliance: Greece and Milosevic's Serbia* (A & M University Press, 2002), p. 51.
3. Crampton, *The Balkans Since the Second World War*, p. 255.
4. Cited in Poulton, *Who Are the Macedonians?*, p. 176.
5. Figures quoted in Jean-Yves Potel, *Les 100 Portes de l'Europe Centrale et Orientale* (Les Editions de l'Atelier, 1998).
6. Michas, *Unholy Alliance*, p. 51.
7. Cited in Woodward, *Balkan Tragedy*.
8. Pettifer, 'The Albanians in Western Macedonia', p. 22.
9. Michas, *Unholy Alliance*, p. 42.
10. David Owen, *Balkan Odyssey* (Harcourt Brace, 1995), p. 80.
11. Michas, *Unholy Alliance*, p. 44.
12. Ibid. p. 48.
13. Poulton, *Who Are the Macedonians?*, p. 177.
14. Evangelos Kofos, 'The Vision of "Greater Macedonia": Remarks on FYROM's new school textbooks', lecture given at the Thessaloniki Chamber of Commerce and Industry Hall, 23 March 1994 (Thessaloniki, 1994).
15. Poulton, *Who Are the Macedonians?*, p. 187.
16. Michas, *Unholy Alliance*, p. 55.
17. 'China, Macedonia resume ties', Reuter despatch from Beijing, 20 June 2001.
18. 'Macedonia: Taiwan's lost gambit', *Asia Times*, 11 July 2001.
19. Mark Almond and John Laughland, British Helsinki Human Rights Group report, 27 June 2001.
20. See Pettifer, *Former Yugoslav Macedonia: The Shades of Night?*, Conflict Studies Research Centre, July 2001, p. 10.
21. Richard Tomlinson, *The Big Breach: Inside the Secret World of MI6* (2001), pp. 143–8.
22. Woodward, *Balkan Tragedy*, p. 507.
23. Correspondence with the author, 2003.
24. Interview with the author, 2002.
25. Owen, *Balkan Odyssey*, p. 355.
26. Eleanor Pritchard, 'A university of their own', *Central Europe Review*, Vol. 2, No. 24, 19 June 2000.
27. Glenny, 'Heading off War in the Southern Balkans', *Foreign Affairs*, May/June 1995, Vol. 74, No. 3.
28. Arben Xhaferi, 'A career', quoted by Beta News Agency, Belgrade, 29 March 2001.
29. Judah, *Kosovo: War and Revenge*, p. 240.
30. 'Milosevic and Operation Horseshoe', *The Observer*, 18 July 1999.
31. Judah, *Kosovo: War and Revenge*, p. 241.

32. Ibid. p. 241
33. John Goetz and Tom Walker, 'Serbian ethnic cleansing scare was a fake, says general', *Sunday Times*, 2 April 2000.
34. Figure cited in *Le Monde*, Bilan du Monde, L'analyse de 174 pays et des 26 regions francaises, Edition 2000, p. 52.
35. Poulton, *Who Are the Macedonians?*, p. 200.
36. Judah, *Kosovo: War and Revenge*, p. 252.
37. Hill interview with Radio Free Europe, 19 April 1999. Hill went on to say: 'What I think Macedonians are worried about is the ethnic mix will become quite changed, and this will in turn cause political changes, and perhaps even efforts to change the constitution... the Macedonian concern is that a humanitarian crisis in Kosovo could cause... a major political upheaval. They are also worried that while we have been very concerned about preventing a Greater Serbia, we have not been concerned enough about preventing a Greater Albania... we're not looking for a Greater Anything, we're looking for a better Balkans, not a Balkans where some ethnic community strives to increase its size at the expense of others.'
38. Figures in this section from *Le Monde*, op. cit., p. 52.
39. See 'Under Orders: War Crimes in Kosovo', Human Rights Watch report, New York, 2001, p. 18.
40. Radio Free Europe interview, 19 April 1999.
41. Pettifer, 'FYROM after Ochrid', Conflict Studies Research Centre, Royal Military Academy, Sandhurst, March 2002, p. 13.
42. Woodward, *Balkan Tragedy*, p. 350.
43. Conversation with the author, 2002.

Chapter 5
1. Macedonian National Statistics Office report, quoted in *Southeast European Times*, 15 December 2003.
2. By 2003, Yugoslavia would be consigned to history and replaced with a looser federation, the Union of Serbia and Montenegro.

Chapter 6
1. Peter was the only British photographer to capture the entire event on film. 'The whole incident took about 30 seconds,' he recalled later. 'I wasn't scared because it all happened so quickly. There's an element of removal from the situation because I was looking through the lens and you don't register the atmosphere and the confusion going on around you. The night after it happened, I went back to my hotel, lay on my bed, stared at the ceiling and thought about what happened,' he recalled later. 'I thought about the way I went about the assignment and wondered if my camera's aperture and shutter-speed were right. All these things ran through my mind. I

thought about the person dying in front of my eyes, how lucky the soldiers were and how lucky we were that that grenade didn't go off.'

2. Translation of NLA communiqué, published in *The Guardian*, 21 March 2002.
3. Marko Georgiev, 'Shrapnels', photo-essay accompanying exhibition of his work during the conflict at the Cix Gallery in Skopje, March 2002. Also on the website www.realitymacedonia.org.mk.
4. Glenny, *The Fall of Yugoslavia: The Third Balkan War* (London: Penguin, 1992).
5. Richard Beeston, 'Macedonia retaliates to seize rebel stronghold', *The Times*, 26 March 2001.
6. *Wall St. Journal Europe*, interview with Hill (then US Ambassador to Warsaw), 11 April 2001.
7. 'Macedonian Army lacking strength', *Jane's Defence Weekly*, 3 April 2001.
8. Pettifer, *Former Yugoslav Macedonia*, p. 8.
9. Churcher, *Kosovo Lindore/Preshevo 1999–2002 and the FYROM Conflict*.
10. 'Ali Ahmeti, politician or terrorist', Beta News Agency, Belgrade, 2 August 2001.
11. Poulton, *Who Are the Macedonians?*, pp. 191, 217; and *Nova Makedonija*, Skopje, 19 May 1992.

Chapter 7
1. Correspondence with author, May 2002.
2. Zoran Kusovac, 'Macedonian army lacking strength', *Jane's Defence Weekly*, 3 April 2001.
3. Correspondence with the author, May 2003.
4. Quoted in 'Newsman killed in Kosovo shelling', *The Guardian*, 29 March 2001.
5. Ibid.
6. Ibid.
7. Richard Beeston, 'Once more, men disappear in Balkans', *The Times*, 30 May 2001.
8. Quoted in 'Two friends stand against forces dividing Macedonia', *Washington Post*, 15 May 2001.
9. *Washington Post*, 10 June 2001.
10. Sixty-four-year-old Zini K. was in his restaurant when the crowds of ethnic Macedonians struck. 'They came inside, destroyed the place and set it on fire. Then they went to another one and they burned it as well. I had a motorbike and they put it inside the restaurant and burned it.' Zini K. managed to extinguish the blaze, but returned to find his restaurant looted and burned to the ground. 'After I left

they came back to the restaurant and burned it again. It is now completely burned. Everything was looted – our kitchen tools, tables, dishes, radio, telephone – there is nothing left.' Zini K. then went home to Tsar Samuel Street and again was faced with a very large mob shortly after 10 pm. After damaging a mosque at the end of his street, they proceeded to select Albanian homes and burned them down. 'They had burned down my nephew's home and another relative's home. Our steel door was locked. They broke it down and started yelling, 'Where are you Shiptar.' I stepped back inside and when they saw me retreat they started throwing flaming objects at the house.'

Hamdi S., 42, was at home on the same street with his wife and children when the mob approached: 'At around 10:20 pm, the lights in the houses suddenly went out. Then we heard a very big noise. First we could hear shooting. I said to my wife that they must have started burning the houses. When I went out I saw that my uncle's house was burning. After they burned his house, they came to my house. I took out my children, my 11-year-old daughter first. At that moment the first [Molotov] cocktail was thrown and I told my boys and my wife to run away.'

A witness saw a 50-year-old former local leader of the Democratic Party of Albanians (DPA) being beaten up together with his 47-year-old wife: 'They broke down the fence and entered inside. First five people entered inside. They were breaking the tables inside, ripping up papers and pouring something out of a bottle. One of them set the home alight. A man and woman were on the top floor of the house when it started burning. The two were taken out of the house. They were taken into the basement and then I couldn't see them any more. After 15 or 20 minutes, they came back outside. They were covered with blood. The Macedonians were slapping their faces.'

Quoted in Human Rights Watch report: 'Macedonia: rioters burn Albanian homes in Bitola', New York, 8 June 2001.

11.   'Macedonia: Albanian rebel abuses of Serb civilians', Human Rights Watch report, 7 June 2001.

Chapter 8

1.   Pettifer, 'The Albanians in Western Macedonia', p. 141.
2.   *Washington Post*, 25 May 2001.
3.   Richard Holbrooke, *To End a War* (Modern Library, 1999), p. 341.
4.   Quoted in *Central European Review*, Vol. 3, No. 17, 14 May 2001.
5.   Ibid.
6.   This and subsequent quotes from interview with author, 7 May 2003.
7.   *Washington Post*, 14 June 2001.

8. Vladimir Jovanovski, 'The Macedonian Hawk', Balkan Crisis Report, No. 255, 13 June 2001.
9. 'Storm Over Macedonian Partition Plan', Balkan Crisis Report, 7 June 2001.
10. Interview with Beeston, *The Times*, 30 June 2001.
11. For details of Leotard's career, see John Lichfield, 'The nearly man of French politics put into Balkan hotseat', *The Independent*, 26 June 2001.
12. Background on Pardew cited in Holbrooke, *To End a War*, p. 83.
13. Quoted in R. Jeffrey Smith, 'Ethnicity distorts Truth in Macedonia', *Washington Post*, 2 July 2001.
14. Paddy Ashdown, 'The West must act now, or face the risk of a wider war in the Balkans', *The Independent*, 3 July 2001.
15. Correspondence with author.
16. Quoted in 'Macedonians attack US Embassy', *Washington Post*, 25 July 2001.
17. 'Massacre in Skopje Quarters of Gazi Baba', *Fakti*, 7 August 2001.
18. *New York Times*, 14 August 2001.
19. 'Macedonia: war on hold', Balkans briefing, International Crisis Group, 15 August 2001.

Chapter 9

1. 'Macedonia Fighting Intensifies', *Washington Post*, 11 August 2001, p. A14.
2. Ibid.
3. Quoted in 'Skopje minister in revenge-raid village', *The Times*, 6 September 2001.
4. Quoted in Jessica Berry, 'Massacre report names Macedonia interior minister', *Daily Telegraph*, 26 August 2001. The security forces had also 'indiscriminately shelled the village, causing the deaths of a six-year-old boy and a 66-year-old man, and contributing to the death of another man who died from shock after a shell hit his home'.
Fasli, 25, a farmer, said, 'There were children playing in the street. Suddenly a grenade hit one of the kids. The boy flew in the air and there was smoke and blood. Everyone ran.' When he tried to escape he reached a checkpoint where, he said, there were 'many police, some wearing balaclavas, and dozens of civilians with guns, axes and sticks'. He was then taken to a nearby police station where he and other men were beaten severely by masked policemen. 'The carpet was covered with blood,' he said. Fasli heard a baying mob outside shouting, 'Let us kill them. Gas chambers for Shiptars!'
Elmas, 55, a paraplegic, told how he watched his 33-year-old son Rami Youssef, die in agony. Unable to move, he could not help him. 'They bombed my gate then they came to my house. There were 20

police in my yard.' An explosion blew out his front door. This was followed by machine-gun fire. He said his son was hit in the side and stomach. 'He died very slowly,' Elmas said. 'It took two hours.'

Aziz Barami said he also saw his son, Suleyman, murdered after they were ordered out of a basement where they had been hiding with other villagers. 'They took us through a small gate where there were eight men face down on the ground with their hands above their heads. We were told to lie down too. A policeman kicked Suleyman in the head. He was in pain and stood up and then the policeman shot him and then everyone was shooting. I heard one say, "This pig is still moving." Then there was another single gunshot. Suleyman tried to flee and then they shot him in the head.'

5. Quoted in Giles Tremlett and Nick Wood, 'Macedonians accused of war crimes', *The Guardian*, 6 October 2001.
6. 'The children were sleeping on the terrace because of the heat, my three and my brother's son,' Sabir said. 'My wife, my brother and I were upstairs. At around 11:30, we heard dogs barking and looked outside to see who was coming. There were 10 of them, around five of them in masks. They just started shooting. We lay down on the floor, but when Tafil woke up he automatically stood up to see what the noise was. He was shot in the stomach. There were so many bullet wounds.' Quoted in 'Macedonia's ethnic cleansers claim first victim', *The Independent*, 12 August 2001.
7. Michael Evans, *The Times*, 16 August 2001, p. 10.
8. 'Why are we in Macedonia? Special Report', *The Guardian*, 23 August 2001. Norton-Taylor continued: 'The mission, says NATO confidently, will last just 30 days. But what happens when the time is up? Will NATO governments take their soldiers away, leaving the heavily armed Macedonian security forces and still adequately-armed Albanians to resume where they left off?

    'The pictures of British soldiers taking the lead in yet another NATO mission in the Balkans is pleasing to the Foreign Office and the Ministry of Defence... It is good, they say, for Britain's image.

    'But what about deep-seated problems back home? It is all very well having a reputation as a "warrior nation", but what about the quality of civil society in Britain?'
9. Frederick Bonnart, 'Macedonia is crucial, and NATO should get ready to react', *International Herald Tribune*, 6 September 2001, p. 4.

    The Guardian itself, in a separate editorial article the same day, was more optimistic. 'NATO's intervention in Macedonia... has been a remarkably smooth and uncontested affair.

    'One reason is that the mission's mandate is narrow and carefully agreed with the contending sides, the Macedonian government and the ethnic Albanian guerrillas. The troops are not peace-keepers in the usual sense.' The model was not the NATO role in Kosovo or Bosnia but events in the Presevo valley of Southern Serbia earlier in the year. 'There NATO brokered a peace deal with the government in Belgrade for ethnic Albanian guerrillas to disband in return for political concessions and an amnesty for the gunmen.' That comparison seemed over-optimistic. The disarmament of the UCPMB in southern Serbia had been successful partly because Albanian guerrillas did not want to risk a major confrontation with the highly professional Yugoslav Army they could not win. The Macedonian armed forces were a softer target for the NLA.

A second reason for NATO's almost relaxed approach, the newspaper wrote, was that it was 'acting, for the first time in its history, as a "coalition of the willing". Not all member countries are taking part, and those that have qualms are not required to contribute. This is an important precedent, symbolised most strikingly by the absence of American ground troops... Arguments between Washington and the Europeans postponed action in Bosnia and Kosovo. This time, at last, the lessons of dissension and delay have been learnt.'

10. 'Russia and Ukraine secretly fly arms to Macedonian forces', *The Times*, 22 August 2001.
11. Reuters despatch from Skopje, 4 October 2001.
12. 'A Para officer on duty in Macedonia', *Independent on Sunday*, 2 September 2001.
13. *The Times*, 28 August 2001, p. 4.
14. Quoted in the *International Herald Tribune*, 30 August 2001, p. 5.
15. *The Independent*, 1 September 2001.
16. *International Herald Tribune*, 30 August 2001.
17. Quoted in Reuters despatch, 4 October 2001.
18. Jovanovski, 'Macedonia: Church enrages Albanians', IWPR Balkan Crisis Report, No. 309, 17 January 2002. The Albanian National Army, a secretive successor organisation to the now disbanded NLA, responded to the church's involvement in the ceremony by threatening a renewal of hostilities. 'The blessing of paramilitary units by the head of the Macedonian Orthodox Church and the buying of new arms from Ukraine, Russia and Croatia forced us to respond,' the ANA communiqué said.
19. Saso Ordanoski, 'In what direction does the Macedonian police go?', *Forum*, 29 January 2002.
20. 'Macedonian official wounds four', AP despatch, 15 May 2002.

Chapter 10

1. Macedonian defence ministry sources put the number of security force members killed at 95. Media estimates of the total number of

people killed range from 'more than 150', from the Skopje daily newspaper *Dnevnik*, to 'less than 100', according to a local staffer of Reuter news agency. Agron Buxhaku, a spokesman for Ali Ahmeti, told me in Tetovo in September 2002 that the total number of people killed in the conflict was around 200. The International Committee for the Red Cross said that a total of 650 wounded were treated in Macedonian hospitals during the conflict.

2.   Brendan Simms of Cambridge University, in his devastating critique of British policy in Bosnia, offered rare approval of the British Labour Government's handling of the Macedonian crisis, saying that the despatch of British troops was essential to contain the ethnic Albanian rebels. Such an expeditious response contrasted with Britain's unhappy record in the Bosnian war marked by pro-Serb bias, he argued. '[Former Conservative Prime Minister] John Major, [former Foreign Secretary] Douglas Hurd and [former Defence Secretary] Malcolm Rifkind would no doubt have clapped an arms embargo on "all sides", told the government in Skopje to cut the best deal it could with the rebels, and generally inadvertently signalled her neighbours to help themselves.' Brendan Simms, *Unfinest Hour: Britain and the Destruction of Bosnia* (Allen Lane, 2001), p. 245.

3.   'Our great Balkan adventure continues,' Geoffrey Wheatcroft wrote in *The Guardian*, for example, 'but all does not go well.' *The Guardian*, leader, 7 September 2001.

4.   Pettifer, 'FYROM after Ohrid', Conflict Studies Research Centre, UK Ministry of Defence, March 2002, p. 1.

5.   Conversation with the author, 2002.

6.   Nina Smirnova and Alla A Yaskova, 'The Balkans and the Mediterranean policy of Russia', in Pettifer (ed.), *The New Macedonian Question*, p. 274. They added that: 'The influence of pseudopatriotic parties and movements on the domestic and foreign policies of some newly created states became evident in the conditions of deepening economic crisis. Experience shows that nationalist ideas and appeals, induced into mass consciousness, are sufficient in such conditions to provoke bloody conflicts... after the end of the Cold War, nationalism has become the main danger in post-communist regions of Europe.'

7.   Beth Potter, 'Kosovo corps officials on U.S. blacklist suspended', Reuter dispatch, 6 July 2001.

8.   Hill interview with European *Wall St. Journal*, 11 April 2001.

9.   Pettifer, 'FYROM after Ochrid', p. 8.

10.   Churcher, *Kosovo Lindore/Preshevo 1999–2002 & the FYROM Conflict*, p. 21.

11.   Judah, *Kosovo: War and Revenge*, p. 301.

12.   Bernd J Fischer, *Albania at War, 1939–1945* (C. Hurst, 1999), p. 274.

13. Woodward, *Balkan Tragedy*, p. 295. She added that 'Bosnia's fate was a consequence of its interior location at the geopolitical and cultural heart of the former Yugoslavia – cordoned off from Europe by the republics of Croatia and Serbia, with no external border except a tiny outlet to the Adriatic Sea at the cluster of fishing huts, tourist inns and villas for Sarajevo politicians called Neum – so its war could not spill over western borders... The great and understandable concern about whether the war in Bosnia-Herzegovina would spread could not be answered without reverting to the causes of war and to the particular political dynamic of unchecked nationalism.'

14. Simms, *Unfinished Hour*, p. 342.

15. Discussion with the author, April 2003.

16. Markovic, *British Perceptions of Serbia and the Balkans*. See also John Phillips, 'Intrepid man from *The Times* kept Victorian Britain in Touch', *The Times*, 17 March 2001.

17. Quoted in Ermira Mehmeti, 'Peace Effort in Macedonia Stalls', *Associated Press*, 16 February 2002.

18. 'Rebels spend drug millions on guns', *Daily Telegraph*, 16 February 2002.

19. Pettifer, 'FYROM after Ochrid', p. 4.

20. Quoted in 'EU military operation in doubt', *Financial Times*, 15 May 2002.

21. 'U.S. Majors consider Balkan pipeline project', Reuter dispatch from Sofia, 15 February 2002.

22. Quoted in AP dispatch, 28 December 2001.

23. Pettifer, 'FYROM after Ochrid', p. 4.

24. Figures quoted in 'Donors pledge aid for Macedonia reconstruction', *Financial Times*, 14 April 2002.

Chapter 11

1. Quoted in Nicholas Wood, 'Violence stirs fear of wider conflict in Macedonia', *Washington Post*, 26 April 2002.

2. 'Macedonian police kill 7 in suspected terror cell', *Washington Post*, 3 March 2002.

3. Correspondence with the author, 2003.

4. 'Albanian language now official in Macedonia', AP, 20 June 2002.

Select
Bibliography

Andric, Ivo, *The Bridge on the Drina* (Chicago: University of Chicago Press, 1999)

Barker, Elisabeth, *Macedonia: Its Place in Balkan Power Politics* (London and New York: Royal Institute for International Affairs, 1950)

Beeson, Trevor, *Discretion and Valour: Religious Conditions in Russia and Eastern Europe* (Glasgow: Collins, 1982)

Churcher, Bob, *Kosovo Lindore/Preshevo 1999–2002 and the FYROM Conflict*, Conflict Studies Research Centre, Ministry of Defence, UK, March 2002

Clark, Victoria, *Why Angels Fall: A Journey Through Orthodox Europe from Byzantium to Kosovo* (London: Picador, 2001)

Clogg, Richard, *A Concise History of Greece* (Cambridge: Cambridge University Press, 1992)

Crampton, RJ, *The Balkans Since the Second World War* (London: Pearson Education, 2002)

Cuddon, JA, *The Companion Guide to Jugoslavia* (London: Collins, 1986)

Cvijic, Jovan, *La Peninsule Balkanique* (Paris: Armand Colin, 1918)

_____, *Questions Balkaniques* (Paris: Attinger Frères, 1917)

Djilas, Milovan, *Wartime* (New York: Harcourt Brace Jovanovich, 1977)

Fischer, Bernd J, *Albania at War, 1939–1945* (London: Hurst and Company, 1999)

Glenny, Misha, *The Balkans, 1804–1999: Nationalism, War and the Great Powers* (London: Granta Books, 1999)

_____, *The Fall of Yugoslavia: The Third Balkan War* (London: Penguin, 1992)

_____, 'Heading off War in the Southern Balkans', *Foreign Affairs*, May/June 1995, Vol. 74, No. 3

Gunther, John, *Inside Europe* (New York: Harper and Brothers, 1938)

Hammett, Dashiell, 'This King Business', in *The Big Knockover and Other Stories* (London: Penguin, 1969)

Holbrooke, Richard, *To End a War* (New York: Modern Library, 1999)

Judah, Tim, *Kosovo: War and Revenge* (New Haven: Yale University Press, 2000)

_____, *Serbs: History, Myth and the Destruction of Yugoslavia* (New Haven, CT and London: Yale University Press, 1997)

_____, 'Greater Albania?', *New York Review of Books*, 17 May 2001

Kofos, Evangelos, 'The Vision of "Greater Macedonia": Remarks on FYROM's new school textbooks', lecture given at the Thessaloniki Chamber of Commerce and Industry Hall, 23 March 1994 (Thessaloniki, 1994)

Krulic, Josep, *Histoire de la Yougoslavie de 1945 a nos jours*, Italian edition (Milan: Bompiani, 1997)

Lampe, John R, *Yugoslavia as History: Twice There Was a Country* (Cambridge: Cambridge University Press, 2000)

MacDermott, Marcia, *Freedom or Death: The Life of Gotse Delchev* (London and West Nyack, New York: Journeyman Press, 1978)

Malcolm, Noel, *Kosovo: A Short History* (London: Papermac, 1998)

Markovic, Slobodan, *British Perceptions of Serbia and the Balkans, 1903–1906* (Paris: Dialogue, 2000)

Mazower, Mark, *The Balkans* (London: Weidenfeld and Nicolson, 2001)

Michas, Takis, *Unholy Alliance: Greece and Milosevic's Serbia* (Texas: A & M University Press, 2002)

Owen, David, *Balkan Odyssey* (London: Harcourt Brace, 1995)

Pavlowitch, Stevan K, *A History of the Balkans, 1804–1945* (New York: Longman, 1999)

Pettifer, James (ed.), *The New Macedonian Question* (Basingstoke: Palgrave, 2001)

_____, 'FYROM after Ochrid', Conflict Studies Research Centre, Royal Military Academy, Sandhurst, March 2002 (available, together with many other useful papers on the region, on the Centre's website, www.csrc.ac.uk)

Potel, Jean-Yves, *Les 100 Portes de l'Europe Centrale et Orientale* (Paris: Les Editions de l'Atelier, 1998)

Poulton, Hugh, *Who Are the Macedonians?* (Bloomington and Indiana: Indiana University Press, 2000)

Silber, Laura, and Allan Little, *The Death of Yugoslavia* (London: Penguin Books/BBC Books, 1996)

Simms, Brendan, *Unfinest Hour: Britain and the Destruction of Bosnia* (London: Allen Lane, 2001)

Stavrianos, LS, *The Balkans since 1453* (New York: New York University Press, 2001)

Tomlinson, Richard, *The Big Breach: Inside the Secret World of MI6* (Edinburgh: Mainstream, 2001)

Ugresic, Dubravka, *The Museum of Unconditional Surrender* (London: Phoenix, 1998)

Velmar-Jankovic, Svetlana, *Dungeon* (Belgrade: Dereta, 2002)

Vesovic, Marko, *Chiedo scusa se vi parlo di Sarajevo* (Milano: Sperling & Kupfer Editori, 1996)

Vukmanovic, Tempo, *Svetozar Struggle for the Balkans*, trans. Charles Bartlett (London: Merlin Press, 1990)

West, Rebecca, *Black Lamb and Grey Falcon, A Journey Through Yugoslavia* (London: Penguin, 1994)

Woodward, Susan L, *Balkan Tragedy* (Washington: Brookings Institution, 1995)

Zametica, Jovan, 'The Macedonian Question among British Contemporaries: Serbophiles, and Bulgarophiles (1897–1920)', in *Europe and the Eastern Question (1878–1923): Political and Civilizational Challenges* (Belgrade: Historical Institute of the Serbian Academy, 2001), pp. 321–335

Index

Dimovska, Dosta 78, 184
Djilas, Milovan 36, 37, 39
Djindjic, Zoran 179
Djukanovic, Milo 172–3
Dnevnik newspaper 128, 131, 132, 185
DOS (Democratic Opposition of Serbia) 180
DPA (Democratic Party of Albanians) 8, 13, 68–9, 74–5, 78, 80; Georgievski and 122–3; role in government 163; and SDSM 184; and Tetovo 97, *see also* Xhaferi, Arben
Drenovec 89–90
Drezov, Kyril 41–2
DUI (Democratic Union for Integration) 178, 187
Dullovi, Lirim 135
Duncan Smith, Iain 150
Durrell, Lawrence 1, 103

ECHAC (European Council of Humanity, Action and Cooperation) 142–3
Efremov, Georgi 123, 124
Eiff, Hans-Joerg 122
Elmazi, Refet 11–12
Emini, Mithat 67
European Commission 186
European Union: and Albanian uprising 98, 130–1, 155, 156; Greek membership of 56, 181–2; interventionism 118, 119; and Macedonia 51, 171–4, 186, 197, 200; and NATO 181–2
Evans, Michael 152
External Organisation (Macedonia) 26, *see also* IMRO

Fakti newspaper 131, 135
Feith, Pieter 6, 125, 126, 130, 136
Ferdinand, King of Bulgaria 25–6, 28
Ferguson, Edward 63
Filipovic, Filip 34
Fischer, Joschka 73
Forum magazine 93, 123, 133, 158–9, 194, 198
Fraenkel, Eran 131–2
France, and peace negotiations 130–1, 144–5

Frasure, Robert 67
Frowick, Robert H. 60, 118–20
Fry, Brigadier Robert 9
FYROM (Former Yugoslav Republic of Macedonia), temporary name 56, 59

Gajre 94, 96
Galevski, Risto 157
Gazi Baba 116, 135
Gemidzhi, anarchist group 26, 134
Geneva, Bulgarian–Macedonian congress (1899) 26
Georgiev, Marko 88–9, 90–1, 93, 128
Georgiev, Vlado 31–2
Georgievski, Ljubco 42, 61, 72, 79–80, 175; and Albanian insurgency 92, 122–4, 134; and Boskovski 158, 159, 185; and Kosovo crisis 76–7; nationalism of 165, 194
Georgievski, Snezana 42
Germany 32, 151; NATO troops 92, 186–7, 193
Germo 95
Gheorgiev, Colonel Kimon 32
Gladstone, W.E. 24
Glenny, Misha 71
Gligorov, Kiro 13, 46–7, 51, 53, 80; and Army 99; and ethnic minorities 65–6, 72; problems of 64, 162; and relations with Greece 54–6; and Serbia 55, 60, 82
Gornja Dzumaja 37, 38
Gostivar 71
Great Britain: and Albanian uprising 93, 150–1; and Kosovo 9; and Macedonia 10, 40, 66, 77; policy in Balkans 10, 28, 118
Greece 21, 27, 29, 40, 53; and EU 51, 56, 181–2; and Macedonia 15, 21, 22, 31, 181–2; relations with independent Macedonia 53–9; Tito's designs on 38–9
Grubacic, Braca 73
Gruev, Damian 24, 26
Guzelev, Dimitar 40
Gypsies (Roma) 65, 80

LPCK (National Movement for the Liberation of Kosovo) 11
LPK (People's Movement for Kosovo) 7–8
LPRK (Popular Movement for the Republic of Kosovo) 8
Lucane 4, 5–6
Lukic, General Sreten 73

Macedonia 17, 21–2, 28, 31, 41–3; and Albania 15, 30, 67–72, 82–3, 180–1; Albanian arms plot 67–72; Britain and 10, 40, 66, 77; and Bulgaria 23–4, 25–6, 31–2, 34, 173, 178–9; and Bulgarian irredentism 40–2; economy 62–3, 75, 185–6; education in 41, 56–7, 69–70, 71; elections (2002) 178; ethnic mix 16, 22–3, 78, 167, 199; and EU 171–4, 182, 200; European interest in 24–5, 182; Grand Coalition Government of National Unity 117, 118; and Greece 15, 21, 22–3, 31, 53–9, 181–2; independence (1991) 48–52, 162; independence movement 15–16, 25–6; international aid 185–6, 197; KLA in 8–9, 10–11; and Kosovo 72–8, 163, 166–71; minority rights (1991 Constitution) 65; origins of religious conflict 19–20; Orthodox Church in 18–19, 41, 42; population 64–5, 79, 168; proposed partition 123–4, 176–7; prospects for 188–99; recognition of Taiwan 61, 172; and Russia 183–4; and second Balkan War 30–1; and Serbia 11, 22, 49–50, 55–6, 80, 81–2, 179–80; Slav ethnicity in 22, 32, 57, 78, 179; war of maps 56–8; as Yugoslav autonomous state 36–43, see also Albanian uprising; Albanians, in Macedonia; IMRO; NLA; Pirin Macedonia; Vardar Macedonia
Macedonian Army (ARM): detention methods 112; equipment 99–100, 110–11; inadequacy of 98–101,

161–2, 172; Kumanovo region 103–10; and Ljuboten incident 137–8; at Tetovo 86–7, 89–90, 93, 96–8
Macedonian ethnicity 15–16, 22, 41–2, 79–80
Macedonian language 22–3, 36, 38, 41, 83
Macedonian nationalism 21–6, 32, 36, 43, 56–8; and future prospects 164–6
Malcolm, Noel 23
Manchevski, Milcho 13–14
Markovic, Slobodan 28, 174
Markovski, Slobodan 147
Matejce 111–12
Mazower, Mark 23, 32
Mehmeti, Kim 135
Meta, Ilir 180–1
MI6, see Secret Intelligence Service
Michas, Takis 52, 54
Mihailov, Ivan (Vanche) 31–2
Milo, Pascal 181
Milosevic, Slobodan 2, 10, 72, 164–5, 167; and Gligorov 60, 82; and Macedonian independence 49–50, 52, 162; and 'Macedonian problem' 54–5, 82; opposition to 5, 9
Milososki, Antonio 133, 137, 141
Mitsotakis, Constantine 54, 55
Mladic, Ratko 52, 174
Monastir (Bitola), Macedonia, as proposed capital of Albania 29
Montenegro 8, 21, 29, 172–3
Mount Sar offensive 96–8
MPRI (Military Professional Resources International) 100, 111
Mürszteg Agreement (1903) 27
Muslim–Slav conflicts 26–7
Muslims, in Ottoman Empire 19
Musliu, Shefket 2, 6
Mussolini, Benito 31

NATO 75–6, 82, 117; and Aracinovo 126–7, 132–3; bombardment of Kosovo 2, 7, 75; British troops 110, 144–50; enquiry into death of Lawton 105–7; and EU 181–2; Macedonian view of 172, 173, 174–